"Complicity with Evil"

The United Nations in the
Age of Modern Genocide

Adam LeBor

Yale University Press   New Haven & London

Set in Minion Roman type by Integrated Publishing Solutions.

Printed in Great Britain by St Edmundsbury Press Ltd, Bury St Edmunds.

Library of Congress Cataloging-in-Publication Data

LeBor, Adam.

"Complicity with evil" : the United Nations in the age of modern genocide / Adam LeBor.

p. cm.

Includes bibliographical references and index.

ISBN-13: 978-0-300-11171-2 (cloth : alk. paper)

ISBN-10: 0-300-11171-1 (cloth : alk. paper)

1. United Nations. 2. United Nations. Secretariat. 3. Genocide. 4. Security, International. I. Title. II. Title: United Nations in the age of modern genocide.

JZ4971.L43 2006

341.23—dc22   2006017319

A catalogue record for this book is available from the British Library.

The paper in this book meets the guidelines for permanence and durability of the Committee on Production Guidelines for Book Longevity of the Council on Library Resources.

10   9   8   7   6   5   4   3   2   1

No failure did more to damage the standing and credibility of United Nations peacekeeping in the 1990s than its reluctance to distinguish victim from aggressor.

—Executive summary of the United Nations 2000 report on its peacekeeping operations

Contents

Part II

Preface

This book takes its title, "*Complicity with Evil*," from the United
Nations' report on its peacekeeping operations during the 1990s,
published in August 2000. The report was commissioned by
Secretary General Kofi Annan, who convened a high-level panel
of diplomats, military officers, and humanitarian officials with
experience of UN operations in crisis zones. The authors proposed new approaches for peacekeeping after the failures in
Srebrenica and Rwanda, so as to confront the challenges of the
post–Cold War world of conflicts fought by rogue states and
anarchic militias. The report's fifty-four pages contain a series
of detailed recommendations about the conduct of future operations, and an outline of institutional and attitudinal changes
needed within member states, the Security Council, and the
Secretariat—the permanent body of UN officials—to make
peacekeeping more dynamic and effective. Probably the document's most important sentence is contained in its executive
summary: "Impartiality for United Nations operations must
therefore mean adherence to the principles of the Charter:
where one party clearly and incontrovertibly is violating its
terms, continued equal treatment of the parties by the United

Nations can in the best case result in ineffectiveness and in the worst may amount to complicity with evil."

This was certainly the case in both Srebrenica and Rwanda, and remains so in Darfur. The Dutchbat battalion of UNPROFOR, the UN protection force deployed in Croatia and Bosnia, stationed in the UN-declared safe area of Srebrenica, was unable to prevent the fall of the town in July 1995 and the subsequent slaughter of up to 8,000 Bosniak (Bosnian Muslim) men and boys. UNAMIR, the UN assistance mission for Rwanda, failed to prevent the genocide of 800,000 Tutsis and moderate Hutus during spring and early summer 1994, despite the valiant efforts of its commander General Romeo Dallaire. By spring 2006 the Sudanese government had been waging a campaign of genocide across Darfur for three years, but the United Nations had not even deployed peacekeepers there, relying instead on a weak and underfunded mission of African Union cease-fire monitors.

But do these actions really make the United Nations guilty of complicity with evil? *Complicity* is an emotive term. The dictionary defines it as "being an accomplice in a criminal act." Complicity can be active or passive. The United Nations did not intentionally assist the Bosnian Serbs to kill the men and boys of Srebrenica, the Hutu militias to slaughter their Tutsi victims, or the Sudanese Janjaweed paramilitaries to burn the villages of Darfur. UN peacekeepers are mandated to save lives, not take them. Secretariat officials believed—and believe—themselves to be acting with the best of intentions, steering the United Nations through a perilous middle path of impartiality and neutrality that by favoring neither side would allow the organization to do the maximum good. When in January 1994 Kofi Annan, then head of the Department of Peacekeeping Operations, refused General Dallaire permission to raid the Hutu arms caches, he believed that such an action was outside UNAMIR's mandate and would imperil both the United Nations mission in Rwanda and the UN's status as an impartial interlocutor.

The members of the Security Council assumed, or at least hoped, in spring 1993 that by passing resolutions declaring Srebrenica a UN-protected safe area, they were taking a meaningful step to protect the innocent. A decade later, the failure of the Security Council and the General Assembly to take any meaningful action against the Sudanese government must be weighed against the need to keep channels open to Sudan and so ensure the continued operation of the United Nations' humanitarian operation in Darfur, which has saved hundreds of thousands of lives.

Thus the argument for the defense. But there is another definition of complicity, which is a nuanced as well as an emotive term. To be complicit in a crime does not necessarily mean actively aiding and abetting the perpetrators. It can also mean failing to act on the knowledge that crimes are being, or are likely to be, committed, or failing to try at least to prevent them happening, despite having the means to do so. This is the principle of "command responsibility" which has evolved through the legal rulings of the UN's own tribunals for the former Yugoslavia and Rwanda. And this is the argument for the prosecution. In this book I show that the United Nations was, and remains, at the very least, passively complicit with evil: in Bosnia from 1992 to 1995—nowhere more than at Srebrenica— in Rwanda in 1994, and in Darfur since 2003.

After declaring Srebrenica a safe area, the Security Council extended that status to another five Bosnian towns and cities, yet its members—all of the UN member states—consistently failed to provide enough troops to provide effective protec-

tion. UN commanders themselves repeatedly refused to authorize NATO air strikes requested by Dutch UN peacekeepers at
Srebrenica, despite having both the mandate and the means to
do so, until it was too late to stop the Serb onslaught. When the
town finally fell, the Dutch UN troops ignored the pleas of
Bosniak men and boys who had taken refuge in their compound and forced them into the hands of their Serb executioners. Rwanda remained a UN member state during the genocide
there and even retained its seat on the Security Council, its ambassador privy to every discussion about how to stop the killings
his government was carrying out. As news of the slaughter
emerged, the Security Council, rather than reinforce UNAMIR,
actually reduced its force from 2,500 troops to 270. Sudan has
enjoyed all privileges of United Nations membership from the
start of its scorched-earth campaign in Darfur in 2003 to the
present day, and remained a member of the UN's Commission
on Human Rights in 2003, 2004, and 2005. All of these decisions
ultimately resulted, whether intentionally or not, in complicity with evil.

The United Nations' defenders reject this. They argue that
the organization is merely the sum of its member states. If they
lack the political will or the economic and military means to
stop a conflict, then there is nothing the United Nations can
do. The world is increasingly complicated, this reasoning goes,
its political and diplomatic realities complex, especially after
the end of the Cold War—which, for all its faults, brought a
sense of stability and balance between the superpowers. The
United Nations itself is composed of competing interest groups
from the General Assembly through the Security Council, and
even within the Secretariat itself, and it is not the United Nations' fault that the international security mechanisms of 1945
have proved woefully inadequate for the challenges of the 1990s

and after. But what this means in practice is that if everyone is guilty, then no one is guilty. If everyone is responsible, then no one is responsible. This circular, convenient argument has undoubted appeal, not least to the consciences of those responsible for the United Nations' failures, from London and Paris to Washington, D.C., and New York, including those working in the United Nations building itself.

But it is not an adequate answer. If the United Nations, whose very raison d'être is the maintenance of international peace and security, does not bear some responsibility for failing to stop the slaughters in Srebrenica, Rwanda, and Darfur, then who does? The United Nations is the primary instrument through which the world makes its stuttering attempts to stop genocide. It is the United Nations that attempted to ameliorate the suffering in those three crises. Whatever factors shape the United Nations' inner dynamics, however responsibility is divided among the Secretariat, the Security Council, and the General Assembly, the United Nations exists and functions not as merely the sum of these parts but as an institution itself, one with a powerful, global, reach. The United Nations is more than sixty years old. It has experience of dealing with conflict zones from Asia to Latin America, from Africa to the Balkans. It has a powerful institutional memory and considerable moral authority—however battered by recent scandals; for many, it remains the institutionalized hope of their dreams of a better world.

The United Nations is the crucial factor that links Srebrenica, Rwanda, and Darfur. In the past decade it has failed twice to stop or prevent genocide, and it is still failing now. I shall in this book detail the reasons for, and the price of, those failures. They are more complex than the arguments that the Secretariat is merely a vast human computer waiting to be programmed by its masters in the Security Council, the Security

Council a mirror of the interests of the superpowers who dominate its proceedings. I shall show how the repeating patterns of appeasement of genocide that ultimately betrayed the victims of Srebrenica and Rwanda still continue today in Darfur. In this sense the United Nations, as its 2000 report on peacekeeping shows, remains at least passively guilty of "complicity with evil." But this pattern can be broken, and I shall examine some proposals for doing so, including the United Nations' own. Recognizing this possibility, changing the way the United Nations works, can only aid and accelerate the process of making it an organization which can prevent and stop genocide, as well as provide succor to its victims.

Acknowledgments

My thanks go first of all to the numerous United Nations officials and international diplomats, both serving and retired, who generously shared their knowledge and experience with me. Some spoke off the record, but of those who can be named, I am grateful to Madeleine Albright, André Erdős, Peter Galbraith, David Hannay, David Harland, Richard Holbrooke, Douglas Hurd, Ed Joseph, Colin Keating, General Lewis Mackenzie, Haile Menkerios, Jim O'Brien, David Owen, Pierre-Richard Prosper, General Sir Michael Rose, Samir Sanbar, Shashi Tharoor, Danilo Türk, and especially Dr. Michael Williams. Diego Arria and Mo Sacirbey were crucial sources in helping illuminate the saga of the United Nations safe areas and its tragic denouement in Srebrenica, while Dr. Mukesh Kapila brought valuable insight into the UN's response to the crisis in Darfur.

The United Nations press corps was welcoming and helpful to a new arrival on their territory, especially James Bone of the *Times* of London, who readily shared his knowledge and experience, Richard Roth and Elizabeth Neisloss of CNN, and Maggie Farley of the *Los Angeles Times*. The Pulitzer Prize–winning journalists Roy Gutman and David Rohde were very generous with their advice, insight, and suggestions. I am grateful to Patrick Bishop, Yigal Chazan, Justin Leighton, Sam Loe-wenberg, Peter Maass, Mark Milstein, John Nadler, Brendan Simms, and Julius Strauss, all of whom have helped with this book and its themes over the years. Thanks also to Martin Fletcher, Richard Beeston, Gill Ross, and Alice Fordham at the *Times* of London, and to Heather Maher of Transitions Online for a useful seminar on the International Criminal Court. Philip Reeker and Janet Garvey kindly helped open numerous doors in New York and Washington, D.C., as did Michael Ward. Steve Crawshaw of Human Rights Watch was especially helpful; so, too, were Peggy Hicks and Joanna Weschler, and John Prendergast of the International Crisis Group. Bjørn Willum generously supplied a copy of his insightful study of the Secretariat's response to the genocide in Rwanda.

Caroline Lam at the Liddell Hart Centre for Military Archives at King's College London and Pavol Salamon and Niall Walsh at the Open Society Archives in Budapest helped me obtain access to many important documents. Peter, Robert, and Sara Green were warm and welcoming hosts in New York, as was Philip Sherwell in Washington, D.C. Alec Russell and Francis Harris generously let me set up camp in the *Daily Telegraph*'s Washington bureau, while Anna Meller and Kati Tordas diligently transcribed numerous interviews. Adrian Brown, Tom Gross, and Erwin Tuil provided many useful leads. Special thanks to Chris Condon and Roger Boyes, for their encouragement, support, and suggestions.

John Kulka, my editor at Yale University Press, has stead-fastly kept faith with this project from its birth to publication. His thoughtful input and careful guidance have been invaluable. Thanks also to Dan Heaton, for his excellent copyediting, and Lindsay Toland; to Robert Baldock, Anne Bihan, and Hazel Hutchinson at Yale in London; and to Bill Swainson and Ruth

Logan at Bloomsbury UK, who first published my biography of Slobodan Milošević—a work which subsequently inspired this book. My agent, Laura Longrigg, has, as ever, been a much-valued source of advice and support, and thanks also to David Riding. Most of all, my thanks go to my family for sustaining me on a dark journey through recent history.

Abbreviations

AMIS	African (Union) Mission in Sudan
APC	armored personnel carrier
AU	African Union
CAS	close air support (targeted air strikes, as opposed to strategic bombing)
DPA	Department of Political Affairs
DPI	Department of Public Information
DPKO	Department of Peacekeeping Operations
EC	European Community (forerunner of the European Union)
ESC	Economics and Social Council
EU	European Union
HRC	Human Rights Council
ICC	International Criminal Court
ICI	International Commission of Inquiry (on Darfur)
ICJ	International Court of Justice
ICRC	International Committee of the Red Cross
ICTR	International criminal tribunal for Rwanda
ICTY	International criminal tribunal for the former Yugoslavia

IDP	internally displaced person (a refugee in one's own country)
JEM	Justice and Equality Movement (rebel force in Darfur)
JNA	Yugoslav national army (Jugoslavenska Narodna Armija)
MONUC	United Nations Mission in Congo (Mission de l'Organisation des Nations Unies en République démocratique du Congo)
MSF	Doctors Without Borders (Médecins Sans Frontières)
NAC	Non-Aligned Caucus
NATO	North Atlantic Treaty Organisation
NIF	National Islamic Front
OCHA	Office for the Coordination of Humanitarian Affairs
OHCHR	Office of the United Nations High Commissioner for Refugees
OLA	Office of Legal Affairs
OP	observation post
PAIC	Popular Arab and Islamic Conference
P5	shorthand for the five permanent members of the Security Council: the United States, Great Britain, France, Russia, and China
P3	shorthand for the United States, Great Britain, and France
RPF	Rwandan Patriotic Front
RSK	Republic of Serb Krajina (Serb-occupied Croatia)
SAS	Special Air Service (British special forces)
SLA	Sudan Liberation Army (rebel force in Darfur)
SPLA	Sudan People's Liberation Army (rebel force in south Sudan)
SPLM	Sudan People's Liberation Movement (political arm of the SPLA)

SRSG	special representative of the secretary general
UNHCR	United Nations High Commissioner for Refugees
UNMIL	United Nations mission to Liberia
UNMIS	United Nations mission in Sudan (North-South)
UNMO	United Nations military observer
UNPROFOR	United Nations protection force for the former Yugoslavia
WFP	World Food Programme
WHO	World Health Organization

"Complicity with Evil"

Introduction

I first encountered the United Nations in the summer of
1992, at its headquarters in Zagreb, capital of the newly independent state of Croatia. I presented a UN official with a
letter from the newspaper for which I worked, the *Times*
(of London), my passport, and two photographs. In return,
she issued me with a small piece of plastic about two inches by
three, emblazoned with a blue stripe marked "Press," and the
emblem of the United Nations, a globe encircled by two olive
branches, symbolizing a peaceful world. I was now officially
accredited to UNPROFOR, the UN protection force deployed
in the former Yugoslavia, able to cross UN checkpoints on the
front lines and fly in and out of the war zone on UN airplanes.

But the world was not very peaceful that summer, especially in the Bosnian capital Sarajevo. Besieged by Bosnian Serbs,
Sarajevo was a giant shooting gallery, ringed by heavy artillery,
mortars, and snipers. Serb gunners lobbed in shells against the
city's hospitals; Serb snipers shot down men, women, and children as they sprinted for safety. The safest way in or out was on
UN relief flights, ironically called Maybe Airlines by the UN
troops who controlled Sarajevo airport. Ours took off from Zagreb, carrying ten tons of food and aid supplies and several

journalists cracking bad jokes to disguise their nervousness. We flew high over the jagged Croatian coastline, its islands scattered across a turquoise sea, banked sharply as we entered Bosnian airspace, and descended hard and fast toward Sarajevo airport. The journey from peaceful Mittel European capital to hell on earth took just forty minutes. As we climbed down onto the tarmac, the blue-helmeted UN soldiers ordered us to leave the area *immediately.* The noise hit us like a wall of sound: the boom of artillery fire, the rattle of machine guns, and the sharp crack of semiautomatic rifles. The airport check-in area was shot to pieces, its floor carpeted with empty bullet cases. We sprinted to a nearby van and roared into town down a side street, avoiding the perilous main road, which had been dubbed Sniper's Alley. As we passed the UN checkpoint that controlled access to the airport, the debris of war was everywhere: wrecked buildings that had collapsed in on themselves, piles of charred rubble, broken glass glittering in the summer sun, houses with their windows shot out, cars riddled with so many bullet holes they looked liked sieves, the streets empty and deserted.

I thought little of the UN checkpoint at the time, but over the next few days it began to bother me. Why was it there? On whose authority? Those without UN papers couldn't even get to the airport, let alone board a relief plane out. I was a British national, yet merely because I had a UN press pass I could enter and leave Sarajevo at will. I was a war zone VIP. Bosnia-Herzegovina was a sovereign state and a member of the United Nations. Yet that same United Nations was preventing Bosnian nationals from entering or leaving their own country. The Sarajevo airport was a kind of mini-Bosnia itself. Bosnian Serbs were dug in at both ends of the runway, while the territory on either side was controlled by the Bosnian gov-

ernment. Butmir, the suburb across the runway, was not besieged. Butmir meant freedom. By late 1992, starving, desperate Sarajevans tried to sprint the several hundred yards across
the runway to Butmir at night. UNPROFOR troops intercepted
them, caught them and brought them to the city. Those few
trying to smuggle food into Sarajevo were taken back to Butmir, and their provisions were confiscated.

And the UN soldiers had night-vision equipment. If they
could not catch the runners, they illuminated them with the
spotlights from their armored personnel carriers. Serb snipers
and machine gunners immediately opened fire. Some of the
runners were killed, but the wounded were picked up by
UNPROFOR and taken to Kosevo hospital in Sarajevo. When
the international press in Sarajevo questioned UN spokesmen
about its actions against those trying to cross the runway, they
said that the rules were set by the Security Council. Challenged
about this claim, and asked for details of the Security Council
session which stipulated that desperate women and children
fleeing the besieged city must be lit up at night, the UN spokesmen were unable to provide details. UNPROFOR then fielded
a spokesman who could barely speak English to dodge difficult
questions. The situation was aptly described by the American
author and journalist Peter Maass, author of *Love Thy Neighbor*, as "a psychotic vaudeville."[1]

The United Nations declared itself neutral and impartial,
but UNPROFOR's actions at Sarajevo airport demonstrated
that these were elastic concepts. In Bosnia, as in every war zone,
the black market flourished, but this one was fed mainly by
stolen United Nations supplies, some of which were looted by
UN soldiers themselves. There was no postal service or international telephone lines, so Sarajevans passed letters to de-
parting journalists to post from outside the country. The jour-

nalists soon learned to hide their friends' letters in their flak jackets to prevent them from being confiscated as "contraband" by the UN soldiers at the airport. The United Nations had paid a high price for the Serbs' permission for aid flights to land: it was helping administer the siege. Some UN officials even denied that Sarajevo was under siege. Instead, they claimed that the Serbs were merely in a "tactically advantageous situation." The United Nations aid operation was keeping Bosnia alive, but whatever its intentions, the United Nations, I soon realized, was not the solution but part of the problem.

This was not what the United Nations' founders had envisaged when the organization was established a few months after the end of the Second World War by a world weary of war and destruction. Fifty countries gathered in San Francisco in June 1945 to sign the UN Charter. Its preamble calls on its members to "save succeeding generations from the scourge of war, which twice in our lifetime has brought untold sorrow to mankind, and to reaffirm faith in fundamental human rights, in the dignity and worth of the human person, in the equal rights of men and women and of nations large and small." These noble principles were reinforced by the Universal Declaration of Human Rights and the Convention on the Prevention and Punishment of the Crime of Genocide. Together, these three documents are the most advanced formulation of the principles of human rights in history, and they have for decades been comprehensively flouted by UN member states, often with impunity.

The United Nations is composed of six principal bodies. The three most important are the General Assembly, the Security Council, and the Secretariat (its civil servants). The other three principal bodies are the Trusteeship Council, which oversaw the independence of United Nations trust territories; the International Court of Justice, which deals with disputes between states; and the Economics and Social Council (ESC), whose various commissions deal with such issues as human rights, development, and sustainable development. The United Nations also has numerous satellite programs. Many of these, such as the World Food Programme (WFP), the United Nations Children's Fund (UNICEF), the United Nations High Commissioner for Refugees (UNHCR), and the Office for the Coordination of Humanitarian Affairs (OCHA), carry out vital work, saving lives and bringing succor in war and disaster zones. The focus of this book is the response of the United Nations to genocide. My conclusions are necessarily critical, but the book is not—and should not be read as—a blanket condemnation of the United Nations organization, and especially not of the UN humanitarian organizations, whose staff in the field frequently work in conditions of hardship and peril, and did so during the three crises examined here. In fact, as will be evident over the following pages, UN humanitarian officials often clash with the powerful Department of Political Affairs (DPA), the secretary general's advisers, and the members of the Security Council, when their ideals conflict with the demands of superpower policy and realpolitik.

There are 191 members of the General Assembly, each with one vote. The assembly is divided into five regional groups: African, Asian, Latin American, Eastern European, and Western European and others. The votes of Bhutan, bordering India (population 2.2 million) and the Palau islands southeast of the Philippines (population 20,000), for example, are equally weighted with those of the United States, Russia, and China. This may be one reason why General Assembly votes have some political significance but are not binding on member states.

The decisions of the Security Council, however, are binding. The Council has primary responsibility for maintaining international peace and security. It can authorize sanctions, peacekeeping missions, the severance of diplomatic relations, the creation of war crimes tribunals, and, crucially, military action against a member state. Power on the Council rests with the permanent five members, known as the P5: the United States, the United Kingdom, Russia, France, and China. Ten nonpermanent members are elected by the General Assembly's regional groups for two-year terms, with five replaced each year. Nine votes are needed to pass a resolution, but any of the P5 can veto a measure it opposes. The veto is rarely actually used, as there is a strong drive to pass consensus measures; as a result, resolutions often are watered down so much that they are meaningless in terms of practical effect. The real diplomatic work is done before a resolution is brought to the meeting, although blunt veto-wielding threats are also rare: the favored formula is that a particular clause is "unacceptable"—code for a veto threat. This archaic structure gives enormous influence to the victors of the Second World War, more than six decades after that conflict ended, and almost none to the ten nonpermanent members. Not surprisingly, the P5 resist any move to broaden the permanent membership, even though pressure is growing from countries such as India, Japan, Brazil, and Nigeria to make the Council's membership more representative.

Once the Security Council has taken its decision, the Secretariat implements its wishes, through the different departments such as Peacekeeping Operations, Political Affairs, or Humanitarian Affairs. The head of the Secretariat is the secretary general, defined in the UN Charter as the "Chief Administrative Officer." This is a vast understatement: the secretary general wields enormous power and influence within the United

Nations, although not always outside its corridors. The "SG," as he is known (a woman has never held the post), is charged with a delicate balancing act between the member states' right to national sovereignty and the United Nations' mission to ensure international peace and security. He has great moral authority, and Article 99 of the UN Charter grants him the power to "bring to the attention of the Security Council any matter which threatens the maintenance of international peace and security." He has many other means of exerting pressure on an issue—for example, by issuing a statement either personally or through his spokesman, by writing letters to specific ambassadors or to the president of the General Assembly, or, more often, through behind-the-scenes diplomacy. The Secretariat's 8,900 officials portray themselves as impartial civil servants, merely waiting for their orders from the Security Council. In fact, the Secretariat is extremely influential. Senior officials, especially in the office of the secretary general and the DPA, can and do help set the United Nations' agenda—sometimes with unhappy results, as will become evident. The relationship between the Security Council and the Secretariat is crucial to understanding the United Nations in the age of modern genocide. Their symbiotic entwining has helped shape the United Nations' failures in Bosnia, Rwanda, and Darfur.

Genocide is the most egregious crime against humanity, and the severest breach of the United Nations' three founding documents: the Charter, the Universal Declaration of Human Rights and the Genocide Convention. In the first part of this book I scrutinize the Bosnian tragedy at some length and in considerable detail, but from a new and hitherto largely unexplored perspective. Other works about Bosnia, and Srebrenica, are recounted from the bottom up—that is, from the perspective of a journalist, aid worker, or victim of ethnic cleansing. I take the opposite, top-down, approach. The book focuses in particular on the relationships between the Secretariat, the Security Council, and the superpowers. It illustrates that the Srebrenica massacre was not an isolated incident but part of a complex of events unfolding in parallel on the battlefield and at the United Nations. The book reveals the insider details of the diplomacy and behind-the-scenes deals in spring 1993 that led to Security Council resolutions 819, 824, and 836, which defined both the so-called safe areas and the limits of the United Nations' response to attacks on them. In addition, I examine the tensions *within* different departments of the Secretariat, especially between the Department of Peacekeeping Operations (DPKO) in New York and UNPROFOR in Zagreb, which so hindered a robust response to the Bosnian genocide. In so doing I hope to bring a fresh perspective to our understanding of the inner workings of the United Nations.

This is intended to be much more than a historical study; it should indeed have a powerful contemporary resonance. By recounting at length the reasons for, and results of, the catastrophe at Srebrenica, I hope to provide a detailed template for understanding why the United Nations has not stopped genocide in Darfur. I shall show that the same feeble response mechanisms, inertia, bureaucratic infighting within the Secretariat, and crucial lack of political will by the Security Council to stop the killing remain entrenched. The philosopher George Santayana was perhaps too optimistic: it seems that even those who *can* remember the past are sometimes condemned to repeat it.

To understand how the past can keep on being repeated, at such an awful human cost, I have stepped inside the building and gone behind the scenes to dissect the United Nations' inner workings. I highlight the Security Council's repeated neglect of its duties to implement the United Nations Charter to protect sovereign nations, and ethnic groups, in favor of a cynical real-politik that sacrifices those deemed inconvenient. Nowhere has this been the case more than in Bosnia. P5 diplomats and politicians and some UN officials still try and portray the Bosnian Serbs' massacre of their Bosniak prisoners as an "aberration," a kind of bloodthirsty Balkan madness, unique in its brutality. In fact, it should have been entirely foreseeable, part of a pattern of mass murder by the Serbs of POWs that began with the fall of Vukovar, Croatia, in November 1991. More than 200 men and 2 women—one of them five months pregnant—who had taken refuge at the hospital were driven to a ravine, lined up, and shot into a mass grave, which was then bulldozed over.[2] The Security Council itself published a preliminary report on the mass grave holding the remains of these prisoners, based on an investigation by Physicians for Human Rights, in February 1993. No modern war was better reported than the Yugoslav wars of the 1990s, and nobody who mattered, whether diplomat or UN official, could claim not to understand the reality of ethnic cleansing and that any male prisoners who fell into the hands of the Bosnian Serbs were in extreme peril.

The crisis in Darfur, the westernmost region of Sudan, began in spring 2003, after rebels took up arms to demand greater rights and an equitable share of Sudan's resources. In response the Sudanese government launched a systematic scorched-earth campaign: not merely to defeat the rebels but to destroy the society from which they came. By spring 2006 two million people had been displaced from their homes and more than 400,000 had died of illness, malnutrition, or exposure or had been killed.[3] The ethnic-cleansing operations were mainly carried out by the Janjaweed, an Arab militia armed, trained, and funded by the Sudanese government and supported in its attacks by the

Sudanese armed forces. The complex tribal and pastoral society of Darfur has vanished, probably forever. The United Nations has sent a peacekeeping force to Sudan, but only to oversee the Naivasha Accords, which ended a separate conflict between the government and south Sudanese rebels. For all the merits of ending that war, the practical effect is that UN troops are deployed in a former war zone that is now at peace, while ignoring a genocide still taking place in the same country.

Perhaps those responsible for the slaughter in Darfur will eventually be brought to trial, although it will be too late for their victims. Like genocide, international criminal justice has been a growth industry in the late twentieth and early twenty-first century. Genocide is not a modern crime, but it is a modern term. The word was invented by a Polish lawyer named Rafael Lemkin. During the 1930s, Lemkin lobbied the United Nations' predecessor, the League of Nations, for passage of international laws against the destruction of a people and its culture. Lemkin, in a legal essay proposing that the crime of "Barbarity" be made an offence against international law, shaped the legal debate about crimes against humanity. Lemkin's arguments were based on his studies of the massacres of the Armenians and Assyrians in the Ottoman Empire during the First World War. The methods used by the Turks were later adopted by both the Serbs in the early 1990s and the Sudanese government a decade later: raising militias composed of former prisoners to commit atrocities; publicly executing notables and community leaders to break the victims' will; destroying not just homes but the very means of life; polluting wells, fields, and water supplies.

Lemkin's proposals were received with interest but were soon overtaken by events when the Second World War broke out in September 1939. He returned to Poland and fought in the defense of the capital, Warsaw, before fleeing to Sweden. Eventually, he made his way to the United States. Lemkin published his most important work in 1944, *Axis Rule in Occupied Europe: Laws of Occupation, Analysis of Government, Proposals for Redress*. Lemkin's detailed analysis of Nazi occupation and its breaches of law was the first work to contain the word *genocide,* from *genos,* Greek for people or race, and the Latin *caedere,* to cut or kill. Genocide is now often defined as the organized extermination of a nation, people, or ethnic group, such as the Nazi Holocaust or the Hutu extermination of the Tutsis in Rwanda in 1994. But this was not Lemkin's definition of the term.

The mass killings of all members of a nation, or the implementation of plans with the intent of mass killings, indeed constitute genocide, but Lemkin gave the word a broader meaning. Genocide, he argued, can also be a coordinated plan of "different actions aiming at the destruction of essential foundations of the life of national groups, with the aim of annihilating the groups themselves. The objectives of such a plan would be the disintegration of the political and social institutions, of culture, language, national feelings, religion, and the economic existence of national groups, and the destruction of the personal security, liberty, health, dignity, and even the lives of the individuals belonging to such groups."[4] Or, in layman's terms, creating conditions calculated to cause the death of national groups, —poisoning water supplies, for example, or destroying the means of life—can be genocide as much as actually executing the victims.

Lemkin's definition was further broadened in December 1948, when the UN General Assembly approved the Convention on the Prevention and Punishment of the Crime of Genocide for ratification by member states. The Convention is an internationally recognized definition of genocide, based on Lemkin's

writings. It expanded his "national" groups and defined genocide as:

> any of the following acts committed with intent to
> destroy, in whole or in part, a national, ethnical,
> racial, or religious group, as such:
> (a) Killing members of the group;
> (b) Causing serious bodily or mental harm to
>   members of the group;
> (c) Deliberately inflicting on the group condi-
>   tions of life calculated to bring about its
>   physical destruction in whole or in part;
> (d) Imposing measures intended to prevent
>   births within the group;
> (e) Forcibly transferring children of the group
>   to another group

Darfur then ranks as genocide, on counts *a*, *b*, and especially
c through the systematic destruction of Darfur's villages and
crops. Srebrenica was a genocide on counts *a*, *b*, *c*, and *d*, as
men were killed to prevent them having more children so that
the "group" would die out. In Rwanda, Hutu militiamen killed
800,000 Tutsis and moderate Hutus in three months with clear
intent to destroy a "national group."

The Convention came into force under international law
in January 1951, but many of the Western powers did not ratify
it for decades: Britain did so in 1970, and the United States, ever
wary of international legal obligations, only in 1988. Article 1 of
the Convention is probably one of the most important clauses
in an international legal document ever to have been published:
"The Contracting Parties confirm that genocide, whether committed in time of peace or in time of war, is a crime under

international law which they undertake to prevent and to punish." The Convention has been breached far more than observed, however. The United Nations, especially the Security Council, is extremely reluctant to use the word *genocide* during a conflict because of the obligation to try and stop it. Neither Bosnia nor Rwanda nor Darfur has been officially declared the site of a genocide by the United Nations during the killing.

Initially, at least, the genocides of the 1990s took the United Nations and the world by surprise. Détente between the superpowers in the 1970s and the collapse of communism in 1989 had ushered in an era of cautious optimism. The zero-sum game between the United States and the Soviet Union, the use of proxies to compete for power and influence, as in the Arab-Israeli conflict, was—in theory—over. Even during the Cold War the United Nations had enjoyed several successes: the Suez crisis of 1956, the 1965 war between India and Pakistan, and the 1973 Arab-Israeli conflict had all been contained and prevented from igniting a superpower conflagration. In later years the United Nations helped end the eight-year war between Iran and Iraq in 1988; negotiated an agreement on the withdrawal of Soviet troops from Afghanistan; and helped wind down the conflicts in Namibia, in Central America, and along the Indian-Pakistani border.

By the early twenty-first century UN peacekeepers and military observers were deployed across the world, from Cyprus to Liberia, from Georgia to the Ivory Coast. Until the wars of the 1990s, most traditional UN peacekeeping operations had three criteria: the force was inserted only after the conflict was over, with the consent of the warring parties and its troops, was armed only with light weapons, and would fire only in self-defense. The underlying causes of the conflicts may have remained unresolved, but the killing stopped, or was at least greatly reduced. The peacekeepers observed rather than enforced.

In fact there is no provision within the UN Charter for peacekeeping as such. Chapter VI of the Charter, which deals with the peaceful settlement of disputes between member states through negotiations and mediation, does not mention the possibility of military operations. Chapter VII deals with enforcement, and ultimately military intervention, through a three-stage process. Article 40 allows the Security Council to call on the offending parties to comply with "provisional measures" to stop conflicts. If these are not observed, article 41 provides for such nonmilitary measures as economic, financial, and cultural sanctions against the offending state. If these prove insufficient, article 42 states that the Council "may take such action by air, sea, or land forces as may be necessary to maintain or restore international peace and security. Such action may include demonstrations, blockade, and other operations by air, sea, or land forces of Members of the United Nations." Article 45 specifically states that member states must make available "national air-force contingents for combined international enforcement action." Dag Hammarskjöld, secretary general during the 1950s, described peacekeeping operations as "Chapter Six-and-a-half."

In September 1988 the UN peacekeepers won the Nobel Peace Prize, and the head of the peacekeeping department, a British diplomat named Marrack Goulding, flew to Stockholm, to represent the United Nations at the celebrations. There Goulding gave a speech on what he called the "noble paradox" of peacekeeping. With hindsight it is clear that what Goulding saw as peacekeeping's strength would, in Bosnia, Rwanda, and Darfur, prove to be its greatest weaknesses. His words now have a macabre resonance: "For peacekeeping soldiers carry arms only to avoid using them; they are military forces but their orders are to avoid, at almost any cost, the use of force; they are asked in the last resort to risk their own lives rather than open fire on those between whom they have been sent to keep the peace."[5] This doctrine, which had some success in dealing with states and governments that respected the norms of international law, has proved woefully inadequate for modern conflicts fought by rogue regimes, militias, and paramilitaries.

The United Nations is the successor to the League of Nations. Founded in 1919 after the end of the First World War, the League comprised forty-four member states that pledged to prevent further armed conflicts through collective security, negotiation, and diplomacy. The League's Covenant called on its members to preserve the territorial integrity and political independence of every member state if threatened by aggression. Any act or threat of war was to be considered "a matter of concern" to the whole League. When in the early 1930s Benito Mussolini, dictator of Fascist Italy, threatened the small east African nation of Abyssinia (now Ethiopia), its ruler, Emperor Haile Selassie, naïvely put his faith in the League, believing it would keep his country safe. The League duly stated that Italy's aggression would not triumph and Abyssinia would be protected. It was not. When Italy invaded in October 1935, the League stood idly by. The Italian air force sprayed fields, villages, and towns with mustard gas, poisoning wells and rivers, polluting fields, and killing thousands of innocent civilians. This would have been classified as a genocide had the word then existed.

The poorly armed Abyssinians were no match for the Italians, and in May 1936 Mussolini's troops marched into the capital, Addis Ababa, and declared the country a province of Italy. The royal family went into exile, and in June 1936 Haile Selassie addressed the League's assembly in Geneva, the first head of state to do so. He spoke with great dignity, and with our knowledge of what soon followed in Europe, his speech is chillingly prescient: "There has never before been an example of any government proceeding to the systematic extermination of a nation by barbarous means, in violation of the most solemn promises made by the nations of the earth that there should not be used against innocent human beings the terrible poison of harmful gases." He called upon the League to implement its promises of collective security and of protecting weak nations against the strong; to help Abyssinia regain its sovereignty; and to take action against Italy. In response the League imposed weak and ineffective sanctions, and several member states recognized Italy's conquests.

This book is rooted in my own experiences covering the war in Bosnia, which also inspired my earlier biography of Slobodan Milošević. Much is recorded in United Nations internal documents, which make a rich paper trail for those delving into the organization's inner workings. Perhaps the most revealing is a cable from the United Nations' most senior official in Yugoslavia, Yasushi Akashi. It records that in May 1995 he refused to authorize air strikes against the Bosnian Serbs, partly in order to strengthen the position of Milošević, the Serbian president, who six years later was charged with war crimes and genocide in Bosnia at the United Nations' own tribunal.

In addition to internal UN documents, the book is based on my own lengthy interviews with dozens of United Nations officials, international diplomats, and statesmen and stateswomen with firsthand experience of the three crises examined here. I conducted these interviews at the UN headquarters in New York, in Washington, D.C., and in London. I also drew upon my own reporting of the Yugoslav wars and that of my colleagues. But the interviews are the core of the book and bring a unique insight, peeling away the usual bland "diplomat-speak." They reveal how superpower politics is really conducted at the United Nations. These voices bring recent history alive. Peter Galbraith, US ambassador to Croatia during the Bosnian war, speaks frankly about his repeated arguments with Akashi over the need for the United Nations to take stronger action against the Serbs. Richard Holbrooke, the chief architect of the Dayton peace agreements that ended the Bosnian war, and Madeleine Albright, the former secretary of state and US ambassador to the United Nations during the Bosnian war and the Rwandan genocide, disclose the inner workings of both the United Nations and the Clinton administration as it struggled to formulate responses to both crises. Albright reveals as well the anguish that still haunts her for their failure.

The British ambassador to the United Nations, David Hannay, and his former boss, Foreign Secretary Douglas Hurd, defend policies that their critics decry as appeasement of genocide but also question, with hindsight, whether they always made the right decisions with regard to Bosnia. David Owen, the European Community negotiator during the Yugoslav wars, argues, perhaps surprisingly, that had NATO fired a couple of well-targeted cruise missiles against the Serb defense ministry in the early years of the Yugoslav wars, many more people might still be alive. A decade after Srebrenica, UN officials themselves speak frankly about the growing split within the organization during the Bosnian war over the increasing calls for military action against the Serbs. A substantial number of those I interviewed are still employed at the United Nations and so were unable to speak on the record. But the cloak of anonymity was often a boon. It allowed those Secretariat officials, many of whom still believe passionately in the United Nations' founding ideals, to speak far more frankly. This was especially true in regard to Darfur. I was fortunate to interview a wide range of officials dealing with Sudan, many of whom had biting and trenchant criticisms of the United Nations' failure to stop the killing.

Nor are the smaller countries denied their say: some of the most telling testimony in the book comes from Venezuela's ambassador to the United Nations during the Bosnian war, Diego Arria, Hungary's envoy André Erdős, and New Zealand's ambassador Colin Keating. Arria and Erdős told me that they were first amazed, then appalled, as they watched the major powers treat newly independent Bosnia as little more than an irritant, inconveniently disrupting the usual smooth flow of business. Erdős outlines the Security Council P5's treatment of the ten nonpermanent members as second-class citizens. Colin Keating reports that the quality of information supplied by the Secretariat during the Rwandan genocide was so dismal that he was forced to attend briefings by such organizations as Human Rights Watch and then relay what he had learned to the Security Council. The most senior United Nations humanitarian official in Sudan from 2003 to 2004, a British doctor named Mukesh Kapila, recalls that the Secretariat ignored his repeated reports of atrocities for fear that they would jeopardize the Naivasha accords that ended the conflict with the south Sudanese rebels. UN officials themselves outline how a culture of "buck passing" and unwillingness to accept personal responsibility has prevented the development of mechanisms for accountability within the Secretariat.

I spent much time at the UN headquarters in New York, a complex in downtown Manhattan that stretches from 48th Street and First Avenue to 42nd Street, across eighteen acres. The thirty-nine-story skyscraper at its center is the world's most concentrated global village, its corridors, cafes, and bars echoing to a myriad of languages. The UN headquarters is a pleasant place to work, especially for those who don't publicly rock the boat. Salaries are attractive, boosted by a wide range of allowances and generous per diems for those in the field. Junior staff working for UNMIK, the UN's mission in Kosovo in 2000, for example, took home more than $6,000 a month. There is an excellent subsidized canteen, a spacious lounge for the delegates, and a restaurant that is one of Manhattan's best-kept secrets. Apart from US nationals, UN staffers do not pay tax, although about 25 percent of their salary is deducted for "staff assessments." While the pay levels do not match those of Wall Street, there are plentiful opportunities for foreign travel, and for relocation to the UN satellite operations in such places as Geneva, Vienna, and Bangkok. Upon retirement, a senior official usually has little difficulty finding a comfortable post at a university or think tank.

Some employees have two bosses: it is an open secret that some Secretariat officials are spies, reporting back to their home intelligence services. The former British Cabinet Minister Clare Short enraged the British government when she claimed in 2004 that she had been given transcripts of some of Kofi Annan's conversations, recorded by British spies.[6] Others in the Secretariat are, at best, happy passengers on the United Nations gravy train. UN insiders complain that many have been given positions for which they lack both experience and qualifications merely so that the Secretariat may reflect the diversity of the United Nations' member states.

The UN headquarters, built in the 1950s, is showing its age. Its carpets are worn, its paintwork grubby and peeling. The buildings, like the ideals of the UN Charter, are neglected. Seventy years after Emperor Haile Selassie addressed the League of Nations, his questions remain unanswered. The League abandoned Abyssinia. The United Nations failed Srebrenica and Rwanda, and a decade later Darfur was still burning. "Is it the Covenant that needs reform? What undertakings can have any value if the will to keep them is lacking? It is international morality which is at stake, not the articles of the Covenant," the emperor proclaimed. His words still echo down the corridors of the United Nations headquarters: "God and history will remember your judgment."

Part I

I
A Safe Area

The main demand is for the United Nations
to be impartial and objective.
—*Slobodan Milošević, Serbian president, 1995*

The video begins with an Orthodox priest blessing the Serb paramilitaries before they go forth. They stand in a row, AK-47 assault rifles in their hands, red berets atop their shaved heads. Flanked by two giant black flags, the priest brushes the soldiers' heads with a handful of greenery as they file past. The date stamp shows that it is 7:30 P.M., 25 June 1995, a few days before the Serbs' final attack on Srebrenica.

The recording then cuts to a road in eastern Bosnia. It is a warm, sunny day, some time after the capture of the town. The soldiers, members of a unit called the Scorpions, are standing around a green army truck. The prisoners scramble out, hands tied behind their backs. They are Bosniak (Bosnian Muslim) civilians. Their faces are gaunt and fearful, their clothes dirty and ragged. One is bleeding heavily from his face. The Serbs sneer and mock, ordering the prisoners to lie in the grass, close to each other. One, Azmir Alispahić, is sixteen years old, another, Safet Fejzić, seventeen. Azmir wanted to be a doctor. He fled Srebrenica on 11 July, the day the town fell, returning briefly to kiss his mother good-bye, before trying to flee north to the city of Tuzla. The boys and men wriggle closer to one another. One man's feet are bare and move from side to side, pale flashes in the dirt.

The Scorpions smoke, chat, and joke. They are completely at ease. and do not mind being recorded, for they believe they are far beyond the reach of any law, with the absolute power of life and death. There is no reason for them to think otherwise. Until recently the prisoners lived in Srebrenica, a United Nations safe area, protected by Dutch peacekeepers. More Serb soldiers appear, and they mingle and talk for a while. They order the prisoners to march around a bend in the road, and to walk off the road into the grass. Azmir, Safet, and the others obey, their heads bowed. The Serbs order them to line up and walk forward, one by one. The first prisoner shuffles ahead. One of the Scorpions shoulders his weapon, peers down its sight, and takes aim at the prisoner's back.

The United Nations' road to Srebrenica begins in the summer of 1991 and the start of the Yugoslav wars. The conflicts were portrayed as impossibly complicated, rooted in arcane "ancient ethnic hatreds" reaching back to the clash of swords on medieval battlefields. The subtext was that nothing could be done to stop the carnage. But there was nothing mysterious about the Serb onslaughts on Croatia and Bosnia. They were carefully planned, and meticulously realized. In many ways, such as the role of Serbia's broadcast media in preparing for war, the secret service's autonomous state-within-a-state, and the sophisticated international disinformation campaign against Croatia and Bosnia, they were very modern conflicts, fought in the most advanced country in eastern Europe.

As communism collapsed, Yugoslavia's neighbors transformed into democracies and began the long haul toward membership in the European Union and NATO. Like Czechoslovakia, Yugoslavia, too, could have dissolved peacefully—into its constituent republics of Serbia, Bosnia-Herzegovina, Croatia, Macedonia, Slovenia, and Montenegro. But war was a deliberate choice for the Serbian ruling elite, to maintain its political power and economic privileges. The dark genius of President Slobodan Milošević was to unite disparate interest groups as the old certainties crumbled. Nationalist academicians found common cause with army generals to resurrect ancient irredentist fantasies. Corrupt local potentates allied with the secret service to protect their business empires. More specifically, the Vojna Linija, or Military Line faction in the Yugoslav army (JNA), delineated the borders of Greater Serbia and annexed the areas in Croatia and Bosnia where Serbs lived. And if some in the JNA were uncertain about firing heavy artillery on their fellow citizens, the doubters' ranks would be filled by the paramilitaries, criminals released from prison, armed and funded by the secret service, free to rape and murder.

The fighting began in June, after Croatia and Slovenia declared independence. After a few days' skirmishing, the JNA pulled out of Slovenia. But Croatia, home to 650,000 Serbs, was a different matter. By winter 1991, with the help of the JNA, rebel Serbs had captured about a third of the country, which

they renamed the Republic of Serb Krajina (RSK). The RSK's
leader was a sinister, baby-faced dentist named Milan Babić.
His forces had committed widespread war crimes, including
mass murder and ethnic cleansing. The United Nations considered Babić a serious negotiating partner. Warlords who should
have been arrested for war crimes—and who later were—were
treated as Balkan statesmen, a pattern that would continue
through both the Croatian and Bosnian wars. Among the UN's
interlocutors was the British diplomat Sir Marrack Goulding,
head of peacekeeping. He recalls in his memoirs: "Babić was a
major thorn in our flesh but I liked him and admired the
power of his intellect and his fearless defence of what he saw as
his people's interests." Babić's "fearless defence" of his people's
interests brought them, and him, nothing but misery. Babić
committed suicide in March 2006 in his cell at the UN Detention Centre in The Hague, sentenced to thirteen years in prison
for crimes against humanity.[1]

   After six months of fighting, under severe pressure from
Germany, the European Community (EC) agreed to recognize
Croatia on 15 January 1992. This left Bosnia with two choices:
declare independence or remain in a Serb-dominated Yugoslavia. The Bosnians asked the United Nations for help. Shashi
Tharoor, Marrack Goulding's bright young special assistant,
and Herb Okun, an American diplomat, met Vice President
Ejup Ganić in Belgrade. Ganić said that the EC had given Bosnia
a week to apply for recognition as an independent state, but to
do so without the consent of all three communities, Bosniaks,
Serbs, and Croats, would violate its own constitution. War would
break out. But, he told Tharoor, "the train is about to leave the
station, and if we don't take a ticket we will miss it."

   Ganić asked for ten thousand peacekeepers. Tharoor said
his delegation would convey his request to the Security Coun-

cil, but he thought it unlikely that the Council would agree.
Tharoor recalls:

> This was the level of expectation from the Bosnians
> based on the pursuance rather fecklessly of a Euro-
> pean decision that had not been formed in the cru-
> cible of the United Nations and had not been dis-
> cussed with the other members. It was unthinkable
> that a Security Council with India and China on it
> would send troops to a sovereign member state of
> the United Nations to help a part of that state secede.
> It was impossible. We said that we understood his
> dilemma, but if the Europeans are pushing you into
> a corner, have them send you ten thousand troops.
> But the Europeans weren't geared up for that.

Tharoor had a point. Germany's insistence on rapid diplomatic recognition of Croatia, and its failure to understand the
consequences for Bosnia, caused widespread alarm among the
Secretariat. General Secretary Javier Pérez de Cuellar, a Peru-
vian diplomat who was coming to the end of his second term,
warned Germany that recognizing Croatia would, by forcing
Bosnia to decide on independence, spread the war. But it was
the United Nations, not the EC, that had a peacekeeping department, with troops deployed across the world. And it was
the United Nations, not the EC, that had the moral authority
to call for emergency action to prevent a conflict of which it
had clearly been forewarned. "When the war started in Croatia,
Hungary and Austria both warned the Security Council that
the very moment this spills over into Bosnia, it will be hell," recalls André Erdős, Hungary's ambassador to the United Nations, who sat on the Security Council from 1992 to 1993. "We

knew the conditions in Bosnia, we understood Bosnia because of our history. But some others did not think like this." On 6 April the EC recognized Bosnia-Herzegovina, and the Serbs commenced their dismemberment of the country. Bosnia joined the United Nations the following month, theoretically protected by article 2 of chapter I of the UN Charter, enshrining member states' territorial integrity, and article 51 of chapter VII, guaranteeing the right of self-defense. The United Nations itself would ensure that this did not happen.

Up in his office on the thirty-eighth floor of the United Nations Secretariat building, with its panoramic view overlooking the East River, Secretary General Boutros Boutros-Ghali seemed little interested in Bosnia. A francophone Egyptian Christian, Boutros-Ghali had succeeded Pérez de Cuellar in January 1992. The sixth secretary general famously dismissed the Bosnian conflict as "a rich people's war." His critics argued that he blended Gallic pomposity with a secretive authoritarianism. He certainly resented the influence and power of the United States within the United Nations. "Boutros-Ghali was an old-style diplomat of the Sorbonne school," says James Bone of the *Times* of London, a veteran UN correspondent. "He resented all the attention that was given to the Balkans, which he thought came at the expense of conflicts in Somalia and elsewhere that were being ignored. I think he was wrong, because rich people's wars are much more dangerous than poor people's wars, and he never really understood that." Boutros-Ghali regarded himself as one of the world's diplomatic elite, licensed to solve all the world's problems, says a United States diplomat then posted to the United Nations. "Boutros-Ghali saw himself as the commissar of the world. He never wanted the United Nations to be involved in Bosnia. He assumed, correctly, that Bosnia would chew up the United Nations and destroy his term as secretary general. But instead of being robust, he went to the opposite extreme."

Boutros-Ghali did not find life in the war zone to his taste. On 31 December 1992 he visited Sarajevo, for six hours. "You have a situation which is better than ten other places all over the world. I can give you a list of ten places where you have more problems than Sarajevo," he proclaimed.[2] His audience was so shocked that nobody thought to ask him to list the ten. The Sarajevo airport seemed to have a peculiar effect on international diplomats. That same month David Owen, the EC negotiator on Yugoslavia, proclaimed there: "Don't, don't, don't live under this dream that the west is going to come and sort this problem out. Don't dream dreams." The Bosniaks saw this as an invitation to surrender, but in a way, Owen's brutal honesty was accurate. In New York, Bosnia's defenders struggled even to make their voices heard. "The Security Council is a nondemocratic body. You have first-class and second-class members. If one of the P5 coughed, the Secretariat went into action. But the ten nonpermanent members were second-class citizens," recalls André Erdős. "You can be qualified, skilled, with expert command of an issue, an informed, eloquent speaker. But if you are a nonpermanent member, it was hard to attract attention. You had to make serious extra efforts to make yourself heard." Erdős and his colleagues perpetually struggled just to find out what was happening on the ground in Bosnia. They complained repeatedly to the Secretariat, to no avail, that information was circulated late, or not at all, and that Secretariat reports were incomplete, a pattern that later repeated itself with respect to Rwanda.

The Security Council chamber is the crucible of the United Nations. The ambassadors of the P5 and the ten nonpermanent members sit around a large horseshoe-shaped table, flanked by

their aides. One wall is covered by a giant peace mural, a gift
from Norway, showing a phoenix rising from its ashes, symbolizing the world being rebuilt after 1945. Stepped rows of
chairs stretch back to the rear of the chamber, while interpreters look down from behind their high windows. The floor
is covered with light brown carpet, the walls lined with darker
brown wallpaper. The resemblance to a large municipal theater is quite apt: most of the dramas that play out here have
been carefully scripted by the P5. By the time Erdős and the
other nonpermanent members arrived, everything had been
decided behind the scenes. "The P5 or the P3 had discussions
among themselves, agreed on a text and presented it to a meeting, saying take it or leave it. It was very difficult to change or
modify it. The whole operation of the United Nations was conducted in this spirit; hence the inability to do anything."

Erdős was horrified at how poorly informed the P5 were.
"The whole atmosphere around Bosnia was very bizarre. I was
flabbergasted by the ignorance of my colleagues about the
historical and geographical realities on the ground. European
ambassadors were just drifting along, not analyzing and wishing to know what was happening in the former Yugoslavia.
One P5 ambassador told me Bosnia-Herzegovina was a 'Titoist invention.' This idea came from Slobodan Milošević, that
Bosnia was an artificial construct." So Erdős brought a 1911 edi-
tion of the *Revai Lexicon*, a famous Hungarian encyclopedia,
to the Council chamber. "I took Volume B of the *Lexicon* with
me to the next meeting. There was a whole section on Bosnia,
fourteen pages and a two-page colored map, almost identical
to the borders of today. I showed my colleague, and said,
'Please look at this, your "Titoist invention."'" This was a very
visual rebuff to some of the foolish ideas that were being

spread around. He did take notice." But not enough to alter his country's policies.

The contrast was sharpest with Kuwait, swiftly liberated after it was attacked by Iraq. Resolution 678, passed in November 1990, called for "all necessary means"—including military intervention—to be used to force Iraq to withdraw if Saddam Hussein did not pull back by 15 January 1991. A "coalition of the willing" was formed under US leadership, the land war began on 23 February, and four days later Kuwait was liberated. But there was no oil in Bosnia. Secretary of State James Baker summed up the US position: "We do not have a dog in that fight"—words that, ten years later, came back to haunt him. Instead, the United Nations imposed sanctions, banning trade with Serbia and Montenegro, as well as sporting, scientific, air, and maritime links. But the Security Council balked at military intervention, arguing that "in the very complex context of events in the former Socialist Federal Republic of Yugoslavia all parties bear some responsibility for the situation," although it was hard to see how the civilians targeted by Serb snipers bore "some responsibility" for their situation. There were no robust enforcement mechanisms to ensure that the sanctions bit. Serbia quickly set up front companies in Greece, Russia, and Cyprus, and the flow of oil into the country barely slowed.

The Security Council then asked the UN Department of Peacekeeping Operations (DPKO) to examine whether peacekeeping would be possible in Bosnia, drawing on Croatia, where UNPROFOR, the UN protection force, was deployed. But UNPROFOR could barely protect itself. Night after night, the few remaining elderly Croats in Serb-occupied areas were murdered. Goulding and Tharoor warned after a trip to the conflict zone in January 1992 that peacekeeping would not work in

Bosnia. There was no consent for peacekeepers, no cease-fire, no suitable environment for peacekeepers to operate in, and no concept of operations acceptable to all the parties. Despite these constraints, UNPROFOR provided a useful fig leaf for the P5, and in June its mandate was enlarged to cover Bosnia—specifically, to keep the Sarajevo airport open.

As the war continued, France dispatched six thousand troops, Britain more than three thousand. London and Paris deployed substantial contingents not because they wanted to go to war with the Serbs but precisely because they did not. The troops were the perfect alibi for not taking more robust action against the Serbs. Their presence allowed London and Paris to exert substantial influence over and control of the UN operation in Bosnia. "Having troops on the ground was a substantial political currency," says a former UNPROFOR official. "My bosses were under no illusions that we had to give special attention to the British and French force commanders."

It was not the DPKO's decision to send UNPROFOR to Bosnia, but it was its responsibility to provide adequate guidance and backup to the peacekeepers in the field. This did not happen, says a former US army liaison officer with UNPROFOR. UNPROFOR's chain of command, under which Sarajevo reported to Zagreb, and Zagreb reported to the Secretariat in New York, was slow and unwieldy. The DPKO was not properly staffed in the evenings and on weekends. Outside of Eastern Standard Time office hours it was impossible to get any decision at all. The US officer recalls that General Philippe Morillon, the French commander of UNPROFOR in Bosnia, "was frustrated dealing with Zagreb and New York. When he called New York on the weekends, there was nobody there to answer his questions. He was left on his own to deal with some very delicate questions, trying to interpret the mandate without the backing of headquarters." And many DPKO officials had never been in a war zone. Bureaucrats did not make good commanding officers, the US officer adds: "You have to talk to somebody who understands where you are, and the operational environment. You need people with experience. If you are a military guy explaining something to a nonmilitary guy who has never been here and only understands things remotely, the culture of bureaucracy means he has little to gain by making a decision that may turn out badly. Better not to make a decision."

In summer 1992 UNPROFOR neither prevented the Serbs setting up a network of concentration camps across northern Bosnia, where men were starved and battered to death and women raped until their bodies gave out, nor forced them to be closed. The media, not the United Nations, revealed the existence of the Serb camps in early August. Information about Serb atrocities and the camps had trickled out into both Western capitals and various UN departments for several months earlier but was ignored or suppressed, according to Roy Gutman, an American journalist who won a Pulitzer Prize for his coverage of the camps. As the news broke Muhamed "Mo" Sacirbey, Bosnia's ambassador to the United Nations, was given copies of two UN memos written in April and May detailing reports of Serb atrocities. When Sacirbey held a news conference about the memos, Marrack Goulding asked him how he had obtained them. Sacirbey in turn demanded to know why the information had never been made public. An official later admitted that the information had been released, says Sacirbey, but only to Security Council members that "needed to know."

The television footage of stick-thin prisoners starving behind barbed wire triggered a wave of revulsion around the world. In response the Security Council passed resolution 770 on 13 August, demanding that the Red Cross have access to the camps. Resolution 770 invoked chapter VII of the UN Charter, known as the "enforcement clause," which provides for potential military action and was used as the justification for liberating Kuwait. Resolution 770 called on member states to take "all measures necessary" to "facilitate"—although not "ensure"—the delivery of relief supplies. Resolution 771, passed the same day, also seemed to point toward the possibility of intervention, calling for all sides to submit information to the Council about breaches of international law. The resolutions were not a direct mandate for a coalition of the willing to liberate Serb-occupied Bosnia. But there was sufficient scope for military action against the Serbs. David Owen agreed. "I wrote a strong letter to [British Prime Minister] John Major arguing for military action, to use air power to interdict the Serb supply lines to the concentration camps. I have never changed my view; I always believed we should have used more force to implement the three peace plans: the Vance-Owen peace plan, the EU action plan, and the contact group map." There was no military response. The Serbs closed the camps, but the war continued.

In September 1992 Yugoslavia, reduced to Serbia and Montenegro, was expelled from the United Nations. Yet UN officials and UNPROFOR officers, fearful of seeming to compromise their impartiality, were still unwilling to implement the mandate granted by resolution 770 to take "all measures necessary" to deliver relief supplies. A single Serb soldier with a gun was enough to stop passage of a UN aid convoy. UNPROFOR refused to use force to get relief supplies through. The United Nations' neutrality had become more important than its actual mission, says the US diplomat who served there during the Bosnian war. "The United Nations would rather be true to its principles than get anything done, be effective, or play a positive role. The United Nations is about the principle of being neutral. In Bosnia the principles of peacekeeping were the opposite of what was needed for the United Nations to play a positive role. When forced to choose, the Secretariat chose principles over effectiveness. In our minds you could not be neutral between the Bosnian Serbs and their victims." Yet what the United States considered a liability was regarded by the Secretariat as its greatest asset. The blue UN flag was the only guarantee of safe passage across the front lines, as Marrack Goulding had proclaimed in his 1988 speech in Stockholm, when he lauded a neutrality that allowed peacekeepers to carry weapons, while avoiding their use "at almost any cost." But what worked then in Cyprus and Kashmir did not work in 1992 in Sarajevo. The cost of the United Nations' obsession with avoiding the use of force soon became clear.

On 8 January 1993 Bosnia's vice prime minister Hakija Turajlic and his escort of French UN peacekeepers were detained by Serb fighters at an illegal checkpoint on the road to Sarajevo airport. The French UN troops stopped as ordered. After the door of the armored personnel carrier (APC) transporting Turajlic was opened, a Serb gunman pointed his weapon inside and shot him dead at point-blank range. The French troops did not return fire, call for reinforcements—less than six hundred yards away—or detain the killers. British troops who arrived on the scene were ordered to leave. By the French. Turajlic's murder clearly highlighted the United Nations' culture of impunity toward the Serbs, says Diego Arria, then Venezuelan ambassador. Arria, a dapper, outspoken former governor of Caracas and newspaper editor, was the spokesman for the 110-member Non-Aligned Caucus (NAC), which did not side automatically with either the United States or Russia. Arria was dubbed the "conscience of the Council" for his defense of Bosnia. He recalls: "It was clear that if you can murder, with the protection of the United Nations, the deputy prime minister of the newest member of the United Nations, you can get away with murder, which actually, they did."

One reason that Arria was in the spotlight over Bosnia was that its own ambassador, Mo Sacirbey, was often obstructed from appearing before the Security Council. The US-born Sacirbey was a lawyer and investment banker with a home on Staten Island. He spoke fluent English with an American accent and understood how to use the media, keeping the pressure on: "The prejudice against Bosnia was already in play: seeing the Bosnians as somehow less than European. The P5 aimed to marginalize Bosnia as a sovereign nation and deny me the right to state its views forcefully and on the record. The legitimacy of Bosnia's government was systematically undermined. Violations of humanitarian law were characterized as 'acts of war.' But Diego and I coordinated fully. He was a close friend and an ally who understood the political and ethical issues at stake. He was Mr. Inside while I was Mr. Outside."

The United Nations' unwillingness to anger the Serbs inspired some bizarre claims. In summer 1993 Brigadier General Vere Hayes, UNPROFOR chief of staff, declared, "There is no humanitarian siege" of Sarajevo. Pressed by reporters, who read out the dictionary definition of the word *siege*, UNPROFOR spokesman Barry Frewer claimed: "The Serbs have encircled the city. They are in a position to bring force to bear on the city. You call it a siege. We say they are deployed in a tactically advantageous position."[3] The representatives of both the UNHCR and the International Committee of the Red Cross (ICRC) immediately disagreed with Frewer.[4]

The circumlocutions of UN spokesmen aside, UN troops did daily risk their lives to keep the UN aid operation going in Sarajevo and across Bosnia. But for some peacekeepers war was highly profitable, as they ran a thriving black market, selling UN food and fuel. "The United Nations operation in Sarajevo was a sieve of corruption," says the American photographer Mark Milstein, who lived in the city for most of the war. "The United Nations sold food to the Holiday Inn hotel, which sold it to the journalists for $20 a meal, and then the United Nations got a kickback. It was an open secret that every restaurant in the city got its food like that. The different battalions ran different operations. The Egyptians ran a taxi service to and from the airport in an APC for anyone with money or a United Nations card. The Ukrainians made a lot of money selling food and fuel." Some French troops traded ration packs for sex. Once sated they could pour themselves a glass of their own specially imported red wine, dubbed Chateau Sarajevo. In New York the DPKO knew nothing about UNPROFOR shining spotlights on those trying to sprint across the airport runway. Shashi Tharoor was eventually informed what was happening by the American writers Susan Sontag and David Rieff. Tharoor sent a cable to UNPROFOR demanding an explanation. UNPROFOR replied that such an incident may indeed have occurred since the force sought to demonstrate its impartiality over the control of the airport. Tharoor then urged UNPROFOR commanders to desist.

By January 1993 more than 60 percent of Bosnia was under Serb control and ethnically cleansed. In the east only Srebrenica and three other enclaves—Cerska, Žepa, and Goražde—held out. With its commanding position in the Drina Valley and bor-

dering Serbia, Srebrenica was an important prize. The Serb attack was planned down to the smallest detail. Srebrenica had
always lacked salt. A JNA research team had analyzed the area's
drinking water and predicted several consequences from salt
deprivation, including a breakdown of the endocrine organs,
as well as "confusion, instability, and aggressiveness, [and] an
inclination toward anarchy and panic and a susceptibility to
psychological manipulation."[5]

Srebrenica was an average Bosnian town: a main street
of drab Tito-era municipal buildings flanked by modern,
square blocks of flats, home to about six thousand people. Surrounded by forests and rolling green hills, the town had been
known even in Roman times for its silver mine—its name
comes from the south Slavic word for silver. This part of eastern Bosnia was a world away from sophisticated Sarajevo or
Belgrade. Women kept their heads covered under floral headscarves and wore long, billowy, Turkish-style pants. At meal-
times, men were served first, while the women retired to the
kitchen. Hamlets survived on subsistence agriculture and were
reachable only by dirt tracks. Many among the older genera-
tion were illiterate and put their faith in charms and amulets.

Srebrenica's commander was a burly weightlifter named
Nasir Oric. Born in 1967 in nearby Potočari, Oric was a policeman and former bodyguard of Slobodan Milošević. When war
broke out in Croatia, the Bosnian authorities sent Oric home
to set up a secret local militia, and train recruits in guerrilla
warfare. Oric launched a string of hit-and-run operations,
ambushing Serb convoys and raiding Serb villages. In the wake
of Oric's fighters came hordes of starving refugees, known as
torbari, bag people, sweeping up anything edible or movable.
Nor could captured Serb civilians or soldiers expect much
mercy. Srebrenica's stubborn refusal to surrender and Oric's

raids enraged General Ratko Mladić, the Bosnian Serb commander. Ratko—"warlike"—was born in March 1942 in eastern Bosnia. Short, stocky, extremely menacing, Mladić cared nothing for the Geneva Conventions or the laws of war. He was transferred to Bosnia from Knin, the capital of the RSK. There and in Bosnia his troops shelled hospitals, civilian homes, and fleeing columns of women and children.

In early 1993 General Mladić attacked. Cerska and the surrounding villages fell, and the survivors fled to Srebrenica. The town's population swelled by ten times. Whole families camped out, sleeping in the snow and burning plastic bottles to try to keep warm. Disease and starvation daily claimed dozens of victims. The streets stank of excrement and filth. People survived on "bread" made from tree buds and corncobs. There were fears of an epidemic of typhoid that could spread through Europe and a sense that Bosnia was on the brink of even greater catastrophe. The French commander of UNPROFOR, General Philippe Morillon, set off to see for himself, arriving in Srebrenica on 11 March. Surrounded by tens of thousands of desperate refugees, he made a promise to Srebrenica that still echoes darkly through the years: "You are now under the protection of UN forces."

General Morillon's bravado caused consternation in the Security Council and anger among senior UN officials. The Security Council chamber echoed to an impassioned debate. The NAC demanded drastic action to protect Srebrenica, while the P5 resisted. "We thought the only way to prevent a massacre was for the major countries to commit their forces. We introduced the resolution on safe areas, after a tremendous conflict with Britain, France, and Russia," recalls Diego Arria. "Russia played the most negative role, but the most intelligent. They were working behind the British and French, blocking every initiative," says Arria. Moscow, the Serbs' traditional ally, skillfully exploited Western fears that the end of the Cold War had triggered a new era of instability, fears that seemed validated by the Yugoslav wars. In August 1991 Boris Yeltsin had led the resistance to a coup attempt by Communist hardliners. But how certain was his grip on power a year and a half later? A failed empire with nuclear weapons and nobody in control was the stuff of nightmares for Western policy planners. Instability in Moscow, war in a former Communist country, the prospect of further ethnic conflicts across the Balkans and the Caucasus—all these factors militated against a robust policy against the Serbs. Saving Boris Yeltsin was judged more important than saving Bosnia, and Srebrenica would pay the price. "The war in Bosnia and the collapse of Yugoslavia took place when there was no certainty that the Cold War was definitely finished," says Colin Keating, New Zealand's ambassador to the United Nations, who sat on the Security Council in 1993 and 1994. "What would have been the impact in Moscow if the United Nations intervened against the Serbs? Would Yeltsin have been able to get support for intervention? Would he have survived another coup attempt? I think the judgment among the P3 was probably that there were indeed real risks if Russia was pushed too far. Some of us argued for a more robust approach by the UN, and I still believe that more could have been done to protect the safe areas. But the Russia factor is always underestimated in analyzing the cautious approach of the P3 at that time."

On 16 April 1993 the Security Council passed resolution 819. The key sentence was that Srebrenica would be "a safe area which should be free from any armed attack or any other hostile act." At first Diego Arria and André Erdős did not realize that they had been completely outmaneuvered. For a "safe" area was something very different from a "protected" area, which demanded robust defense, as would a "haven." The declaration that Srebrenica "should," rather than "shall," be safe, was also crucial. After all, everywhere in the world "should" remain safe. But "shall" would have implied a duty to ensure that it did. "We thought we had achieved a very important, significant accomplishment with this resolution," says Arria. "But Britain and France were in favor of the safe areas because actually safe areas were a totally meaningless concept. Little did we know at the time that this was the case." Playing with words is an art on the Security Council, argues Erdős:

> It is a school of drafting of things which can be interpreted in various ways. When I understood a statement or resolution unequivocally, I was surprised to learn that others had a quite different interpretation. We discussed the terms *safe* and *protected*, and an ambassador from a P5 power said, "Safe, yes, but that does not mean that we will protect Srebrenica or send armies and troops." When I saw a certain situation and said action must be taken on account of our resolutions, others looked at the same text and said they did not see it at all, that they did not see any urgency or obligation by the United Nations to respond.

UNPROFOR brokered a deal under which Srebrenica would be demilitarized but not occupied by the Serbs. The Bosnian army would surrender its weapons in exchange for a cease-fire and access to relief supplies. Resolution 819 also authorized members of the Security Council to visit Srebrenica and report back, the first such Council mission of its kind. Journalists were banned from accompanying the diplomats. Once the diplomats arrived in Srebrenica, they understood why. They were shocked to the core by what they saw. "It is one thing when you read about something or see it on your television screen. It is quite another to go there and see the physical reality," recalls André Erdős. "I remembered newsreels that I had seen of 1944, when Allied troops entered Belgium and the Netherlands and the people lining the streets, cheering and applauding. They did the same for us in Srebrenica, because they thought we were coming as liberators. But I knew they were deadly mistaken. The most we could do was publicize their situation so the world might listen more carefully."

Arria's delegation was treated with utter contempt by the Bosnian Serbs. This was the price of the "neutrality," so jealously guarded by the Secretariat and the P5. When the convoy was delayed by the Bosnian Serbs and Diego Arria argued for the right to pass, the gunner on a Serb vehicle pointed his weapon directly at Arria's car. The mission passed a Norwegian aid convoy, which was stopped by the side of the road by a single Serb soldier. Once inside Srebrenica, UNPROFOR officers tried to keep to a tightly controlled itinerary. UNPROFOR had its own agenda: total cooperation with the Bosnian Serbs. Arria refused. "I told them I wanted to go to the school where a Serb bomb killed fourteen children. They said there was not much time left. I insisted, and we went there. There were the mothers of the children, and there were still the remains of the bodies of the children on the ground."

As the day wore on, it became clear who was in charge at Srebrenica, the United Nation's first "safe area" in Bosnia: the Serbs. "That's when we understood perfectly well that there were two United Nations," says Arria: "one in New York, and one on the ground, which was not really the United Nations operation. It was British and French. The commanders on the ground were following the directions of their governments, not the UN Security Council, which was theoretically the conductor of the operation. It was very shocking." The mission's report to the Security Council described conditions inside Srebrenica as a "slow-motion" genocide. Much worse was to come.

II

Master Drafters

The safe-areas policy was real back-of-the-envelope
stuff, a complete absurdity, one of the worst decisions
the United Nations has ever made.
—*David Owen, EC negotiator for Yugoslavia*

Diego Arria's most powerful opponent on the Security Council was David Hannay, Great Britain's ambassador to the United Nations and the de facto leader of the P5. Even his colleagues admitted that Hannay, supremely confident and a master of his brief, did not suffer fools gladly. He often lectured the Security Council like a British public schoolmaster forced to teach a particularly dim group of pupils. "He is one of the most gifted and combative people I have seen in my life," says Arria. "He had very strong views and we did not see eye to eye at all. The United Kingdom was, through the whole process, the only one with a clear view of what it was going to do. When the Bosniaks refused to play their role of passive victims and their resistance grew, the British and the French became very irritated. They were desperate for it to be finished, but the Bosniaks would not cooperate."

Nor did Hannay's impatience with those less intellectually gifted always endear him to his diplomatic colleagues. "Hannay is extremely effective and has very strong views. Some of them found him slightly too much of a tutor," recalls one senior British official, who cited as an example US Ambassador Madeleine Albright. "He did not think he was making policy, but he was quite good at saying, 'If this is what you really mean you should do it this way.'"

Hannay understood that the steadily building pressure among the NAC for military intervention against the Serbs had to be defused. The Security Council mission to Srebrenica had recommended that safe-area status be extended to the other besieged enclaves. The safe areas provided a useful alibi for the P5—it gave the appearance of humanitarian action while doing nothing to halt or reverse ethnic cleansing. After further lengthy debate, on 6 May 1993 the Security Council passed resolution 824, which again invoked chapter VII, and declared Sarajevo; Tuzla, in the north; Bihać, in the northwest; and the two other enclaves of Žepa, and Goražde, as "safe areas." Like Srebrenica, the five additions were some of the most dangerous places in the world. The NAC's draft resolution, including robust enforcement measures, was rejected.

The United Nations did not even have a guaranteed right to inspect the safe areas. Despite this, Srebrenica was theoretically disarmed, and about 170 peacekeepers, mostly Canadian, were deployed. But the NAC, fearful that the disarmed Bosnians would be annihilated by the Bosnian Serbs, had scored one small victory. Under instructions from the DPKO, UNPRO-FOR did not pursue the demilitarization of the Bosnian forces with undue zeal. There were no house-to-house searches, and most of the materiel collected was unserviceable or lacked ammunition. But what was a safe area? What did it mean? Nobody really knew. In November 1992 the Security Council had passed resolution 787 inviting the secretary general and the UNHCR to carry out a study on the viability and practicality of safe areas. This report was produced, but was not classified as an official document, entering a category known in UN parlance as a "non-paper." Its contents and analysis were so dire that influential members of the Security Council insisted that it be discussed only informally, that it be given no official status, and that it not be entered on the record, according to Shashi Tharoor. Safe havens for the Kurds had worked in Iraq, because Saddam had been defeated and the Allied troops were mandated to use force. The ban on Iraqi military flights, establishing a no-fly zone, was rigorously enforced. Resolution 781, passed in October 1992, had established a no-fly zone over Bosnia. But there was no enforcement clause, merely a call for member states to provide information about violations. There were extremely strict limitations on when NATO planes might open fire, and the Serbs ignored the ban: when on 9 April General Ratko Mladić attended a meeting with General Philippe Morillon of UNPROFOR, he arrived by helicopter.

The safe-areas concept in Bosnia was flawed from the start. The Bosnian Serbs had not been defeated by the West, nor even engaged. There was no credible threat of force, so there was no reason for General Mladić to respect the status of the safe areas. Thousands more UNPROFOR troops would be

needed to properly protect the six safe areas, but despite lobbying by both Boutros-Ghali and the DPKO, most member
states refused to commit their soldiers. Turkey's repeated offers
were refused for fear of inflaming the Serbs. "From that moment on, March 1993, there was a warning about Srebrenica,"
argues David Owen. "Every serious person knew about it,
every single one of those UN Permanent Representatives who
negotiated about it, particularly those two very able people
David Hannay and Jean-Bernard Mérimée, who understood
the significance of a comma here and a comma there. And in a
way we were the victims of two very successful diplomats who
produced a form of words that satisfied capitals that they were
not actually committed to defending these safe havens, but
gave the impression to the rest of the world that we were."

The P5 earned their seats as the victors of the Second World
War, and when it came to Bosnia, they sometimes seemed still
to be fighting it. Diego Arria recalls: "During the whole crisis,
we were told repeatedly, by the British, the French, and the
Russians, that 'we know the area much better, we know the history, we know the Serb, from our First World War, then they
finished off Hitler, so you must listen to us . . . '" The P5 knew
neither "the Serb," nor Yugoslavia during the Second World
War. The Nazis never fully conquered Bosnia, but the anti-
Nazi fighters were multinational Communist partisans, not
solely Serbs. Their commander, Josef Brož, known as Tito, was
half-Croat and half-Slovene. Among his young officers was the
Croat Franjo Tudjman, Croatia's president after it declared independence in 1991.

Nor did the P5 understand 1990s Yugoslavia, says André
Erdős. "If I asked my colleagues on the Council the difference
between Slavonia, Slovenia, and Slovakia, none of them, apart

from the Austrian ambassador, would know." In fact, the term
P5 was somewhat of a misnomer. Practically speaking, it was a
P2: David Hannay and his French counterpart Jean-Bernard
Mérimée. "The French and the British were as close as they
ever could be," says David Owen. "Their military operation in
Bosnia had unbelievable, unparalleled cooperation between
their commanders. By and large they were following the same
policies. [French] President [François] Mitterrand told me the
day I was appointed, 'Forget any bombing or military activity
against the Serbs; you won't get any.' Prime Minister John
Major was the same. They would do everything for the humanitarian effort, but would only commit to a fighting role if
NATO and the Americans were there."

Critics of this hazy nostalgia, for a wartime world that
never was, dubbed it the Fitzroy Maclean factor. Maclean, who
was probably the inspiration for James Bond, was a swash-
buckling Scottish aristocrat who parachuted into Yugoslavia to
lead Great Britain's liaison mission to the partisans. Maclean's
advice was still sought by the grandees of the British Foreign
Office. Before he took up his post as spokesman for UNPRO-
FOR, Michael Williams, a British academic, attended briefings
at the Foreign Office. He was shocked at what he heard. "The
Fitzroy Maclean factor was very strong. There was a real unwillingness to address the war and its causes. The prevailing attitude, with the exception of a few colleagues, was that this was
a terrible war and all parties were to blame, and we had to
manage it as best we could. Now clearly there were faults on
all sides, and to some extent violations on all sides, but the
primary causes of the conflict were very clear: this was well-
organized violence, initiated from Belgrade and carried on
with particular aggression by the Bosnian Serbs."

With Great Britain and France setting the agenda, where

were the other great powers? China's main concern was that the break-up of Yugoslavia not set any precedents for the sensitive issue of Tibet, which Beijing had illegally invaded in 1950 and annexed. Russia, Serbia's traditional ally, automatically opposed any move to stop the Serbs. Moscow was also wary that any intervention on humanitarian grounds would set a precedent for action against its own scorched-earth campaign in Chechnya. The United States, the one country which could have made a difference, stood aside. In the summer of 1992 Bill Clinton, Democratic nominee for president, made much of Bosnia. There was talk of "lift and strike": lift the arms embargo and launch air strikes against the Bosnian Serbs. Once in power, Clinton changed his mind. The United States, it seemed, still did not have "a dog in this fight." Instead, Clinton bought into the "ancient hatreds" theory, as expounded by his secretary of state, Warren Christopher, who proclaimed in March 1993: "The hatred between all three groups . . . is almost unbelievable. It's almost terrifying and it's centuries old. That really is a problem from hell. And I think the United States is doing all we can to try to deal with that problem."[1] The Clinton administration refused to support the Vance-Owen peace plan, drafted by Cyrus Vance, a former US secretary of state, and David Owen; that plan, the administration claimed, rewarded ethnic cleansing, but it could offer nothing else except lukewarm support for the safe-areas resolutions.

General Ratko Mladić and Mohammed Farah Aideed never met, but the Somali warlord was one of Mladić's greatest de facto allies. The debacle in Somalia cast a long shadow over Bosnia. President George Bush, Clinton's predecessor, had opted for intervention in Somalia because the African country seemed to offer a far higher probability of success for a quick humanitarian operation. Television crews filmed US troops landing on the beaches, and at first, all went well. By the end of 1992 the United Task Force (UNITAF), commanded by US troops, had secured major relief depots, while the United Nations Operation in Somalia (UNOSOM) protected aid deliveries and worked for a political solution. But America's good intentions soon turned sour. When senior members of Aideed's clan gathered in Mogadishu to discuss a possible peace agreement with the United Nations, US forces bombed the building, killing more than fifty people. A raid by US troops on Aideed's headquarters ended in disaster. Two Black Hawk helicopters were shot down, eighteen soldiers were killed, and seventy-nine were wounded. Television footage of a jubilant Somali crowd dragging the bound corpse of an American soldier through the streets triggered revulsion across the United States. Aideed's forces braced for a ferocious counterattack, but instead, to their amazement, the US troops were pulled out. Once again, Clinton lacked the courage to stand firm, a pattern that would soon repeat itself in Rwanda.

The Somalia disaster had a profound effect, says Richard Holbrooke, President Clinton's envoy to Yugoslavia and chief architect of the Dayton accords that eventually ended the war in Bosnia. "The administration was burned and traumatized by what happened in Somalia. Congress was up in arms, and the United States was reeling. This was a very critical point. History is continuous, and you are always affected by what has just happened. Somalia took out all the will for action, both in Rwanda and Bosnia."

Clinton's lack of political will produced a disconnect with his own United Nations mission. The new US ambassador, Madeleine Albright, herself a refugee from Czechoslovakia, was a passionate supporter of Bosnia. Albright had a seat in the cabinet, but she lacked the political clout to persuade

Clinton to be consistent. "President Clinton had been very critical of President Bush and James Baker before he was elected. It was an issue in the campaign," she recalls. "But when we got into office, there were a lot of other things that came up. We were dealing with Bosnia hour by hour, but I was very frustrated by the rest of the State Department, and I sensed that the assistant secretaries for Europe were not as much into this as we were. I was UN ambassador, not secretary of state." Albright's humanity worked against her, says a Western diplomat who frequently worked with her. "She was quite an emotional person and allowed it to show. She was completely committed to Bosnia but could not produce the policies that would reflect that commitment."

Albright's arguments in cabinet meetings for a robust response were swept aside by General Colin Powell, the chairman of the Joint Chiefs of Staff. She recalls:

> The national security adviser or the secretary of state would ask what was the military plan and what could be done. General Powell was a brilliant briefer. He would come in with maps and a little red laser beam. And he would say, we can do this and that, move this division and fly helicopters or whatever. But it would take 50,000 troops or 500,000 troops and it will take many months, in fact years, and what are you going to do when Sergeant Smith steps on a land mine, how are you going to tell his mother why this happened? Watching this made me feel terrible. You would be led up the hill of possibilities then dropped off the side with a reality check. It was a decision, if you thought the Balkans were worth an American life. We came at this in dif-

ferent ways, to oversimplify, from my Munich context and their Vietnam context. I would say this was
important for the United States, and for them it was
just another place.

As Clinton stood aside, others took the initiative. Pakistan's UN ambassador, Jamsheed Marker, submitted a memorandum to the Security Council on 14 May 1993. In it he called
for all six safe areas to be robustly defended by UNPROFOR
and said that even though UNPROFOR had been established
under chapter VII, its function had been narrowly interpreted
to focus on providing relief supplies. Once again, the key question was not UNPROFOR's mandate but its *interpretation*.
The Secretariat also presented its own paper on the safe area,
with three options: a token force of up to 2,000; a sizable force
of up to 12,500, to protect the safe areas; or 15,000 troops to defend the safe areas. The distinction between "protecting" and
"defending" was not clear. Boutros-Ghali's questions to Security Council members—in particular, when United Nations
troops would be expected to use force if the Serbs did not comply with the resolutions—went unanswered. The safe areas, he
predicted, would not be safe at all.

Draft resolution 836 was introduced by France, Great
Britain, Russia, the United States, and Spain at the beginning
of June. It did not call for the robust measures demanded by
Marker and the NAC. Instead, it proposed that UNPROFOR's
mandate be extended to "deter attacks against the safe area." It
authorized the use of force but, crucially, only for UNPRO-
FOR "acting in self-defense," *not* to defend the enclaves. Arria
and Marker knew that they could not stop the draft resolution's eventual passage, but they could abstain, and the more
abstentions there were, the more embarrassing it would be for

the P5. "Britain, France, Russia, and the US were very concerned that Venezuela and Pakistan would oppose the resolution. We were among the original promoters of the safe-areas concept, although as proper, protected areas. If we voted against their resolution, the media would jump on it," says Arria.

London and Paris went into action to ensure that the vote went their way. British and French diplomats stationed in the capitals of the nonpermanent members launched a highly coordinated lobbying campaign, using promises of aid and trade, as well as subtle threats of future potential difficulties, to make sure that these countries duly voted for resolution 836. "There is intense work between New York and the Foreign Office, and the time difference of five hours is very useful," recalls Douglas Hurd.

> Hannay could give us his recommendations, we could deal with them in the morning, and by the time he got to his office he got his instructions. The main discussion about the text of resolutions would be done in New York. Security Council discussions move so fast that you have to be expert in wording. It has to be right and needs to be done there. Once it is clear, the Foreign Office sends a telegram to all posts represented on the Security Council, saying go to the foreign ministry, saying we think this is the right formulation and we hope you will support this.

It worked. Mo Sacirbey recalls: "One by one, the NAC countries acceded to London and Paris, which both wanted unanimity on the resolution, to show their diplomatic wisdom and principled position and that Bosnia did not care about its own people." Only Pakistan and Venezuela held out.

Draft resolution 836 was formally brought before the Security Council on 4 June. Hannay and Mérimée both looked worried as Arria walked in, recalls Sacirbey. "It was clear from his face that Venezuela had succumbed to the pressure. But Diego had not." The Venezuelan foreign minister had been trying to reach Arria all morning, to instruct him to vote for the resolution. Arria refused to answer his telephone. "I had inside information that British and French ambassadors in Caracas were with our foreign minister, pushing him to lean on me to vote for the resolution," Arria recalls. "The foreign minister then called my deputy, but he told him I was not taking calls. Hannay was on the phone to the British ambassador in Caracas, telling him I was not taking calls."

In a long and impassioned speech, Arria criticized the P5's view that all that was needed to stop the war in Bosnia was the adoption of such containment and prevention measures as sanctions, no-fly zones, and border monitors. "Collective security," Arria said, "demands the right to self-defense." Pakistan's Marker went farther, calling for the invocation of chapter VII and the use of all necessary measures, including air strikes, and the reversal of Serbian ethnic cleansing. But resolution 836 was passed by thirteen votes with two abstentions: Venezuela and Pakistan. It was a superb example of the diplomat's craft: it sounded sufficiently martial but in reality promised nothing, except that UNPROFOR could fire back or call on NATO airpower—but only to defend *itself*, thanks to Hannay and Mérimée's determination. Hannay now admits that resolution 836 was flawed: "There was a great deal of fuss over the word *protect* and whether the troops should be there to protect themselves and their mandate, or protect the safe areas.

We favored the former. The British troops were there for humanitarian intervention, to enable the delivery of supplies, not to fight a war. The negotiations were designed to ensure that the concept would be as effective as it could be, despite its considerable defects. I don't think that straddle was very successful."

The Secretariat was just as dismayed as the Bosnians about the safe-areas resolutions, although for different reasons. UNPROFOR commanders had already warned that the concept was unworkable. Now the Security Council had declared six towns to be safe areas without committing the troops to make sure they were in fact safe. Shashi Tharoor argues: "The Council was particularly bizarre because it called on the parties to treat the areas as safe, without actually doing anything to make them safe; secondly, it consciously and deliberately avoided the use of the words *protect* or *defend,* so there was no obligation, and they said so explicitly at the time, on the UN troops to protect or defend these areas. But at the same time they wanted the UN to deploy in these areas in the hope that their mere presence would deter attacks." After the vote on resolution 836, Arria was recalled to Caracas for some time. But he had no regrets. "I told Hannay and Mérimée that they were in effect asking my government to end my post. They told me that 'business was business.' But Marker and I do not have to carry on our conscience what happened later." Just 7,500 UNPROFOR troops were eventually dispatched to "deter attacks" on the six safe areas. No NATO country would deploy troops to Bihać, the isolated pocket in the northwest of Bosnia, despite sustained lobbying by officials in the DPKO. Eventually a battalion of Bangladeshi troops was dispatched—with summer uniforms, useless in a Balkan winter.

"From that moment on, we knew that Bihać was not defendable, nor Žepa nor Srebrenica," says David Owen. "Maybe we could defend Tuzla and Sarajevo. Safe areas are a way forward only if you are serious and have enough troops to defend them." With hindsight, when it became clear that the extra troops were not going to be available, Great Britain should have said that the resolutions no longer applied, argues Douglas Hurd. "We should have pulled the rug out then. It would have been awkward, but we should have said it was no longer valid, because of the original assumptions on which this rested, that there would be enough troops. The drafting of the telegrams show a very convoluted piece of drafting because there were different concepts at work. It was a mess. What is not true is that the Bosnian government was deceived; they knew the weaknesses, but you can argue that the inhabitants of Srebrenica did not."

It was the inhabitants of Srebrenica who ultimately paid the price for the United Nations' incoherence. The Security Council lacked both the necessary vision and the understanding of how to respond to genocidal violence, says Danilo Türk, a former assistant secretary general for political affairs and Slovenian ambassador to the United Nations during the early 1990s. As a representative of a former Yugoslav republic, he had a better grasp than most of the causes of the Bosnian wars.

> The Security Council approached Bosnia in a very piecemeal way. The policies, the overall political understanding, and the political will at that time were quite inadequate. I would go to the Security Council and tell them that the first thing they had to do was get rid of this rhetoric about "centuries-old hatreds." It was either intellectual laziness or obfuscation. You needed to look at the core of the

problem and then figure out how to manage a robust response. That was my second point, a *robust* response. It was not very popular at the time and very few Europeans supported it, although Iran and Saudi Arabia did.

Meanwhile, President Clinton decided that the US must intervene, but he changed his mind after reading *Balkan Ghosts*, a travel book by Robert Kaplan, which seemed to reinforce the "ancient hatreds" theory. "It was absurd, a nightmare dealing with the Clinton administration; initially they had a different policy every week," recalls David Owen. "They moralized from thirty-five thousand feet; they said they would come into Bosnia, through NATO, but not to enforce a settlement. It was naïve in the extreme. OK, maybe you don't want to enforce a peace plan, but you don't have to tell General Mladić and Radovan Karadžić that you are not going to. The Serbs always knew that the United States was not committed. As long as that was the case, they would call their bluff." Clinton dispatched Secretary of State Warren Christopher to London to lobby for "lift and strike," but London would not support this strategy. "Washington came up with a policy that involved no commitment at all. At the United Nations it was known as 'lift and pray.' It was not at all clear what the results would be," recalls David Hannay. Eventually, the United States would break the arms embargo itself, and NATO would finally strike the Bosnian Serbs, but by then it would be too late for Srebrenica.

Secretariat officials, especially those serving in the DPKO, understandably continue to emphasize the warnings they issued to the Security Council that the safe areas were not tenable. But others dealing with the United Nations during the Bosnian war, or reporting on it, argue that some Secretariat officials and UNPROFOR officers were playing a more insidious role. They charge that some UN staffers supported London and Paris's policy of nonintervention in order to preserve the United Nations' neutrality, and even that some Secretariat officials elided the distinction between aggressor and victim, blurring the lines of responsibility for atrocities, to preempt and prevent calls for the United Nations to take a more robust role.

This was especially true of the Secretariat's briefings to the Security Council on Bosnia, says a United States diplomat then stationed at the United Nations. The Secretariat seemed to consistently support the P5's policies, shaping the flow of information in a way that would persuade the ten nonpermanent members that the P5's approach was correct. The nonpermanent members may have been second-class citizens, but their votes mattered. It was crucial for London and Paris that there be as few abstentions as possible on their resolutions so they could—wrongly—represent their Bosnia policies as the authentic will of the United Nations. "Britain and France were set in their position, but the middle ground, some of the ten nonpermanent members, was open to argument," according to the US official. "But the way the Secretariat conducted themselves made it difficult for us to argue for a more robust position. There was a sense in the Security Council that the Secretariat is neutral and supplies facts. The smaller countries had no embassies in the Balkans; they relied on the Secretariat for advice and information. But for us the Secretariat was an obstacle to be overcome."

The reports filed to Zagreb from British and French UNPROFOR commanders in the field, and forwarded to New

York, often did not reflect the reality on the ground, the diplomat says.

> The Secretariat tried to justify its neutrality by saying that all sides are committing atrocities and asking us why we were making such a fuss about the Bosnian Serbs. We knew that UNPROFOR would not allow certain things to be reported, such as some Serb violations of safe areas. They were soft-selling Serb atrocities and emphasizing the Bosniaks' response. In our minds you could not be neutral between the Bosnian Serbs and their victims. But the United Nations felt neutrality was the paramount response, and that is how they presented things in the Security Council.

Boutros-Ghali rarely attended Council discussions on the crisis, usually sending Chinmaya Gharekhan, his special political adviser, to brief the members. Gharekhan was a veteran Indian UN diplomat of the old school. His performances were not impressive, says the US diplomat. "During the war the Security Council discussed Bosnia three times a week. Gharekhan would brief us, but we knew from our own sources that the briefing was not true or left out a lot of things. We asked him questions that we already knew the answers for, about what was happening in places occupied by the Serbs, such as Žepa or Brčko, to try and get these issues on the table, to discuss what we thought was really going on. The Secretariat hated this, because then they had to do a lot of work."

In an absolute sense it was true that all three sides were guilty. The Bosnian government forces, like every army in his-

tory, contained soldiers who breached the laws of war. The question was how many Bosnian government soldiers committed
war crimes in proportion to those committed by the Croats
and the Serbs? General Lewis Mackenzie, the UN commander
in Sarajevo in summer 1992, testified before a US congressional
committee that the United States should not intervene because
"a good deal of what is going on by the Bosnian government
forces is to convince you to get involved."[2] He compared the
Bosnian armies to three serial killers, one who has killed fifteen
people, one who has killed ten people, and one who has killed
five. His proportions were far from the truth. The UN International Criminal Tribunal for the former Yugoslavia (ICTY)
has indicted 162 people: of those only nine are Bosniak commanders, barely 5 percent of the total.

Some UN officials and commanders suggested to correspondents that the Bosniaks were staging incidents to boost the
world's sympathy. They cited as an example the mortar attack on
a funeral of a young Bosniak girl at Sarajevo's Lions cemetery in
early August 1992, television coverage of which was seen around
the world. Officials pointed out that each time an international
negotiator came to speak with President Alija Izetbegović, a "convenient" mortar barrage exploded nearby. Some even blamed
the Bosnian government for the notorious "bread queue massacre" in May 1992, when a mortar exploded among shoppers
on Vase Miskina Street in Sarajevo, killing twenty and injuring
dozens. They argued that the explosion may have been caused
by a remote-controlled bomb.

In August 1992, after conversations with several senior
UN officials, including General MacKenzie, Leonard Doyle, the
correspondent for the British newspaper the *Independent*, wrote
one of the most controversial articles of the Bosnian war:
"United Nations officials and senior Western military officers

believe some of the worst recent killings in Sarajevo, including the massacre of at least 16 people in a bread queue, were carried out by the city's mainly Muslim defenders—not Serb besiegers—as a propaganda ploy to win world sympathy and military intervention." He continued: "The view has been expressed in confidential reports circulating at UN headquarters in New York, and in classified briefings to US policymakers in Washington. All suggest that Sarajevo's defenders, mainly Muslims but including Croats and a number of Serb residents, staged several attacks on their own people in the hope of dramatizing the city's plight in the face of insuperable Serbian odds. They emphasize, however, that these attacks, though bloody, were a tiny minority among regular city bombardments by Serbian forces."[3]

Doyle's article was the single most damaging report for the Bosnian cause during the war, especially as the *Independent* was strongly supportive of Bosnia, and Doyle had written extensively on the Serbian rape camps. Doyle's article was seized on by Belgrade and still features on Serb Web sites. The debate shifted from the need for air strikes against the Serbs to whether the Bosniaks were shelling themselves. A United Nations investigation later established that there were two splash-mark craters on the pavement and that the bakery walls were pockmarked: the precise signs of a mortar explosion, but the whispers continued that Bosnian forces may have fired the mortar themselves.[4]

By spring 1993 the DPKO had a new chief: an emollient Ghanian named Kofi Annan. Annan joined the UN in 1962. Fluent in English, French, and several African languages, Annan was descended from tribal chiefs. There was a certain noblesse oblige in his courteous, if remote, manner. Following a brief interlude in the mid-1970s as Ghana's tourism director, Annan returned to the United Nations. After stints in the UN's human resources and finance departments, he led the first UN team negotiating with Iraq on the sale of oil to pay for humanitarian aid, known as "oil for food." From there he was moved to the DPKO in 1992, before being promoted to under–secretary general and department chief. Annan worked with Shashi Tharoor, now DPKO team leader for Bosnia, and Peter Schmitz, a German who was the Yugoslavia desk officer.

Tharoor's old boss, Marrack Goulding, had been moved sideways to head the new Department of Political Affairs (DPA). The most senior official dealing with Yugoslavia in the field was Boutros-Ghali's special representative, Yasushi Akashi. Akashi, the first Japanese to join the Secretariat, was immensely powerful. As the political chief of UNPROFOR, he could turn the United Nations' half of the "dual key" it shared with NATO to authorize air strikes. Akashi had formerly run the United Nations mission to Cambodia and had helped steer the country toward democracy.

But in Cambodia, Akashi had taken the principle of impartiality to unprecedented levels: two Khmer Rouge soldiers with a strip of bamboo across a road were enough to stop him from proceeding.[5] Over the next months Akashi's obsessive nonconfrontationalism would, according to his critics, make him a de facto ally of the Bosnian Serbs.

"Akashi had a somewhat different view of how the United Nations should behave," says Madeleine Albright. "While I understood we had to deal with Milošević, I did not feel we had to be excessively neutral. I knew what had gone on in Bosnia and I think it was very hard to be neutral." But Akashi was just what the P5 wanted. "He was put there because people knew what his character was like," says journalist James Bone.

"These things are engineered behind the scenes. The French were very influential over Bosnia policy at that point and were in cahoots with the Brits." Other Security Council members were also puzzled. "Akashi was a strange appointee, a devotee of a very old-fashioned approach to problems," says Colin Keating, New Zealand's ambassador. "The Secretariat was incredibly cautious then. That worked when you had twenty United Nations observers on each side of the cease-fire line and they monitored situations and were totally evenhanded, because that was the Charter's original vision of peacekeeping. But it was inappropriate for the 1990s, conflicts pursued with total savagery and no respect for the rules of war. Some people were better than others, but Akashi, I think, was particularly devoted to the old-fashioned way."

The new commander of UNPROFOR also believed in the "old-fashioned way." General Michael Rose was a former commander of the British SAS regiment, the elite special forces. The diminutive Japanese diplomat and the tall, brisk British officer found much to agree on. Crossing the front lines on his first day in Sarajevo, Rose witnessed government forces firing mortars at Serb artillery emplacements, which soon responded. General Rose's anger was roused. Such cynical tactics—by the *Bosnian* government—would have to stop. "Obviously my first task would be to tell President Izetbegović that this grim strategy of inflicting horrors on his own people would never succeed. I would do all in my power to prevent the United Nations from becoming engaged in a war in Bosnia as a combatant," he records in his book *Fighting for Peace*.[6]

The first crisis of 1994 came shortly after noon on Saturday, 5 February, when a mortar crashed onto a table in Sarajevo's main market, killing sixty-eight and wounding more than two hundred. By now Washington, London, the Serbs, and

UNPROFOR each had a well-honed response routine. President Clinton called for air strikes but refused to commit American ground troops, London refused to support air strikes because of its soldiers in the field, the Serbs blamed the Bosnian government, and UNPROFOR equivocated. Still, it was clear that a line had been crossed. Boutros-Ghali wrote to Manfred Wörner, NATO's secretary general, calling on NATO to "prepare urgently for the use of air strikes to deter further such attacks." Akashi met with Radovan Karadžić and told him that unless the Serbs pulled back their guns some twelve miles from Sarajevo, the United Nations would support air strikes. Eventually, the Serbs and Bosnian government forces signed a ceasefire. The Bosnian Serbs pulled back their guns the required distance, and UNPROFOR troops were positioned between the lines, which was now declared a "total exclusion zone." For a while Sarajevo enjoyed peace, of a sort.

But the reason why—because for once UNPROFOR *had* taken a robust stand, with credible threats of NATO air strikes—was soon forgotten. General Rose was obsessed with what he called "crossing the Mogadishu line"—the danger that United Nations troops would become combatants, as had happened to United States soldiers in Somalia. But Rose's position was based on a misinterpretation of UNPROFOR's mandate. Two separate issues were blurred: strategic air strikes and the passage of aid convoys. Certainly the Bosnian government wanted nothing more than for NATO to bomb the Serbs into defeat. There was an argument that resolutions 819, 824, and 836, which mandated UNPROFOR to "deter attacks" on the six safe areas, were sufficient justification for this response, as all these resolutions invoked chapter VII, the enforcement clause of the UN charter. The second issue was aid convoys. General Rose argued that attempting to force passage would be an "act of war."

But if there was room to debate the scope of 819, 824, and 836, resolution 770 was clear: it authorized member states to take "all necessary measures" to get relief supplies through. This clearly covered the potential use of force. But without an agreed definition, "all necessary measures" was a meaningless formula, says the US army officer who served as liaison with UNPROFOR. "One country would take that and run with it, transferring into a combat operation, but another would say, 'We will use all necessary measures' within the confines of how we view humanitarian assistance."

As Britbat, the British UN armored infantry battalion stationed at Vitez, in central Bosnia, showed, a robust approach was perfectly feasible within UNPROFOR's mandate. The war around Vitez, between the Bosnian Croat army (HVO) and government forces, rumbled through late 1992 and early 1993. The commander of Britbat, the charismatic Colonel Bob Stewart, did not agonize over the nuances of resolutions but stormed into the fighting, rescuing civilians on both sides of the front line. On the morning of 16 April Colonel Stewart was on patrol when he heard reports of a massacre at the village of Ahmići. He was stopped outside by HVO soldiers asking whether he had permission to enter. His reply has gone down in history: "I don't need the permission of the bloody HVO, I'm from the United Nations," he proclaimed, driving through the barricade into a scene of horror: the HVO had killed more than one hundred civilians, including women and children, many burned to death.

Nordbat, a Swedish, Danish, and Norwegian battalion based in the northern city of Tuzla, had twenty-four NATO Leopard tanks. When the Serbs fired artillery at its base, Nordbat fired back dozens of rounds. The Serbs stopped shelling. "Two or three days later we had talks in Pale with Mladić and

Karadžić," recalls Michael Williams. "General Rose said we would face real difficulties. But Mladić was quite relaxed; he said, 'Yes, there was an incident,' and he clearly regarded it as fair game. The lesson the Serbs drew was that the Danes would shoot back. Even within the mandate there was very considerable room for a robust response." Meanwhile Akashi further honed the concept of UN "neutrality," allowing seven Serb tanks to pass through the heavy weapons exclusion zone around Sarajevo to reposition elsewhere.

The Bosnian Serb onslaught on the safe area of Goražde began in late March 1994.

Strung out along the banks of the river Drina, Goražde, like Srebrenica, was surrounded by the Bosnian Serbs, although soldiers and civilians passed in and out on a perilous mountain path. The Serb assault coincided with the return of General Mladić after the suicide of his daughter Ana, a medical student in Belgrade. Mladić's own loss did not nurture any human sympathy. By early April his troops were advancing toward Goražde's town center, raining down tank and artillery shells. Initially many in UNPROFOR argued that the Serbs did not intend to take Goražde but merely to "shrink" the enclave. There were no UN troops in Goražde, but there were UN relief workers and UN military observers (UNMOs), who were not part of UNPROFOR. The UNMOs listened with disbelief to UNPROFOR's analysis. The UNMOs told their headquarters: "It is a grave situation. . . . Saying it is a minor attack into a limited area is a bad assessment, incorrect, and shows absolutely no understanding of what was going on."[7] Their reports on the Serb attack were leaked to the press, sparking General Rose's anger.

The Goražde crisis was problematic for the United Nations. If the town fell, there would be no choice but to launch

strategic air strikes against the Bosnian Serbs. NATO was willing
to do this, but many in the United Nations were not. NATO's
role in the Bosnian war was increasing, bringing commensu-
rate political influence and fueling a growing policy disagreement. NATO combat patrols enforced the no-fly zone. The
North Atlantic Council (NAC), NATO's decision-making body,
had already approved plans for massive air strikes to break the
siege of Sarajevo. On 28 February 1994, US F-16s shot down
four Serb jets flying over Bosnia. NATO's first-ever combat action was judged a resounding success. Many, including Secretary General Wörner, wanted much more. There was a growing sense that the world's most powerful military alliance was
impotent, hidebound by UN bureaucrats, unwilling to enforce
its own mandates.

On the morning of 10 April, Goražde's defenses collapsed
completely and the Bosnian Serbs smashed through the front
lines. US intelligence intercepted a message from General Mladić
that he did not want "a single lavatory left standing." Fears
grew of massive civilian casualties. From Vukovar in November 1991 to eastern Bosnia in 1992, the fate of every town captured by the Bosnian Serbs proved that the only question was
not whether war crimes would take place but what would be
their extent. General Rose authorized "close air support" (CAS).
CAS was not a strategic air strike but comprised pinprick targeted attacks on specific tanks or gun emplacements. The planes
flew back and forth, unable to find a tank to attack because of
poor light, bad weather, and the targets' movement. General
Rose then ordered an attack on the Bosnian Serb artillery command post. It was destroyed and nine Serb officers killed.

The next day the Bosnian Serbs resumed shelling, and
NATO planes were again dispatched. General Rose ordered the
planes to attack, and they destroyed a tank and two armored

vehicles. The assault slowed, but General Mladić dramatically upped the stakes: his troops took 150 UN soldiers and aid workers hostage. Akashi and Shashi Tharoor traveled to Pale to meet Karadžić to try and negotiate the hostages' release. This was quite courageous, considering that NATO had just killed several Bosnian Serb officers. While Akashi and Tharoor parleyed, several UNMOs were hit by machine-gun fire in Goražde. General Rose asked Akashi for more air strikes to try and save the UNMOs. Akashi refused.

The fighting continued, the Serbs advanced, and on 15 April the Bosnian Serbs shot down a British Sea Harrier fighter plane. By now it was clear that Goražde was totally unprotected and could be taken whenever General Mladić wanted. The United Nations, the Security Council, and NATO were all in an uproar. Washington and NATO pushed for strategic air strikes to stop the Serbs, but London and Paris resisted. Cables flew back and forth, while the press reported that tens of thousands of civilians were in peril. Boutros-Ghali wrote to NATO Secretary General Wörner, asking NATO to examine the feasibility of air strikes against the Bosnian Serbs in all six safe areas.

On Friday, 22 April, the North Atlantic Council set a deadline of noon Saturday for the Serbs to pull back. Many UN officials felt that the situation had passed out of their control. Either the Serbs would capture Goražde or NATO would stop them. But Akashi decided to travel to Belgrade to meet with Milošević and the Bosnian Serbs. Several members of his senior staff argued against this. "Most of us had fairly strong reservations about using Milošević to restrain the Bosnian Serbs," recalls Michael Williams. "We were increasingly depressed, and many of us felt there was nothing further we could do. The role of the United Nations was becoming increasingly marginalized. We felt this would not work and that it would interfere with Boutros-Ghali's appeal to NATO to take action." Neverthe-less, that afternoon, Akashi, Williams, other UN officials and the French General Bertrand de Lapresle, UNPROFOR commander for the former Yugoslavia, flew to Belgrade. "There was keen interest in Zagreb and New York whether we were going to be able to secure a Serb agreement for a cease-fire. Otherwise, it was clear what was going to happen. NATO bombers would hit the Serbs and hit them on an extensive scale," Williams recalls.

Late on Friday evening the negotiations ended without agreement. On Saturday morning Williams showed Akashi a cable from Boutros-Ghali, warning the UN delegation to leave Belgrade by noon. Akashi replied that he wished Williams had not shown him the cable and insisted on more negotiations. NATO fighters readied for strategic air strikes. Milošević blinked first. About 10:30 A.M. the Bosnian Serbs agreed to a cease-fire. Coffee and *slivovitz*, plum brandy, were served. Both sides re-laxed, until General de Lapresle warned General Mladić that the deal must be adhered to or NATO would bomb. General Mladić turned red with rage, the veins in his neck popping out. "It's up to you to restrain them, and you should be aware that if there are any NATO attacks, we will be absolutely merciless to your people on the ground," he shouted. The UN delegation left soon after, escorted at top speed to Belgrade airport.

Akashi's relief was short-lived. Noon came and went, the Bosnian Serbs carried on firing. Manfred Wörner telephoned Akashi, pressuring him to authorize air strikes. Akashi resisted. Akashi instead offered to call Radovan Karadžić for further talks. Wörner was furious, but could do nothing. Events had descended into farce. The Bosnian Serbs had signed a cease-fire and immediately broken it. NATO planes were on standby, the target lists drawn up. The P5 had reluctantly accepted that Goražde could not be allowed to fall. Yet still Akashi would not budge. Wörner and his officials were incredulous. A Japanese civil servant was stopping NATO from going to war.

Yet how had NATO gotten itself into this mess? The United Nations was designed to make peace; NATO was configured for war. Akashi sincerely held that the United Nations must remain impartial peacekeepers. But the most senior UN official in the field was far out of time and place. The United Nations' role in Bosnia demanded new ways of thinking, but Akashi could not, or would not, make the mental leap. The Serbs eventually pulled out of Goražde, but the town remained under siege. The Goražde crisis was extremely significant for Srebrenica. It nearly ruptured relations between the United Nations and NATO. It highlighted how UNPROFOR's cumbersome chain of command prevented decisive decision making. It showed how reluctant was the United Nations to use any meaningful force to stop the Serbs. The poverty of the safe-areas policy was clear. NATO's pinprick air strikes, General Mladić understood, were no threat at all.

III
Countdown

It is deeply disquieting, if not humiliating, that United
Nations peacekeepers in Goražde are being transported
by horsecart, and that reports of civilian starvation are
beginning to emerge from Srebrenica.
—Shashi Tharoor, confidential memo to
Kofi Annan and Yasushi Akashi on the
future of UNPROFOR, 6 December 1994

I n view of later events it was ironic that the Netherlands
offered a battalion of peacekeepers precisely because it
thought the United Nations should take far more robust
action against the Serbs. The 570 troops of Dutchbat I
arrived in Srebrenica in early March 1994, replacing the Cana-
dians deployed the previous April. Dutchbat was a much larger

mission. It included two infantry companies, reconnaissance
and security troops, engineers, and explosives experts. But the
Srebrenica enclave covered about fifty square miles, and Dutchbat was spread thin on the ground. The town itself was on the
eastern side, almost two miles from the front line. Dutchbat's
compound and operational headquarters were located in Potočari, more than four miles north. To the west was a string of
villages and isolated hamlets, and the enclave reached another
three miles south. There were eight UN observation posts strung
out along the thirty-mile-long border, although nobody agreed
where the safe area began: the UN, the Bosniaks, and the Bosnian Serbs all had their own lines of demarcation. The exact
border had been delineated in May 1993, but UNPROFOR had
lost the map.[1]

Dutchbat's mission had three objectives: to deter attacks,
as outlined in the resolutions of spring 1993; to facilitate humanitarian aid; and to demilitarize the enclave. But the troops
were poorly prepared. The Dutch ministry of defense's training was based on bizarre orientalist clichés. Videos showed
actors in white robes and turbans clicking prayer beads and
shouting, "You are disturbing our prayers" and "Allah will punish you." Serb soldiers in the videos screamed and stamped
their feet and wore Russian-style fur hats. Dutchbat's standing
orders instructed male soldiers not to make eye contact with
Muslim women, speak openly to them, or shake hands, advice
more suitable for Saudi Arabia or Iran. No Bosnian Muslims
wore white robes, and only the *hodjas,* local Islamic leaders,
wore turbans. No Bosnian women wore veils, which was why
the old Turkish proverb said, "If you want to see your wife,
then go to Bosnia." Nor did Serb soldiers wear fur hats. It was
certainly a poor start for a mission that would end in disaster.[2]

By now the Serbs had learned that as long as they let a

small proportion of aid and supplies through, they could do as they wished with the rest. Dutchbat's weapons, ammunition, fuel, and supply convoys were delayed, obstructed, and turned back. The Dutch troops were often forced to patrol on foot. Their generators broke down, which meant that fresh food could not be stored and hot water was scarce. Even so, Dutchbat contributed much: it cleared roads of snow, dredged wrecked cars from the river, and helped restore municipal services. Dutchbat's doctors treated local people, although strictly speaking they were not supposed to, except to save lives or limbs. Dutchbat's presence helped stabilize the situation and ensure that at least some relief aid got through.

Despite the demilitarization agreement, sporadic fighting continued. Nasir Oric's troops continued raiding into Serb territory. A favorite tactic, which infuriated the Dutch soldiers, was for Oric's men to position themselves next to the Dutch posts and fire at the Bosnian Serbs, hoping to draw Dutchbat into the conflict when the Serbs fired back. Serious questions over Dutchbat's security remained unresolved. Prime Minister Ruud Lubbers could not get answers from Boutros-Ghali to questions about when air support would be authorized if the Dutch troops were attacked.[3] But Boutros-Ghali could not supply information he did not have.

Inside Srebrenica, just as the JNA's analysis had predicted, the lack of salt was taking effect. Mladić's troops deliberately removed the boxes of salt from the little relief aid that was allowed through. Srebrenica's inhabitants were indeed experiencing "confusion, instability, and aggressiveness" and "an inclination toward anarchy and panic." The bland diet of relief supplies made them crave any kind of taste. Eventually they broke into the municipal warehouse holding stocks of road salt, scoured the dirt from the grey lumps, and boiled them down

to a fine powder. "We were becoming more and more like animals, as if the salt was the only thing that had once made the
difference between animals and us," recorded Emir Suljagic,
author of *Postcards from the Grave*.[4] The road salt was nutri-
tionally worthless. It contained no iodine, essential to prevent
goiter.

Life, or rather existence, in Srebrenica was medieval. More
than twenty-two thousand people were crammed into the town,
almost four times its prewar population, while another twenty
thousand were scattered through the enclave in remote villages. There was no work except for the few employed by the
United Nations or relief organizations. Prostitution, preferably
with a Dutchbat soldier, black marketeering, or looting on the
raids into Serb territory were the only other sources of income.
There was only sporadic running water and barely any food
apart from relief supplies. Electricity was generated by water-
wheels. Corn husks were ground down to bake a barely di-
gestible "bread." Most lived on a few hundred calories a day.
The common social bonds broke down. All that mattered was
survival. The isolation exacted a heavy psychological toll. The
war had rent families asunder, scattering them across the world.
Every morning long queues formed outside the ham radio
operator's office, Srebrenica's only link with the outside world.
Some traveled for days on foot or horseback, from the ends
of the enclave, for five minutes of radio time talking to their
loved ones.

The town was split between indigenous locals and refugees.
Locals held every key position in the municipal administration, police, and army. The military commander Nasir Oric and
the war president, Osman Suljić, controlled most of the supply
of relief aid. Flour and rice were distributed, but little else. The
cynicism and corruption of the municipal leaders knew no
limits. They stockpiled aid to create shortages and keep prices

high in the black market, which they controlled. The United Nations stopped delivering children's toys after even they were stolen. Fabric set aside for refugees to make clothes was turned into new uniforms for the police. "The first conclusion I reached during my initial stay in Srebrenica in May 1993 was that it was the largest refugee camp in the world, and the poorest run one at that," wrote a UN civil affairs officer after a visit in September 1994. "I still maintain that conclusion. No one is in charge."[5] Cigarettes, diesel fuel, and gasoline were smuggled in from the Ukrainian peacekeepers in nearby Žepa, coffee and salt were bought from the Serbs—sometimes along with weapons and ammunition. The profits were substantial: a packet of Marlboro cigarettes fetched 10 deutsche marks ($6.60), two pounds of coffee DM70 ($46), and two pounds of salt DM30 ($20).

While the town's leaders invited peacekeepers for dinners served by waiters with white cloths draped over their arms, crowds gathered each morning around the Dutchbat garbage dump, scrabbling through the empty cans and leftovers. "And how happy they were with a discarded piece of meat from the kitchen," wrote one Dutch peacekeeper to his girlfriend. "Sometimes there would be two or three grown men tugging at a rubbish bag. No, I will not forget that in a hurry."[6] Health conditions were appalling. Homes were infested by lice, fleas, and cockroaches. The UN civil affairs officer recorded 530 cases of yellow fever, a mosquito-borne disease usually found in Africa; more than 3,000 cases of intestinal disease; 14,500 cases of scabies, and 26,000 cases of lice.[7] It was impossible to keep the vermin at bay as the Serbs refused to allow sufficient soap and disinfectants through. The director of the local hospital spent much time performing abortions, for a fee of DM100 ($66), and feuding with the staff of the aid agency Médecins Sans Frontières (Doctors Without Borders, MSF), who refused to give him control of their pharmacy for fear that the prescription drugs would immediately be sold on the black market. Little was reported, for by 1994 Srebrenica had slipped off the outside world's radar.

There was a massive psychological gap between Dutchbat and the local population. Coming from a prosperous and peaceful country, the young soldiers had no idea of the effect of war: the degradation, apathy, and depression it induces. They found the poverty and misery hard to deal with. Children gathered outside the Dutch base asking for *bon-bon*, sweets, sometimes serenading the soldiers with songs. Many soldiers wanted to give them chocolate but were forbidden, as dozens more children would instantly appear. The Dutch soldiers were angry at the Bosniak men who spent their days listlessly walking back and forth. Many of these men had been separated from their families and were lonely and depressed. There was no work and their poor diet deprived them of energy. They shared cramped, miserable accommodation where beds were used on a rotation basis. Food disposal was a major problem for Dutchbat. Eventually it was decided that any leftovers would be given to the old people's home or the communal kitchen. Municipal leaders were furious, as the donations drove down prices on the black market. Understandably, the Dutch soldiers were disgusted by the corruption of the local authorities. Their anger turned ugly. One soldier had a T-shirt produced in Holland showing a Dutchbat soldier grasping by the throat a small boy who is asking for *bon-bon* and replying "Nema"—there aren't any. Some in Dutchbat preferred to deal with the Serbs: they at least had a command structure and a proper army with officers and ranks. Ultimately, Dutchbat reflected the society from which it was drawn: some soldiers were kind and humane, others dismissive or prejudiced.

Srebrenica was not alone in being run by criminals. At the start of the war in Sarajevo mafia gangs led the defense of the city. Eventually, when their power became so great that it threatened the government, they were wiped out. But Sarajevo had no control over Srebrenica. There taking a stand often had fatal consequences: when the refugees elected a representative to deal with aid supplies, he was immediately murdered. A slogan scrawled on a wall proclaimed, "Welcome to the biggest concentration camp in the world," though conditions were perhaps more reminiscent of the wartime Jewish ghettos, such as Łódź in Poland. In Srebrenica, as in Łódź, suffering did not ennoble—rather, it made people cynical, selfish, and bitter. And absolute power corrupted absolutely, whether in Bosnia in 1994 or Poland in 1944. Mordechai Rumkowski, leader of the Łódź ghetto, built a squalid kingdom of privilege, even deciding who would live or die in the Nazi roundups. In Srebrenica, too, empire building was all, noted the UN Civil Affairs official: "Municipal officials have shown reluctance in initiating any new or additional projects that they can not directly control, to improve their living conditions." The Łódź ghetto, like Srebrenica, was divided between the locals and newcomers. An influx of bourgeois German and Austrian Jews cornered the ghetto's black market in bread, angering the local Jews. A rhyme from wartime Łódź could just as well apply to Srebrenica:

> When we had nothing to eat,
> They gave us a turnip, they gave us a beet,
> Here, have some grub, have some fleas,
> Have some typhus, die of disease.

The men of Srebrenica would soon die, but not of disease.

The Dutch troops who preferred the Serbs were not alone. The Serbs were boisterous hosts, at least while they were winning. The cover photograph of *Unfinest Hour,* Brendan Simms's au-

thoritative dissection of Britain's Bosnia policy, shows General
Rose smiling and shaking hands with a laughing General Mladić
on 1 January 1995. United Nations visitors to Pale were plied
with roast lamb, *slivovitz,* and wine. Meetings with the Bosnian
Serb leadership began in the afternoon and lasted for hours, the
Serbs often descending into drunken near-chaos. "We had to
have discussions with the Bosnian Serbs, but I did not like the
atmosphere in which these meetings were conducted; it seemed
to me to border on incorrect behavior," says a UN official who
was present at many such meetings.

Sarajevo could not compete. Bosnian government ministers greeted their visitors with drawn faces and bitter expressions. They sat in cold, dark rooms with the windows blown
out and served Tang, a powdered orange drink. "I once asked a
UN official why they don't like the Bosnians," recalls the photographer Mark Milstein. "He said because they don't wear
uniforms. I never forgot that comment." Peter Galbraith, then
US ambassador to Croatia, concurs: "There was a real antipa-
thy toward the Bosnians at the United Nations in Zagreb and
Sarajevo. They saw the Bosnians as always whining and com-
plaining. But the Serbs were winners, and they were good
hosts."

Wearying of Europe's appeasement of the Serbs, President
Clinton launched a new twin-track policy, one overt and one
covert. The overt track was based on the Washington agreement, brokered by Galbraith, which ended the Bosniak-Croat
war and created the Federation of Bosnia and Herzegovina, allowing the Bosniaks and Croats to focus on their common
enemy: the Serbs. The covert track had US military advisers se-
cretly training the Croatian army, while Washington tacitly approved an illicit arms supply from Muslim countries, including Turkey and Iran, through Croatia to Bosnia. Other NATO

countries knew what was going on but turned a blind eye, it seems. "If the Americans were prepared to do that on the side that was their business," says Douglas Hurd, former British foreign secretary. "Latterly we knew a certain amount. We were not told but we guessed. I knew that arms were reaching the Croats with American connivance."

In autumn 1994 the Bosnian 5th Corps broke out of the safe area of Bihać, in northwest Bosnia, and recaptured considerable territory. But the Bosnian Serbs soon counterattacked with an all-out assault. The Bihać crisis was a rerun of Goražde, six months earlier. Bihać town was starving—only 5 percent of UN aid got through. As the Serbs advanced, General Manojlo Milovanović, Mladić's chief of staff, issued a chilling warning: "I have already called on you to surrender. You failed to obey and were punished. If you fail to obey this time I will not be able to guarantee your lives, since many of you have committed horrible crimes against the Serbian people." Lacking tanks and artillery, the government troops could not hold their new conquests. The defense line collapsed and they retreated. On 19 November, Serb airplanes killed many civilians in a bombing raid, violating the no-fly zone. General Mladić deployed sophisticated antiaircraft missile systems and radar which could "lock onto" NATO aircraft. NATO and the United States pushed for strategic air strikes, now clearly justified, to destroy the Serb antiaircraft system. UNPROFOR refused, and the two organizations bickered and argued over targets and the scope of CAS. General de Lapresle, UN commander for all the former Yugoslavia, authorized only a low-level attack on the runway of Udbina airport, from where the Serb airplanes had taken off. The planes themselves were not touched.

In Zagreb, Peter Galbraith went straight to the UN headquarters and headed for Akashi's office. Galbraith, the son of the economist John Kenneth Galbraith, was a hawk on Bosnia. He had seen genocide at first hand. In the late 1980s he had uncovered Saddam Hussein's Al-Anfal (spoils of war) campaign against the Kurds. His reports on the use of chemical weapons against Kurdish villages led the US Senate to pass sanctions against Saddam's regime. "I was Akashi's main interlocutor with the United States. We had arguments all the time about UNPROFOR's response," recalls Galbraith. "I was often pushing for military action against the Serbs, urging that the dual key be turned, or there be air strikes. I told him the bombing of Udbina airport was not enough. They had avoided bombing the planes because of UNPROFOR's appeasement of the Serbs." But Akashi was as adamant as ever.

Bihać began to collapse. The mayor said that 300,000 refugees were pouring in, while the UNHCR estimated 180,000. At one stage the Serbs were firing on Bihać hospital from eight hundred yards. Ed Joseph, a former US army officer serving in UNPROFOR's civil affairs division, had managed to cross the front lines and enter the town. He briefed the international media by satellite telephone, which helped keep the pressure on for NATO to intervene. Joseph urged the UN commander there to send peacekeepers to defend the hospital, as hospitals were protected under the Geneva Conventions. "He was hesitant about deploying until I reminded him of the hospital's special status, and then to his credit he deployed the Bangladeshis, whose presence had an immediate impact." But Joseph was opposed by a UN legal official. "He came out with the astonishing argument that UNPROFOR should not deploy, as the United Nations was not party to the Geneva Conventions." This was technically true but completely irrelevant and morally bankrupt.

General Rose eventually ordered CAS to support UNPROFOR. US A-10 tankbusters were dispatched from Aviano air base to attack the Serb tanks. General Rose had a team of British SAS commandos inside Bihać, acting as forward air spotters, to relay the coordinates of Serb tanks and guns to the US planes. Despite this action, the A-10s returned home without finding any targets, causing anger in both Sarajevo and Washington.[8] A UN official alleges that General Rose instructed the SAS team not to cooperate. For unknown to General Rose, US intelligence was apparently eavesdropping. The UN official recalls: "The Americans said that there was some evidence that General Rose deliberately misled the planes, as his people on the ground did not identify the targets." General Rose denies these claims: "Official records of the time (NATO's included) show that I ordered the forward air controllers to the south of the Bihać pocket to where the Serb attacks were being launched, and that it was the NATO pilots, who could not find the targets, who called off the attacks because of increasing bad weather."[9]

Generals de Lapresle and Rose wore United Nations berets, but their first loyalties often seemed to be to their own governments. The split was widening between Akashi and General Rose on one side and the United States and NATO on the other. "We did not hold General Rose in high regard, especially those of us in the United States government on the more hawkish side," recalls Peter Galbraith.

> We believed that military force had to be used to enforce the United Nations, to protect the safe areas, to stop attacks, and to ensure the delivery of relief supplies. There was a tactical and strategic question here. The tactical one was that this appeasement of delivering threats and not following up was encouraging the Serbs to engage in more and more outrageous behavior. The Serbs were classic bullies and

would back down if you responded with force. The strategic question was that we thought we could not be neutral. There was an aggressor, violating international law, and a victim. This was about the international community using force, including air strikes, or Bosnia would become like Israel and Palestine, a sixty-year cesspool. But it was solvable. That was the fundamental point.

Eventually, the Serbs stopped shelling and pulled back. But the Bihać crisis, like the Goražde crisis, ended without resolution, and the enclave remained surrounded and under siege. General Mladić had now launched two major attacks on UN safe areas. Neither had fallen, but neither had NATO seriously attacked the Bosnian Serbs. Srebrenica, Mladić understood, was there for the taking.

As the United Nations approached 1995, its fiftieth year, its critics argued that in Bosnia, at least, it was no longer primarily a moral instrument of the international community, working to further peace and human rights. It was true that the UN humanitarian organizations had helped save many thousands of lives, feeding and housing the victims of ethnic cleansing. UNPROFOR's *humanitarian* record was praiseworthy. Without the UNPROFOR headquarters in Sarajevo, the city would probably have fallen. By the winter of 1994 there were more than twenty-four thousand UN troops deployed across Bosnia. More than one hundred had been killed, and hundreds more wounded and injured, not always at the hands of the Serbs. UN troops did bring valuable succor, escorting aid convoys that otherwise would never have made it through; repairing water and electricity supplies, building bridges and roads, clearing minefields, repairing schools and hospitals, evacuating the sick and wounded, and exchanging POWs. General Rose argues: "The United Nations did heroically come to the aid of the Muslims. They stopped Bosnia from being overrun by the Serbs, fed the Bosnian people during three years of civil war, and were instrumental in bringing about the halting of the fighting between the Croats and the Muslims. Indeed if it had not been for their presence, Dayton [the US-brokered peace accord that ended the war] would never have happened."[10]

UNPROFOR treated the symptoms of the Bosnian war. But the political causes of the conflict remained largely unaddressed, the necessary robust strategic response to the Bosnian Serbs neither formulated nor implemented. The Security Council members had ensured that the United Nations' founding principles, to save humanity from the "scourge of war," had been sidelined for their own expedient aims, often with the support of those Secretariat officials who were more concerned about preserving the United Nations' impartiality and neutrality than its mission to save lives. But as Peter Galbraith and others have argued, neutrality and impartiality in the face of sustained, organized aggression did not mean steering a middle course: they meant de facto appeasement, the aiding and abetting of genocide and ethnic cleansing, and complicity with evil. Doubtless, neither the Security Council nor the Secretariat intended this, but this was the result.

As the war in Bosnia ground on, divisions within the Secretariat itself widened: in Zagreb, Akashi continued to follow an ultrapacifistic, slavishly "neutral" position. But in New York, the growing pressure from NATO, especially the United States, and the widening split between the Western alliance and the United Nations was forcing the DPKO into a more robust position, however unwillingly. Kofi Annan and Shashi Tharoor realized that UNPROFOR's passivity was starting to exact a high political cost to the United Nations and strain its relations with its most important paymaster, the United States. They began to shift position.

This may have been one reason why Boutros-Ghali generally refused to let Annan brief the Security Council, sending instead his special political adviser, Chinmaya Gharekhan. But when a serious crisis erupted, the Security Council insisted that Annan appear, says Colin Keating. "When things got tough and hard decisions had to be taken, for example on the use of airpower in 1994, the Council insisted on Annan coming. They took seriously what he and Iqbal Riza [a senior DPKO official] said. They had well-thought-out and credible recommendations, and we felt well served by the Secretariat. I would not put Annan at the end of the spectrum which was for peace at all costs. He was quite willing to come to the Council, and say this is a time when it is essential to use force."

Akashi sensed that things were shifting in New York. He could not control NATO's increasing exasperation, but he could control what New York knew about the situation on the ground. Akashi and his staff were highly selective about the flow of information to New York, quick to call attention to misdemeanors by the Bosnian army while downplaying Serb felonies, says a former UNPROFOR civil affairs officer. "If any reports detailing Serb misdeeds managed to get through the bureaucracy, UNPROFOR Zagreb made a concerted effort to massage them so that what they sent to New York always maintained the 'all three sides are guilty' premise and thus staved off the pressure for air strikes." This is confirmed by another UN official who worked in Bosnia:

> A lot of information either got converted or didn't really end up the way it should have in New York.

There was a certain prevalent view in Zagreb about how this information should be passed on to New York. Sometimes it was, and sometimes it wasn't, because I think there was a decision that there are certain things that just can't be done. In the case of Srebrenica, for example, we should have taken action much earlier. And when we didn't, I am not sure that the level and extent of what was happening on the ground was being reported as such.

Akashi himself denies this, countering that the staffers at the United Nations headquarters were too influenced by the media. "In no instance did we 'shape' information we sent to New York, certainly not consciously. It was our impression, however, that New York's information was frequently shaped in the political climate and media views prevalent in New York City."[11]

But UNPROFOR's strategic and political response to the war was ever weaker, as the United Nations cracked under the contradictions of its Bosnia policy. The split between NATO and the United Nations mirrored Washington's split with London and Paris. The P5 refused to recognize that the UN troops were increasingly being drawn into a combat mission for which they had neither the mandate, the equipment, or domestic political support to properly fight. Inside the DPKO there was a growing sense that the mission had become untenable. There was an increasing sense of looming disaster. In many areas UNPROFOR was "unable to supply itself, unable to protect the delivery of humanitarian aid, unable to deter attacks, unable to fight for itself and unable to withdraw," noted Shashi Tharoor in his confidential memo to Kofi Annan and Yasushi Akashi. "Our usual arguments (UNPROFOR withdrawal would lead to war, international community has no better alternative, something is better than nothing, etc.) cannot be responsibly

made if we are unable to perform most of our existing mandates as a result of Serb non-cooperation, and there is no peace
process worth protecting."[12]

Tharoor concluded by recommending the "assertive delivery of supplies to UNPROFOR and to civilians in the safe
areas" as a mean of breaking the stalemate, which could "transform the functioning of the Force and restore credit to the
United Nations' often unjustly-maligned record in Bosnia and
Herzegovina." Tharoor was right, but why had this realization
taken two and half years? Resolution 770, authorizing "all measures necessary" for the delivery of relief supplies, had been
passed on 13 August 1992. Meanwhile, Boutros-Ghali submitted a report on the safe areas to the Security Council. He admitted that the "light option" and air strikes alone could not
effectively protect the safe areas. However, Serb surface-to-air
missiles now constrained the use of NATO air power. The missiles could not be attacked, though, because the Serbs might
then attack UNPROFOR. So the United Nations could not
protect the safe areas because of the Serbs. But the United Nations could not do anything about the Serbs, because they might
attack the United Nations. Sometimes it seemed as though the
United Nations' Bosnia policy was a cross between *Alice's Ad-
ventures in Wonderland* and *Catch-22*.

In January 1995 Dutchbat II handed over command of
Srebrenica to Dutchbat III, commanded by Lieutenant Colonel
Thom Karremans. While the changeover took place, the Bosnian Serbs advanced into the enclave and set up new positions
on the front line formerly patrolled by Dutchbat II. Srebrenica's defenders demanded that Dutchbat retake the positions,
for which their comrades had died, but Dutchbat refused. Rumors, which have never been fully verified, flew back and forth
that the Bosnian government was considering swapping Sre-

brenica in exchange for Serb-held suburbs of Sarajevo. British intelligence officers at UNPROFOR warned that Srebrenica was a tinderbox. "Srebrenica has to be dealt with before the situation further deteriorates," wrote Lieutenant Colonel C. A. le Hardy on 24 February 1995. "Srebrenica will not simply go away. It needs high level attention."[13] In April 1995 Nasir Oric, who strongly opposed trading the enclaves, was recalled to Sarajevo by the Bosnian government, never to return.

The new UNPROFOR commander, General Rupert Smith, traveled to Srebrenica to observe conditions for himself. General Smith, like General Rose, was British, but the two men were very different. General Smith was a former assistant chief of the Defense Staff in London, and during the 1991 Gulf War had commanded the UK armored division. Rose dealt in tactics, Smith in strategy. "To be fair to Rose, the situation had developed when Smith arrived. I think he felt from early on that the situation in Bosnia was untenable and that there were limited options for the United Nations," says a former UNPROFOR official. "One was a pull-out, and if governments did not want to entertain that, they had to confront the realities of Bosnia. This was that Bosnian Serb forces were willfully, and repeatedly, attacking civilians and safe areas that were allegedly under United Nations control." General Rose's approach had not worked, says Douglas Hurd. "Rose did not want his terms of reference enlarged. He thought that what he had, used with vigor and imagination, could actually produce a transformation. From time to time he got results, a cease-fire. He thought it could be done from bottom up, but it didn't work out. Smith did not think that." General de Lapresle, the overall commander of UN forces in the former Yugoslavia, was replaced by another French appointee, chosen by President Mitterrand: General Bernard Janvier. The winter cease-fire brokered by Akashi and former US President Jimmy Carter ended, and Bosnia was once again at war.

On 8 May 1995 Yasushi Akashi sent cable Z-740 to Kofi Annan.[14] The previous day several mortar or artillery rounds had landed in Sarajevo, killing and injuring several people. The shells were fired by the Bosnian Serbs, who were also threatening to fire on any UN vehicles that approached the area, and so preventing UNPROFOR from carrying out a proper investigation, noted Akashi. The Serbs were considered in violation of both resolution 836, mandating UNPROFOR to "deter attacks" on the safe areas, and NATO's ultimatum of February 1994 that declared a total exclusion zone around Sarajevo. General Smith, wrote Akashi, had recommended that NATO carry out air strikes. It seemed an open-and-shut case. But not while Akashi controlled the United Nations' half of the dual key. After consulting General Janvier and others, he wrote, "I have decided we should not at present proceed with the request for an air-strike." He continued:

> In addition to the normal concerns raised in such circumstances (UN hostages, blockages of convoys, supply problems to the enclaves), a number of other concerns relevant to the present situation were considered. Our greatest concern was the possibility that an air-strike now would de-rail the stabilization process begun in Croatia, undermine the moderates in the Knin leadership, encourage adventurism on the part of Martic and Karadzic and weaken Milosevic, rendering the possibility of the FRY [Yugoslavia] recognizing Bosnia and/or Croatia more remote.

Every one of the clauses in this second sentence was wrong. There was no stabilization process in Croatia. On 1 May the

Croatian army launched Operation Flash, recapturing a Serb-held strip of land in the west of the country, sending thousands of Serb refugees over the border into Bosnia. There were no "moderates" in the rebel Serb leadership in Knin. The warlord-dentist Milan Babić had been sidelined by a portly former policeman named Milan Martić. In early May, Martić twice ordered long-range Orkan rockets, fitted with cluster bombs, to be fired into downtown Zagreb, a war crime for which he was later indicted. American diplomats were negotiating with Milošević about a peace deal, but the talks, one of many sets of negotiations, eventually collapsed without resolution. The most startling phrase is that air strikes might "weaken Milošević." It seemed it was now United Nations policy to help keep in power the Serbian commander in chief, who supplied General Mladić's tanks with gasoline, his artillery with shells, and his snipers with bullets, whose own army fought alongside the ethnic cleansers, whose intelligence service instructed the paramilitaries in the art of murder and rape, and whose state coffers paid all of their salaries.

Even Great Britain balked at this. Partly under the influence of General Smith, and partly for fear of splitting NATO, London and Paris were shifting position. There was talk of pulling out UNPROFOR and launching strategic air strikes against the Bosnian Serbs. Douglas Hurd wrote to Boutros-Ghali protesting Akashi's decision. "The dual key tended to produce a negative result because the UN people and Akashi were worried about the consequences. But it was not meant to be a veto which was always and automatically exercised," recalls Hurd. "I thought on this occasion it should have been possible to turn the dual key, and I said so. It seemed to me they were getting into the attitude that in no circumstances was bombing justified. I thought that was wrong. The policy was that air strikes should be examined by both NATO and the United

Nations. I was trying to get the policy back where I thought it should be, a genuine look at each case, and not an automatic assumption there could be no bombing." NATO's exasperation was clearly explained to Boutros-Ghali and Annan. The split between the Secretariat in New York and UNPROFOR widened. Boutros-Ghali's five-year term expired at the end of 1996. Annan coveted his job. It was an open secret that Boutros-Ghali and Madeleine Albright loathed each other. By attacking Akashi, Annan would both distance himself from a policy that was now clearly a failure and put himself in Washington's good graces.

An opportunity came on 8 May, the same day as Akashi's cable Z-740. Muhamed Sacirbey wrote an angry letter to the Security Council after returning from Sarajevo. Together with vice president Ejup Ganić, Sacirbey had been promised that UNPROFOR would send an APC to transport him from Mount Igman down the most dangerous section of the road out of Sarajevo, which was exposed to Serb machine-gun fire. But when he and Ganić arrived at the meeting place, they were informed that UNPROFOR was not coming. They had to make their own way out on foot. It was an extremely perilous journey. When Sacirbey and Ganić eventually made it across the lines, they were furious. "We found the UNPROFOR armored personnel carriers and soldiers in a sheltered area," wrote Sacirbey. "They informed us that although their orders had been initially to pick us up at the top of Mount Igman, their orders were subsequently verbally changed not to proceed." Annan wrote to Akashi the next day, including a copy of Sacirbey's complaint: "We would, in particular, appreciate an explanation of the circumstances surrounding the Ambassador's transportation to Sarajevo. In case you judge that an apology is warranted, we would also appreciate a draft letter for my signature. The larger issues he raises should be covered in the draft review report we are expecting from you by 15 May."[15]

The growing rancor between New York and Zagreb was noticed in other departments. Samir Sanbar, an engaging Lebanese UN veteran, was head of the Department of Public Information (DPI). Sanbar's antennae were twitching over Bosnia. He dispatched a DPI official to try to find out what was happening on the ground, but without much success, as UNPROFOR was not cooperative. Sanbar decided to go himself. "I had the feeling that something was going on, that something might happen in Srebrenica. I talked about it with Annan. He was encouraging." Sanbar flew to Zagreb. He was royally received by a coterie of UN officials and taken to the Intercontinental Hotel in Zagreb. He passed a pleasant evening with Akashi.

The next morning Sanbar was packed and ready. A three-car convoy came to pick him up, UN pennants fluttering in the breeze. Sanbar was driven straight to Zagreb airport and put on a plane to Geneva. "It meant it was none of my business and I should stay out of their work." As Akashi fought his turf wars, morale plummeted. Michael Williams resigned as head of UN-PROFOR public affairs and left the United Nations. "I was increasingly apprehensive about the direction of the UN operation, and I had growing misgivings and fears. Each time I heard about a Serb attack, on Goražde or Bihać or Sarajevo, I felt increasingly fearful. The Serbs were pushing things to the limit."

In Srebrenica, General Mladić would show there were none.

IV
The Fall

urgent   urgent   urgent

bsa [Bosnian Serb Army] is entering
the town of srebrenica will someone stop this
immediately and save these people thousands
of them are gathering around the hospital there
is nothing to be confirmed any more please help at
least half the enclave has been taken
please help with any means

—Cable sent at 4:06 P.M. Monday, 10 July 1995,
from UNHCR Srebrenica to UNHCR offices

As spring moved to summer, General Mladić squeezed Srebrenica hard. The Serbs humiliated the United Nations. They blocked the passage of all fresh food, dairy products, flour, and meat. No engineering equipment, spare parts, or fuel reached Dutchbat, and the soldiers lived off combat rations. The health of those trapped inside the enclave further deteriorated—the sticky heat of a Balkan summer was a perfect breeding ground for cockroaches, fleas, and lice. The Serbs prevented any troops from entering or leaving after 26 April. Dutchbat was 150 soldiers short. Day by day the sense of impending disaster grew. Those living in the outlying villages moved into Srebrenica town, further straining the meager supplies. The UNMOs stationed inside the enclave informed UNPROFOR headquarters in Zagreb of the arrival of Arkan's Tigers, the most notorious and brutal of the Serb paramilitaries, a sure sign of impending conflict. Dutch politicians warned Muhamed Sacirbey that the Serbs were reinforcing and preparing an assault. Srebrenica's last days were approaching. The only question was when?

The countdown began on 1 June, when a Serb raiding party entered the enclaves and killed several civilians. The Serbs demanded that Dutchbat surrender its observation post (OP) Echo in the southeast, to facilitate the capture of a road south of the enclave. Dutchbat refused, and the Serbs attacked with mortars and antitank weapons. Dutchbat's request for close air support (CAS) went unanswered. This was an open-and-shut case—the Serbs were directly targeting UN peacekeepers. The request for CAS, stalled at UN regional command at Tuzla, did not even reach UNPROFOR headquarters in Zagreb, let alone New York. Dutchbat commanders were puzzled that soon after, the Serbs allowed a convoy carrying 100,000 liters of fuel through to the enclave. But the Serbs' purpose was soon to become clear.

The final assault began shortly before dawn on Thursday, 6 July. Serb guns rained down shells on the southeastern, eastern, and northern parts of the enclave while troops advanced. OP Foxtrot, near OP Echo, was hit by Serb tank fire. The Dutchbat OPs measured about fifty yards by thirty and were reinforced with sandbags. Their tents, containers, and bunkers were all painted regulation UN white, making them an easy target. The observation posts were not strong enough to withstand a full-blown assault. The Bosniaks fired back with small arms but were outgunned. The new Bosniak commander, Major Ramiz Bećirović, asked Lieutenant Colonel Karremans, the Dutchbat commander, to hand back the weapons the Bosniaks had surrendered to UNPROFOR in 1993, when Srebrenica was demilitarized. Karremans refused, on the grounds that it was UNPROFOR's job to defend the enclave, even though this was technically not part of the mandate. This was the first of many decisions by UNPROFOR that would have tragic consequences.

As the Bosnian Serbs continued firing on OP Foxtrot, Dutchbat went on a state of red alert, and soldiers took to the bunkers. Karremans again requested CAS from Tuzla. Colonel Charles Branz, also from the Netherlands and the regional UNPROFOR commander, approved the request and passed it to Sarajevo. But Mladić had timed his assault well: General Smith, who almost certainly would have approved the request, was on leave.

Instead, the request was handled by UNPROFOR's chief of staff, Major General Cees Nicolai, also Dutch. Nicolai refused. He later told UN investigators that he believed that the criteria set by General Janvier, his superior officer, had not been met. The Serbs continued their sporadic but targeted shelling on the UN base and OPs until around 3 P.M., when the firing stopped. That day's attack was a probe, a prelude to an all-out assault. General Mladić had learned everything he needed to know: Dutchbat had not returned fire, and no NATO planes had been dispatched.

As night fell in Srebrenica, in New York the Secretariat met with representatives of countries contributing troops to UNPROFOR. But the Secretariat knew nothing of the attack on Srebrenica, so it was not discussed. UNPROFOR's reports remained sitting on desks in Srebrenica, Tuzla, Zagreb, and Sarajevo.[1] The following day, Friday, 7 July, the Bosnian Serbs fired almost three hundred shells into the enclave. Colonel Karremans told the UN regional command in Tuzla that he believed the Serbs wanted to "neutralize" the enclave, as a prelude to its conquest. Karremans again called for CAS. Once again, his request was stalled at UN regional command in Tuzla. The Serbs moved forward. OP Foxtrot was hit by several Serb shells, while artillery, rocket, and mortar fire slammed into the town.

That afternoon, Karremans repeated his request for CAS. This, the fourth call since 1 June, was again refused and the danse macabre continued. General Nicolai ordered Dutchbat to withdraw from OP Foxtrot. UN commanders in Zagreb and Sarajevo argued that the Bosnian Serbs did not want to take the whole enclave, but only strategic ground in the southern part—echoing the claims during the Goražde and Bihać crises that the Serbs wanted only to "shrink" the enclave.

Even without the benefit of hindsight, the repeated refusals of Karremans's requests by Cees Nicolai and his bosses seemed inexplicable. Srebrenica had been under direct attack for two days, and Dutchbat's positions had been repeatedly and deliberately targeted. The UN troops were in extreme peril.

The attack came after months of humiliation and blockades by the Bosnian Serbs, in themselves clear grounds for air strikes. Whether or not the Serbs wanted only to "shrink" the enclave was anyway irrelevant. All of its territory constituted a safe area under resolutions 819, 824, and 836. Any assault should have been met with robust force, whether General Mladić attempted to capture the town in whole or in part.

DPKO officials in New York said in off-the-record briefings to the press corps that the Serbs wanted only the south of the enclave. Once again the lessons of Goražde and Bihać were conveniently ignored. "It is not clear to me whether the DPKO desk officers were distorting things themselves or were the victims of distortion by UNPROFOR," says James Bone. "It's possible that if somebody said they did not believe the Serbs really wanted to take Srebrenica, they might have genuinely believed that, based on information fed to them by Brits and French." Shashi Tharoor recalls: "We were getting cable traffic about possible Serb movements and analysis from the generals. They believed it was merely a feint and there was no intention to seriously erode the integrity of the safe areas." When the final assault began, several senior DPKO and UN officials were absent. The department head, Kofi Annan, was away. That week Shashi Tharoor, after addressing the NATO Council of Ambassadors in Virginia, took a few days' leave. Iqbal Riza, Annan's deputy, was in left in charge, while Peter Schmitz, the Yugoslav desk officer, covered for Tharoor. General Rupert Smith was also away, while Boutros-Ghali was traveling in Africa. Madeleine Albright demanded on Friday, 7 July, that the DPKO report on whether the Serbs were still advancing and firing on Srebrenica, and whether there had been air strikes in response. She got no answer for three days. Just as General Morillon had complained in 1992, it seemed that there was still nobody available at the DPKO office on the weekends.

Soon after 2 P.M. on Saturday, 8 July, a Serb tank smashed its way through the Bosniak front line near OP Foxtrot and stopped about one hundred yards away. The Dutch soldiers watched nervously as twenty Serb troops marched in, including members of Arkan's Tigers. Unlike the usual local Serb soldiers, they were disciplined, well armed, and extremely menacing. They stole the Dutch soldiers' personal items and demanded their guns, which the Dutch handed over. Some five hundred yards away, the Bosniak troops watched angrily as the Dutch abandoned OP Foxtrot. Lieutenant Colonel Karremans and Major Ramiz Bećirović had agreed that if the Dutch withdrew from an OP, the Bosniaks would quickly advance and take it over. Their comrades had died for these hills, which the Dutch had given up without firing a shot. The armored personnel carrier of the fleeing Dutch did not get far. The path down the road was blocked by a makeshift barricade, manned by a local Muslim farmer. As the APC drew nearer, he primed his grenade.

The Serb attack on Srebrenica was not an isolated battle but part of a strategic push by the Bosnian Serbs that began in spring 1995 against the safe areas. The United Nations stood by as Sarajevo, Srebrenica, Goražde, Bihać, and Žepa were regularly shelled. Less than one-third of aid supplies were getting through. On 24 May, General Smith announced that unless the Serbs pulled back their heavy weapons from Sarajevo—as agreed under the NATO ultimatum of the previous year—he would launch air strikes. Akashi had little choice but to authorize strikes: the Serbs were in clear violation of the 1994 exclusion zone agreement. On 25 May, NATO planes bombed an ammunition dump in the Bosnian Serb capital of Pale. In response General Mladić ordered all six safe areas to be shelled. That evening an artillery shell slammed into downtown Tuzla, which was packed with young people enjoying the spring weather. Seventy-one were killed and more than 250 wounded, in the worst single attack of the Bosnian war. The Bosnian Serbs then took 350 UN troops hostage across Bosnia, declaring them to be "human shields."

The United Nations buckled quickly. London, Paris, and other countries with UN troops on the ground blocked any further air strikes, fearful of television pictures of soldiers coming home in body bags. This decision was a massive strategic mistake, both cowardly and counterproductive. It was cowardly because it showed once again that the United Nations and the Western powers were weak, and that General Mladić called the shots. It was counterproductive because there is little doubt that had Mladić started executing the hostages, the Bosnian Serbs would have been hit with waves of strategic air strikes. The United States was already straining at the UN's leash. It is inconceivable that Washington would have stood by while NATO soldiers were killed, says a senior former UNPROFOR official. On 29 May, General Janvier issued new guidelines on air power. OPs were to be abandoned if they came under fire. The authority to call for CAS was removed from General Smith and given to General Janvier. Any strategic air strikes would now have to be personally approved by Boutros-Ghali. Perhaps most crucial of all, the guidelines made explicit that "the execution of the mandate is secondary to the security of UN personnel."[2] These guidelines helped explain why all four of Karremans's requests for CAS had been rejected.

As the Dutch APC headed back to the base, a loud bang resounded through the trees. The farmer manning the roadblock had thrown a grenade at the vehicle, hitting the gunner Raviv van Renssen. He collapsed, blood pouring from a large head wound, and died soon after. Dutchbat's first fatality, at the hands of those it was sent to protect, caused fury among the soldiers and a significant psychological shift. While Dutchbat medics fought in vain to save van Renssen, Boutros-Ghali, Akashi, Annan, Generals Janvier and Smith (who had been recalled from his holiday), and other UN senior officials all met in Geneva to discuss the situation in Bosnia. News reached them of van Renssen's death, but it was decided that General Smith should go back on leave.

The Serb attack intensified. Early on Sunday, 9 July, OP Uniform, also in the southeast, fell. The Serbs sent the Dutchbat troops to nearby Bratunac, in Serb-controlled territory. Lieutenant Colonel Karremans dispatched an APC on a reconnaissance mission. It was captured by Bosnian Serb soldiers. OPs Kilo, Mike, and Delta all reported that they were under attack. It was clear that the UN troops could not protect themselves, let alone the safe area. Panic swept through the enclave as civilians poured into the town center. By now the United Nations leadership in Geneva had finally been informed that Srebrenica was under attack. General Janvier and Akashi left Geneva for Zagreb. Janvier asked UNPROFOR to prepare target information for CAS. OP Delta fell next. By the evening of 9 July, three Dutchbat OPs had fallen and several more were under attack. The Bosnian Serbs had advanced to within a mile of the town, and thirty Dutch troops were held hostage by the Bosnian Serbs. Not a single NATO plane had been dispatched. General Janvier ordered Dutchbat to set up a "blocking position" against the Bosnian Serb advance. Troops manning the position were expected to fire back if attacked, and close air support would be dispatched if necessary. Janvier and Akashi sent a fax to the Serbs demanding that they stop their offensive, pull back, and release all Dutchbat personnel. If Dutchbat's blocking position was attacked, NATO planes would be dispatched. But the fax did not make the same threat if the Serbs attacked the enclave itself. This was a crucial distinction. Karremans then changed his mind about CAS. He decided that CAS would trigger a massive barrage from the Bosnian Serbs, which could be stopped only if all their weapons were simultaneously destroyed. This was, he believed, unlikely.

B Company set up the blocking position soon after dawn on Monday, 10 July. Fifty soldiers and six APCs closed the approach road to the town. The soldiers were armed with antitank weapons and machine guns and ordered to return fire if the Bosnian Serbs attacked. By early evening, B company, which was holding the blocking position, reported that Serb troops were advancing on the high ground overlooking the town. Captain Jelte Groen ordered mortar flares to be fired, while Dutchbat also fired its machine guns, but only over the heads of the Serbs. The second warning flare landed precisely on target, over the head of the Serb soldiers.

Then came one of several moments when, had Dutchbat acted differently, the men of Srebrenica might still be alive. Dutchbat now had the Serbs perfectly ranged for a live mortar round. "There were 120 Serbs soldiers on the ridge. A live mortar would have probably killed a dozen and wounded more," says a former UNPROFOR official. "It was never going to be great if Dutchbat had stood and fought, as they did not have the operational capacity to defeat the Bosnian Serbs. It would have made the Serbs very mad. But it also would have made it very difficult for UNPROFOR not to authorize full and immediate air support. Dutchbat certainly had the capacity to delay the Serbs and give them a bloody nose, had their calls for air support been supported." It was not to be. As dusk fell, Groen

ordered B Company to fall back, fearful that it would be out-
flanked in the night. As B Company retreated, in New York
a member of Boutros-Ghali's staff finally briefed the Security
Council, attempting to answer the questions asked by Madeleine
Albright the previous Friday. The briefing was a disaster, the
latest link in a chain of incompetence and miscommunication
that reached from Srebrenica to Tuzla to Zagreb to New York.
The UN official claimed that the Serb shelling had stopped, although it had resumed that morning. He could provide no
clear chronology of requests for air support. He did not report
that Dutchbat had repeatedly asked for air support between 6
and 8 July, and that these requests had been turned down in
Tuzla and Sarajevo. "Neither he nor anyone in the Secretariat
appears to have been aware of those requests," the United Nations report on Srebrenica notes.[3]

By Monday evening it was clear that only air power could
save the enclave. Dutchbat troops fired warning flares and again
fired over the heads of the Bosnian Serbs. Karremans again requested CAS. Despite the risks to Dutchbat, the Dutch minister of defense, Joris Voorhoeve, authorized CAS. He appeared
on Dutch television warning that air strikes seemed inevitable,
with a "strong possibility" of casualties. This time Karremans's
request was approved in both Tuzla and Sarajevo and was
quickly passed to General Janvier. Srebrenica's fate now hung
on his signature.

At 7:00 P.M. Janvier was informed that NATO aircraft
were on standby and were "night capable," meaning that they
could be deployed at any time. Janvier stalled. His decisions
that crucial evening, probably the last hours that the Serbs still
presented a clear target, proved fatal. He convened his crisis
team at 7:55 P.M. Janvier requested NATO aircraft to be "cock-
pit ready" but also claimed that there were no targets to hit.

This was disputed by one of his own staff, who argued strongly that tanks and artillery had already been identified. Meanwhile, Dutchbat's blocking position had proved as useful as France's Maginot Line in 1940. The Serbs had simply bypassed it and continued their advance. By 9:00 P.M., four thousand refugees had poured into the town, and public order was collapsing. At 9:25 General Janvier called Mladić's headquarters, "to tell them that the situation was impossible and that he would do everything he could to avoid the use of force, but that there were limits," according to the UN Srebrenica report. UN peacekeepers had been deliberately targeted for four days, and the first safe area had virtually fallen without a single NATO plane being dispatched. Yet the highest-ranking UN officer in the former Yugoslavia was reassuring General Mladić that he would do his best *not* to use force. Janvier then told his staff that he had not authorized CAS, as it was dark and Dutchbat was better placed to stop the Serbs. "Janvier seemed to be determined not to allow any military operation to take place at all," says one senior Western diplomat. Soon after Janvier spoke with Mladić, Karremans changed his mind again. He told UNPROFOR that he did not want CAS at night, but that it should be ready for 6:00 A.M. the next day.

At the Dutch headquarters in Potočari, Karremans and the Bosniaks coordinated a joint defense plan at a midnight meeting. Karremans said that NATO would launch massive air strikes the following morning if the Serbs did not pull back. Once they did, Dutchbat would retake the fallen OPs. His optimism was not shared by the Bosniak commanders.

In Sarajevo the Bosnian government demanded that the United Nations either retake Srebrenica by force or announce its unwillingness to do so, thus showing the hollowness of the safe-areas policy. President Izetbegović contacted municipal leader

Osman Suljić and told him to fire the antitank missiles which
had been smuggled through earlier. But none of Srebrenica's
defenders knew how to use them. The Bosnian government
made no meaningful military efforts to save Srebrenica. Bosnian army intelligence had warned of the attack a month before it began, but no precautions had been taken. No attempt
was made by the Bosnian army 2nd corps, based in Tuzla, to attack south to relieve Srebrenica.

UNPROFOR's incompetence on the morning of Tues-
day, 11 July, sealed Srebrenica's fate. At 4:00 A.M. Dutchbat telephoned regional headquarters in Tuzla, which reported that
forty targets had been identified and that NATO planes would
be overhead by 6:50 A.M. Dutchbat took to its bunkers, the
Bosniaks to the cellars. Seven o'clock came and went, and there
was no sign of any air strikes. Dutchbat again telephoned Tuzla
and was told that despite the earlier promises, no planes had
been dispatched, because no new request had been received for
either close air support or larger air strikes. Dutchbat filed a
fresh request to Tuzla around 7:45 A.M., which then took two
hours to reach Sarajevo. The reasons for the delays remain unclear, but they may have included failure to fill out the form
properly, use of the wrong form, or a problem with the fax line.
At 10:45 A.M. UNPROFOR in Sarajevo finally confirmed that it
had received the request for air strikes from Tuzla and was now
forwarding it to UN headquarters in Zagreb. In fact, the NATO
planes *had* been in the air since 6:00 A.M., just as Karremans
had requested, but because they had not been ordered to attack,
they needed to return to base to refuel. Five hours had been
wasted. That morning General Smith finally ended his leave,
and he spent the next thirty-six hours traveling to Sarajevo.

General Mladić watched and waited. No NATO planes
appeared, and at 11:00 A.M. he ordered the Bosnian Serbs to
continue the attack. By now thousands of frightened civilians

were huddled around the Dutchbat bases, vainly hoping that the bases would offer some protection as shells and mortars smashed into the town. Still UNPROFOR in Zagreb equivocated. At 12:20 P.M. General Janvier and Akashi finally signed Dutchbat's request for the close air support that had been expected since 6:00 A.M. and had been resubmitted at 7:45. Even as the Serb guns pounded Srebrenica, Akashi and Janvier stood firm against the meaningful use of force. NATO's response would be minimal, Akashi cabled Annan in New York. "Close air support is now on station, but will be employed only if UNPROFOR personnel come under actual attack. There will be no pre-emptive use of NATO aircraft."[4]

The endgame began. Dutchbat abandoned OP November in the north of the enclave. Serb tanks opened fire on B Company, hitting its compound in the town where thousands of civilians were sheltering. The Bosnian defenses collapsed. The tanks rumbled forward, Serb infantry in their wake. Soon after 2 P.M., the Serb flag was raised over the bakery in the south of the town. Mladić's troops advanced into the center, shooting wildly, cheering and swigging slivovitz. As the Serb ensign flapped in the wind, eighteen NATO aircraft were finally dispatched. But Srebrenica had fallen.

Around 2.40 P.M. two NATO planes dropped two bombs on the Bosnian Serbs' armor. General Mladić knew precisely what to do. The Bosnian Serbs threatened to kill the Dutchbat soldiers that they held, and to shell the Dutch compound at Potočari. The threat worked perfectly. Joris Verhooeve quickly called Akashi and asked that close air support be stopped. NATO withdrew. These two bombs were the sum total of NATO's efforts to defend Srebrenica. The Dutch abandoned their base in the town and sped north to Potočari, driving so fast that they hit several civilians on the way. A vast human col-

umn, more than twenty thousand strong, trudged out of Srebrenica. Most were terrified women, children, and elderly men,
clutching whatever they had managed to grab before fleeing.

Dutchbat troops cut a hole in the side of the fence to
allow civilians easier access, but after several thousand people
poured through, swamping the base, they refused entry to any
more. Between fifteen thousand and twenty thousand people
spent the night outside, in scenes of terror and chaos. Most of
Srebrenica's men said good-bye to their families and gathered
in a large column in the northwest of the enclave. The plan was
to trek thirty miles north to government-controlled territory,
picking their way through the minefields, hiking through the
forest, and fighting their way through the Serb lines. The one-
third who were armed led the column. A much smaller group
headed on a much shorter journey east, to cross over the Drina
into Serbia proper, a decision which saved many of their lives.
Meanwhile, UNPROFOR ordered Dutchbat to withdraw from
all its OPs, concentrate its forces in Potočari to take "all reasonable measure to protect refugees and civilians" and defend
themselves "with all possible means."

That evening General Mladić summoned Lieutenant Colonel Karremans to Bratunac. A pig was brought into the room.
While an aide held the squealing animal down, Mladić grasped
it by its neck and cut its throat. As the pig writhed in its death
throes and the blood gushed over the floor, Mladić turned to
Karremans and said, "You have to be able to watch this before
we can talk." Dutchbat's commander tried to explain the desperate situation of the thousands of civilians at Potočari. Mladić
promised to respect the Geneva Conventions but demanded
the Bosniaks hand over their weapons or he would shell the
base. On his return Karremans sent a report to Tuzla, Zagreb,
Sarajevo, and the Dutch crisis staff at the ministry of defense

in The Hague. The situation was desperate, he wrote. He could defend neither Srebrenica's people nor his own battalion.

While Mladić was spelling out his terms, Akashi, General Janvier and other UN officials met in Zagreb. Srebrenica's fall occasioned not soul-searching but self-exculpatory explanations. Akashi was rightly concerned that the United Nations would be blamed for NATO's feeble response, but he and Janvier agreed that CAS would not have been effective, as the targets were "too close" to the UN troops.[5] The reason they were too close was that Janvier had refused to authorize air strikes when the Serbs could still be stopped. Even though Dutchbat had not fired directly at the Bosnian Serbs, Akashi claimed they had put up a "strong defense." The British NATO liaison officer disagreed, reporting that American NATO commanders believed targets had been identified and that timely use of air power would have worked. As the author David Rohde notes, when the Serb bombardment was at its most intense, "only four Serb tanks and several hundred infantry led the main attack up the narrow asphalt road, something NATO jets or well-organized defenders could have held off for several more days." By now Janvier even seemed to be out of sync with Paris. The new French president—Jacques Chirac, a former mayor of Paris— appeared to take a much harder line against the Serbs. Chirac called President Clinton, proposing that French troops, transported by US helicopters, retake Srebrenica, recalling the dashing gallantry of General Morillon.

In fact, this was probably just grandstanding, perhaps even a cover for a cynical French agreement with the Bosnian Serbs, probably decided a month earlier, when General Janvier had held a secret meeting with Mladić in Zvornik on 4 June. At this time the Bosnian Serbs were holding almost three hundred UN troops hostage, many of them French. There have been persistent rumors that a deal had been struck: the hostages would be freed in exchange for assurances that there would be no more NATO air strikes.[6] France denied having made any deals, but the circumstantial evidence is strong. On 6 June, Janvier's predecessor, General de Lapresle, traveled from Paris to the Bosnian Serb capital of Pale. The following day the Bosnian Serbs released 111 hostages. On 13 June twenty-eight hostages were released. The Bosnian Serb "foreign minister," Aleksa Buha, announced that Milošević had relayed to him a promise that there would be no more air strikes. The remaining hostages were freed soon after. Akashi, who authorized the meeting between Janvier and Mladić, then announced that the United Nations would abide strictly by peacekeeping principles, which was understood as shorthand for "no more air strikes." He later said: "For us, liberating our hostages was our highest priority. When you are the official most responsible for safety and security of all your personnel, of course getting freedom for all those who are detained or had hostage status had the highest priority for me."[7] When NATO commander Admiral Leighton Smith requested permission from General Janvier to carry out air strikes after Bosnian Serb aircraft violated the no-fly zone, he was refused.

Janvier had made his position clear at a meeting on 9 June in the Croatian port of Split with Akashi and General Smith. The United Nations' record of the discussion highlights the division between the two sides. Smith refused to have any more dealings with the Bosnian Serbs. He argued that massive air attacks should be considered if a United Nations base was targeted, and the Security Council should designate United Nations routes into the enclaves. The "Mogadishu line" had already been crossed, Smith argued, and the United Nations needed to be prepared to fight across "a range of threats. If we are not prepared to fight, we will always be stared down by the BSA [Bosnian Serb Army]." Janvier completely disagreed. "It is just for this that we must establish contact with the Serbs, to show, to explain to them that there are some things they cannot do." Smith ended with a prophetic analysis: "But because we have some enforcement obligations, either we fail, or we act and will be the enemy of the Serbs. I think that we will be forced to make a decision within one month."[8]

In New York the DPKO again moved to distance itself from Akashi and General Janvier. On 15 June, Annan wrote to Akashi:

> We have all been troubled as we are sure you must be
> by the profusion of press reports that UNPROFOR
> has adopted a "negative mentality" and is unable or
> unwilling to carry out any of its mandated tasks.
> Some of these reports appear to be based on indi-
> cations from unnamed UN officials that the force
> has been told to take no actions whatsoever with-
> out Serb approval. You know well that we have is-
> sued no such instruction, but we would be grateful
> for your views on these reports. In particular, we
> would appreciate your clarifying, if you can, the basis
> on which the Bosnian Serb "FM," Aleksa Buha, claims
> he has received reassurances through President Milo-
> šević that there will be no more airstrikes.[9]

As the Serbs celebrated their capture of Srebrenica, the Security Council prepared to meet in emergency session. A draft resolution on Srebrenica was faxed through to Akashi in Zagreb on Tuesday, 11 July. The resolution seemed to raise the possibility of the use of force to recapture the town. Point G1 demanded that the Bosnian Serbs "cease their offensive and withdraw from the safe area of Srebrenica immediately." Point G6 requested that the secretary general "use all resources available to him" to restore Srebrenica's status as a safe area. Still Akashi cabled back the next day: "Our reaction to the draft resolution has been pretty much as you would expect. The resolution again raises unrealistic expectations and its failure to take into account reality on the ground will inevitably lead to further disillusionment and disappointment among the international community."[10] Even with the benefit of a decade's hindsight and our knowledge of the United Nations' inner workings, it is hard to comprehend Akashi's continuing obsession with neutrality. The "reality on the ground" was that more than twenty thousand civilians, mainly women and children, were now at the mercy of the most brutal army Europe had known since the Second World War. Their men so clearly understood their fate if captured that they were trekking for days through minefields to avoid falling into Serb hands. Akashi's suggestions were ignored, and resolution 1004 was passed on 12 July.

Yet in a way, Akashi's forecast was right. No military action was taken to recapture Srebrenica. Only now were the consequences finally made clear of those hard-fought debates in the Security Council in the spring of 1993, when Ambassadors Hannay and Mérimée had ensured that the word *protect* was not included in resolutions 819, 824, and 836, defining the six safe areas. The capture of Srebrenica was not General Mladić's triumph alone but could be shared with London, Paris, and a vacillating President Clinton. David Hannay was not present to see the ultimate consequences of his robust diplomacy—he had retired. In 1993 Diego Arria had described Srebrenica as a "slow-motion genocide." It was about to speed up.

The Bosnian Serbs entered Potočari shortly before 1:00 P.M. on Wednesday, 12 July, and took up positions around the Dutchbat compound. Vehicles began arriving: at first mainly military vans and trucks, then later in the day vast numbers of civilian buses. Soon after, the Serbs entered the compound. The Dutch troops were disarmed. General Mladić's arrival sent a wave of fear through the crowd. Surrounded by Serb journalists and television cameramen, he was clearly enjoying the attention. The reporters filmed Serb soldiers handing out bread and water, giving sweets to the frightened children clinging to their mothers. Mladić promised the women and children safe passage to the front line, where they could cross into government-controlled territory. He patted the head of a terrified young boy. "Let women and little children go through first. Do not let any of the children get lost. Don't be afraid. Nobody will harm you." Few believed his reassurances, especially when the Bosnian Serbs began to separate the men and boys, some as young as twelve, from their families. Mladić had a different message for his soldiers later as he surveyed his captives. "There are so many. It is going to be a meze [an Arabic feast of many small dishes]. There will be blood up to your knees," he proclaimed, then nodded at the many young women in the crowd. "Beautiful, keep the good ones over there. Enjoy them."[11]

Mladić reassured Dutchbat that the men would be properly treated, but said that they had to be screened for "war criminals," even though many were teenage boys or elderly and incapable of fighting. Everyone understood what would happen next, except those with the power to try to stop it. The

Dutch troops watched the men try to comfort their sobbing relatives, promising to meet up eventually in Tuzla. Some of the Dutch soldiers felt ashamed. Others argued that there was nothing they could do. Petrified mothers draped headscarves over their young sons, hoping to disguise them as girls, and hid them deep among the crying women. The men outside the compound were taken away, the Serbs screaming abuse and beating them as they were forced onto trucks and buses. About three hundred Bosniak men remained inside the compound. The mystery of the recently arrived 100,000 gallons of diesel was finally solved. Srebrenica's men would be taken to their deaths in buses powered by UN fuel. When the television cameras were gone, the Bosnian Serbs took back the food and sweets they had handed out.

Finally, "Nema bon-bon."

V

Recently Disturbed Earth

A safe area for animals.
—*Yasushi Akashi, joking at a lunch with*
Slobodan Milošević and General Janvier at a
hunting lodge outside Belgrade, 8 August 1995

On the morning of 10 August, a month after Srebrenica's fall, Madeleine Albright began her presentation to the Security Council. Her voice was calm and controlled, for any hint of emotion, she knew, would allow the assembled diplomats to doubt or dismiss the evidence in front of them. She drew support from Diego Arria, who sat nearby. Albright reported that the whereabouts of some six thousand Bosniak men and boys from Srebrenica was unknown. But their fate was not. "We have enough information to conclude now, however, that the Bosnian Serbs beat, raped, and executed many of the refugees," Albright said. The information she presented was based on several CIA satellite photographs of an area around Nova Kasaba, a town about fourteen miles northwest of Bratunac, and on testimony gathered by John Shattuck, assistant secretary of state, who had interviewed survivors.

The first photograph showed a soccer field with a dark shape in the middle. Vehicles were parked near the road, and small dots around the perimeter were identified as guards. American intelligence experts believed that the shape was a group of at least six hundred people. Albright then moved to another set of photographs, showing the soccer field and a second field, less than a mile away. The second field had several open areas, clearly visible. "The earth in those spots was not disturbed several days earlier," Albright said. Several dozen men had been beaten to death in the soccer field, she said, while the rest had been loaded onto trucks and driven to the second field. The refugees had been lined up in groups of twenty to twenty-five and machine-gunned. The details were related to Shattuck by a sixty-three-year-old man who had survived by falling as the shooting started. He hid for hours under the bodies and trekked through the woods for ten days until he reached safety.

By now Albright had the undivided attention of the room. Once Shattuck had relayed the survivor's account to Washington, the spy satellites took fresh pictures of the same locations. "The difference is more striking in the enlargements I will show you now. You can see the disturbed earth. One section is about one hundred meters [110 yards] square, the other about fifty meters square. There are tracks from heavy vehicles leading from the road to the disturbed earth," Albright explained. These

patches of earth were believed to be recently made mass graves:
there was recently disturbed earth, with no vegetation, where
refugees were known to be; heavy vehicle tracks where there
were none before; no apparent alternative reason for the tracks
or disturbed earth; multiple, confirming reports from survivors.
The Russian ambassador asked how Albright knew that the dots
were really people and that the marks on the ground were tire
tracks. Albright had been well briefed. There was enough granu-
larity in the pictures to be able to discern details, and the pictures
had been taken over a long enough period of time to be certain
of the images, she explained.[1] The Russian ambassador nodded.

The Bosnian war had probably been the most photo-
graphed, televised, and documented conflict in human history.
For more than three years journalists had broadcast footage of
ethnic cleansing and atrocities, while newspaper reporters and
photographers recorded the bloody details of the war in fine
detail. Yet no images had as much impact as these grainy black-
and-white pictures of obscure fields in eastern Bosnia, images
almost meaningless without expert interpretation, seen only
by a select few. Somehow their very mundaneness—views of
earth and fields, trees and hedges—made them even more
chilling. The expressions on the diplomats' faces were clear:
this was a massacre too far. Perhaps some even felt ashamed.
Bosnia's fate had been decided in the Security Council chamber in 1993, and now it would be decided there again. The
Bosnian Serbs had crossed a line and would soon pay the price.
For Albright it was a bittersweet triumph, if a triumph at all.

"We kept trying to find evidence that could be presented
at the Security Council," she recalls. "We knew that satellites
were overhead at various times, and the combination of the
pictures and the report by a survivor who had hidden beneath
the bodies was absolutely key. It was exactly the evidence that

we needed. I had mixed feelings that day. You can't say you're glad you have proof of a massacre. But it was a key moment."

Soon after the fall, Peggy Hicks, an American civil affairs officer in UNPROFOR, traveled to Tuzla to meet with other UN officials and try to get to Srebrenica. Hicks worked in Akashi's office as part of a small team set up in May 1995 to deal directly with human rights. "We knew there was a human rights crisis of large proportions, but we didn't know at first that there had been mass executions," she recalls. Hicks and her team stayed in Tuzla for more than a week, conducting seventy interviews. The survivors' reports were consistent and numerous. "By then it was absolutely clear that there were executions and that thousands of men were missing. We weren't sure if one thousand had been executed and six thousand were missing, or the proportions thereof. But we knew that something massive had happened."

Even by the standards of the Bosnian war, the accounts gathered by United Nations and human rights workers were shocking in the savagery they detailed. Once Mladić had left the UN compound and the television cameras had gone, the Serbs had begun drinking heavily. Many wore the insignia of the Chetniks, the ultranationalist Serb paramilitaries. Their terrified prisoners were their playthings. Neither age nor youth was a defense. A Bosniak woman recounted to Human Rights Watch how most of her family was killed. One son, Elmadin, fifteen years old, was taken away by the Serbs. She saw him in a circle of prisoners guarded by soldiers and dogs, but she could not get through. She asked a United Nations interpreter for help, but he said he could do nothing, because all the Dutch troops had been disarmed. The following afternoon, her husband was taken away. The Serb soldiers then threw their son,

three years old, and young daughter on the ground. Another
son, Esmir, was killed in front of her. "I was holding him in my
arms. He was my son from my first marriage. We were hugging
but they took him away. They grabbed him and just slit his
throat. They killed him. They made me drink his blood. I just
can't say any more, I just can't; you have to understand that it
is breaking my heart."[2]

The killing had begun as soon as the Serbs arrived in
Potočari. A Dutchbat soldier watched a Bosnian Serb lead a
group of prisoners down a dirt track. The next day other Dutch
soldiers found the bodies of nine men, all shot in the back at
heart level. Sporadic executions continued around the compound, well within earshot of the UN troops. As women, children, and the elderly began streaming out of Srebrenica, Dutchbat commanders tried to place a soldier on each bus carrying
civilians, but they were overwhelmed by the speed and extent
of the exodus. Instead they dispatched soldiers in UN escort
vehicles to follow the convoys, but the Bosnian Serbs hijacked
thirteen of their fourteen vehicles and confiscated them, together with the UN troops' weapons and equipment. Inside
Srebrenica the Dutchbat troops were disarmed by the Bosnian
Serbs and left powerless and humiliated. While some Dutch
troops did intervene directly to save lives, a substantial number, together with their commanders, seem to have suffered a
collapse of will, courage, and, sometimes, simple humanity.
After the Bosniak men outside the UN compound were taken
away, deputy commander Major Robert Franken ordered those
still inside to present themselves to the Bosnian Serbs. They
protested, telling Franken that the bodies of other prisoners
had already been discovered. Many of the men and boys began
to cry, telling the Dutchbat soldiers that they would be killed.
But Franken had ordered a list to be drawn up of the 239 men's

names to be forwarded to the Red Cross. Franken asserted that this was sufficient protection and believed that the men would be treated in accordance with the Geneva Conventions.

When UNHCR staffers reached Srebrenica that day, they witnessed a chilling sight: "UNPROFOR and Serb soldiers working together to bring the last groups of Bosniaks from the UNPROFOR compound to the waiting Serb buses."[3] None of the 239 men was ever seen again. Other UN officers, it seems, better understood the likely fate of all the men and boys of Srebrenica, especially when the Bosnian Serbs ordered their captives to pile their identity documents on the ground and leave them there. Joseph Kingori, a Kenyan UNMO, intervened for several teenage boys, asking the Bosnian Serbs that they be removed from the adult captives. He later testified at the ICTY: "You could see the fear. There was a lot of fear. They didn't know what would happen. They felt . . . that . . . something bad was actually going to be done to them. . . . They were crying. You know, men—you can imagine men crying in front of you and seeking assistance from you, assistance which you cannot give."[4]

The Bosnian Serbs killed their prisoners by rifle and machine-gun fire. They threw grenades at men locked inside buildings. Many of the killers enjoyed their work. The prisoners were made to walk through two lines of Serb soldiers. The Serbs broke their bones with crowbars and chopped them with axes before slitting their throats. They beat the prisoners, taunted them, shot them in the limbs to prolong their agony. They dragged out young women and raped them until they died. These were scenes Europe had not witnessed since the SS Einsatzgruppen, the Nazi extermination squads, had executed Jews and partisans. United Nations and Western officials still portray the massacre at Srebrenica as a unique event, something unpredictable and unforeseeable, outside the usual paradigm of armed conflict. But few events in recent history have been more foreseeable than the murder of the Bosniak men separated from their families. "We never had any doubts about what would happen after the men and women were separated," recalled José Maria Mendiluce, then a senior UNHCR official. "In particular in Srebrenica, where the cruelty would be worse because Mladić wanted to avenge the Bosnian offensive of 1992. Only a fool would not have expected it, or someone badly informed. I don't know whether the force commander [General Janvier] was a fool or badly informed, but he shares the responsibility for the genocide."[5]

The killings of Srebrenica were not carried out by battle-enraged soldiers who had seen their comrades die. This was cold-blooded, methodical slaughter, planned and organized in great detail, for executing almost eight thousand men and boys demands extensive logistical preparation. Holding locations must be secured, transport arranged to move the victims, units deployed to carry out the killing, arms and ammunition stockpiled, bulldozers brought in to dispose of the bodies. Only one of the low-ranking executioners has been brought to trial, an infantryman named Dražen Erdemović. His story and testimony to the ICTY bring new insight to the mechanics of genocide and its perpetrators. Born in Tuzla in 1971, Erdemović was a Croat with a wife and young son. When war broke out, Erdemović spent three months in the Bosnian government army before joining the Bosnian Croat forces. He also worked as a people smuggler, helping Serbs cross over to Serb-controlled territory. Arrested in late 1993, Erdemović was sent to prison, and fled to Republika Srpska, the self-proclaimed Serb Republic within Bosnia, after two weeks.[6] In April 1994 he was called up to the Bosnian Serb army. He joined the 10th Sabotage Unit, which operated mostly behind the lines in government-controlled territory. On 16 July part of Erdemović's unit was sent to Branjevo farm, in eastern Bosnia. Commander Brano Gojković announced that buses would soon be arriving, bringing Muslims from Srebrenica. The orders were to shoot everyone on board. The vehicles started arriving soon after 9:30 A.M. They were filled with men, the youngest in their teens, the oldest in their seventies. Inside each bus were two Bosnian Serb military policemen. Gojković told Erdemović how to form an execution squad, and the men were brought out in groups of ten to the meadow by the farm.[7]

It was a bright, warm morning, the sun shining in a clear blue sky over the fields and rolling hills of eastern Bosnia. The pastoral scene was about to turn into a killing field. The first group of men were lined up with their backs to the Serb troops, who stood about twenty yards away. Gojković ordered them to open fire. Erdemović resisted at first, but Gojković said that if he felt sorry for the Muslims, he should line up with them. Erdemović began shooting, and the rapid crack of automatic weapons resounded across the fields. The men fell and died. When the second group was brought forward and the men saw the corpses, they began to beg for their lives, promising that their families in Austria would send the Serbs money. They pleaded in vain. More shots rang out, and they too crumpled onto the ground. The killing continued all day. The executioners sometimes broke for a cigarette or a slug of slivovitz. The air was momentarily still in what the Hungarian Nobel laureate and Auschwitz survivor Imre Kertész called the "moments of silence while the firing squad reloads." The Serb commanders set up a machine gun to speed the killing, but the heavy-caliber bullets caused hideous wounds without killing the prisoners, who then begged to be finished off. Erdemović and several others, unable to bear the sounds of the wounded men, argued with the commanders to put the machine gun away. The executioners then reverted to their AK-47s. Some of the prisoners insulted their killers, others prayed quietly or tried to bribe them. One man complained vociferously when he was led out of the bus, Erdemović recalled. "He said that he had saved Serbs from Srebrenica who were now in the Federal Republic of Yugoslavia, and that he had the telephone number of those people and he begged to be allowed to live."

Erdemović asked Gojković to spare the man. "I wanted to save that man. I was sorry for those people simply. I had no reason to shoot at those people. They had done nothing to me." Gojković refused, saying that there could be no witnesses. The man, like all the others, was quickly killed. Even the bus drivers, who had been told that the men were being brought to a prisoner exchange, were forced to take part. Each was handed a gun and forced to kill at least one prisoner. By the end of the day between one thousand and twelve hundred men had been shot. The field was carpeted with bodies and awash with blood.

The executioners walked through the bodies, checking whether anyone was still alive, and shooting the living in the head. Their work done, they looted the bodies, gathering money and jewelry, prizing wedding rings from the dead. Each had been promised four or five deutsche marks—about three dollars— for each person he shot. Erdemović was unsure how many men he had personally killed, perhaps about seventy. He told the court, "I do not know exactly. I cannot estimate but, to be quite frank, I would rather not know how many people I killed." He had fired single shots rather than long volleys.[8] A Bosnian Serb officer then arrived, ordering the unit to go to the nearby town of Pilica, where another five hundred Bosniak men were held in a hall awaiting execution. But this time Erdemović refused. Others in his unit also said no. The soldiers from Bratunac did not object. When Erdemović and the others arrived in Pilica, they heard shots and hand grenade explosions. Back at the unit's base in Bijeljina, the Serbs compared their booty and boasted loudly between drinks of their marksmanship.[9] Soon after, Erdemović returned home to his wife and child. He was later shot and seriously injured by a man who had boasted of killing 250 prisoners. The decision seems to have been made to silence Erdemović, lest he might one day testify. Erdemović was eventually sent to the Belgrade military hospital, where doctors saved him.

The dark history of the twentieth century shows that it is not difficult to turn men into mass killers. From the Russian front in 1945 to eastern Bosnia in 1995, the extreme conditions of war spawn an alternative universe, one where events unimaginable in everyday civilian life become the norm. The 10th Sabotage Unit can be compared to German Reserve Police Battalion 101, which carried out mass killings of Jews in Poland during the Second World War. Most of the members of Battalion 101 were not fanatical Nazis, records the historian Christopher Browning in his study *Ordinary Men*.[10] They were working-class, middle-aged career policemen from Hamburg. Many hoped to return to their jobs after the war. Just as Erdemović and several others refused to go to Pilica, a small minority of Battalion 101's members refused to kill Jews. But overall, the battalion, like the 10th Sabotage Unit, did as it was instructed. In October 1942 it cleared the Jewish ghetto Końskowola, in eastern Poland. The old, children, and the sick were shot on the spot. The remaining Jews were herded to the marketplace. Some of the able-bodied were shipped to work camps. Those left were marched to the wood. The men were forced to lie down and were shot, then the women and children. In Końskowala, as in Srebrenica, such acts constituted the culmination of what Browning calls "atrocity by policy." The enemy no longer comprises human beings but mere objects.

Where did it come from, this hatred of Bosnian Muslims, enough to kill a child in front of its mother or mow down a row of elderly men with a machine gun? "Atrocity by policy" meant that the Bosniaks were not human beings but "Turks." When Mladić first walked through newly conquered Srebrenica, he proclaimed: "I return the city in the tradition of the Serbian struggle against the Turks as we have overcome the Dahije," the title of the governor under the Ottoman Empire. In the dark recesses of Mladić's mind he was reliving the Serb struggle against their former Turkish masters. Yet there is no hate like self-hate. In many ways, from the food they ate to the language they shared, much more united Bosnian Serbs and Muslims than divided them. Serbs and Bosniaks spoke the same language, lived in the same country, and shared the same Mediterranean easygoing approach to life. Serbia and Bosnia were culturally far more similar than Croatia or Slovenia. Serbia's national dish, small grilled sausages known as ćevapčići, is originally Turkish, rooted in the Arabic word *kebab*. Coffee is drunk in Serbia the Turkish or Arabic way: the grounds are boiled up with water in a small brass pot, and the coffee served thick and black.

Even the sawing rhythms of the ultranationalist Turbofolk music sung by Ceca, wife of the paramilitary leader Željko Ražnatović, better known as Arkan, have strong echoes of the Middle East. No matter how ardently the Serb demolition squads blew up the Ottoman mosques and tombs or destroyed the libraries and municipal records, they could not escape their centuries-old entanglement with Bosnian Islam, preserved in Bosnia's very toponomy. Mladić's headquarters were sited at Han Pijesak, outside Sarajevo, *Han* a Turkish word for cara-

vansary or traveler's resting place. The Serb suburb of Sarajevo
was called Ilidža, Turkish for spa. Karadjordje, leader of the
first Serbian uprising against the Turks in 1805 and founder of
the Serbian royal dynasty, was born Djordje Petrović but took
his nom de guerre from the Turkish word for black, *kara.*

The lawlessness and corruption of Serbia under Milošević's rule, its cronyism and plundering of public coffers, its
casual brutality resembled nothing so much as the Ottoman
Empire in its last years. The ethnic cleansing of the Bosnian war
mirrored the Turkish genocide against the Armenians in 1915,
or the massacres of the earlier Balkan Wars. The Ottomans had
deployed the bashibozouks, wild and undisciplined irregulars,
many of whom had been released from prison, who lived off
plunder and looting. Milošević opened Serbia's jails to provide
recruits for the paramilitary units that committed many of the
atrocities. When the campaign against the Armenians began,
the Turkish troops had rounded up community leaders, intel-
lectuals, and people of standing and publicly executed them to
encourage a mass exodus. When the Bosnian Serbs took a town
or village, they already had lists, drawn up many months before, of community notables to be killed. Where the Serbs and
Bosniaks parted was in their readiness for war.

As the men of Srebrenica died, in New York the DPKO floun-
dered as it tried to find out what was happening. Scant news
was coming from Akashi and his team in Zagreb. On 14 July,
Peter Schmitz, Yugoslav desk officer, told US diplomats that
Srebrenica appeared to be a ghost town but that UN personnel
sent into Srebrenica the previous day had not been able to confirm the reports of human rights abuses already appearing in
the press.[11] A confidential US diplomatic cable from the US
embassy in Zagreb, sent the same day, noted: "A senior UN

official also told Charge [d'Affaires] late July 13 that so far as the UN was able to determine, there had been no significant mistreatment of the refugees by the Serbs, although he conceded that with limitations imposed on the movement of the Dutch battalion by the Serbs a lot could happen that might not be observed."[12] Back in the field, for UNPROFOR it was still business as usual. On 15 July the EU and UN negotiators on the former Yugoslavia, together with Akashi and General Smith, met Milošević and Mladić in Belgrade for what the UN report describes as "a largely ceremonial meeting over lunch." The UN officials were, according to the report, "aware of reports that grave human rights abuses might have been committed against the men and boys of Srebrenica, but unaware that mass and systematic executions had commenced."[13] Both sides agreed that the Red Cross would be able to register the Bosniak men as POWs. This would not have been a lengthy process, for while the UN officials ate and drank, Mladić's soldiers continued executing their prisoners.

After a six-day trek, the first soldiers of the column that had fought its way north from Srebrenica began to arrive in Tuzla. Strafed by machine-gun fire, shelled, repeatedly ambushed, and filthy and bedraggled, the survivors of the "marathon of death," had seen their comrades die all around them. They had walked through freshly laid minefields hand-in-hand, one step at a time, each following the man in front. Many had been lured down from the hills by Bosnian Serb troops dressed in stolen UN uniforms. Fathers had been forced to call their sons down from the hills, to be taken away together for execution. A gloating Serb television crew followed an elderly Bosniak as he walked toward the soldiers. "Are you frightened?" the journalist asked. "How could I not be?" the man replied. The wounded had killed themselves rather than fall into the Serbs' hands. Yet even though they were starving, outnumbered, and outgunned, the Bosniaks had still managed to break through two Serb cordons as they battled their way to Tuzla.

When they finally approached the front line near the city, the column's advance guard attacked a Serb command post from behind. The Srebrenica fighters captured two tanks and a heavy machine gun. Turning the Serbs' weapons against them, they smashed through the first rows of Serb trenches, but more troops were dug in ahead of then. The Bosniaks signaled across no-man's land to the Bosnian Army's 2nd Corps. If the 2nd Corps attacked the Serbs, it could pin them down while the column broke through. The 2nd Corps, which had not moved to save Srebrenica, again was of little help. But Nasir Oric, Srebrenica's former commander, was waiting on the Bosnian side with a group of fighters. Oric had not forgotten his comrades. He signaled to the Srebrenica fighters to attack the Serbs from behind, while his men advanced from the front. Hit from two directions, the Serbs fled. The column smashed through and crossed into government-controlled territory. But it was a bitter triumph. Of the twelve thousand to fifteen thousand who had set off on the marathon of death, less than half survived.

The 450 members of Dutchbat finally pulled out of Potočari on 21 July, together with its Bosniak UN staff. Those Bosniaks whose names were included on Dutchbat's list of its local staff survived. Those whose names were not listed died. Ibro Nuhanović, a Bosniak man, had accompanied Major Franken on his negotiations with the Bosnian Serbs on 17 July. One of Nuhanović's sons, Hasan, worked as a translator for Dutchbat. Both Ibro and Hasan were on Dutchbat's list, but Ibro's younger son was not. Despite their desperate pleas, Franken refused to add his name. Hasan stayed on the base, but Ibro chose to go with his wife and younger son. All three were taken away and are presumed dead. Hasan survived. Had Franken added his brother's name, he, too, would almost certainly have lived. In a final humiliation, Dutchbat's soldiers left behind their weapons, helmets and flak jackets, and medical supplies for the Serbs. Dutchbat arrived in Zagreb to a heroes' welcome from Defense Minister Joris Voorhoeve and Crown Prince Willem Alexander. They celebrated with a drunken party and danced in a chorus line. By then most of the men of Srebrenica were dead.

In New York diplomats demanded information from the Secretariat about Srebrenica's fate and the location of the men. The media were full of accounts of atrocities. Akashi warned of "unconfirmed" reports of rapes and executions. Yet by 18 July, seven days after the fall, the Secretariat still had not received a single report from UNPROFOR about the atrocities. The DPKO sent an angry cable to Akashi: "You will no doubt have read and heard the extensive accounts of atrocities committed by Bosnian Serbs during their takeover of Srebrenica. While many of these reports emerge from refugees, they are widespread and consistent, and have been given credence by a variety of international observers, including UNHCR. We have, however, received nothing on this subject from UNPROFOR." The DPKO demanded that Akashi interview Dutchbat officers, continuing: "Our inability to corroborate (or authoritatively contradict) any of the allegations currently being made, many of which involve events of which UNPROFOR in Potočari could not have been unaware, is causing mounting concern here." Akashi responded that Dutchbat soldiers had been debriefed in Zagreb. He claimed that the debriefings "did not reveal any firsthand accounts of human rights violations."[14]

Even now, some UN officials still seem keen to pass on, rather than accept, any share in the blame for the internal information breakdown and the Secretariat's failure to publicize in the world's media the atrocities taking place. When the final assault began, Iqbal Riza called Shashi Tharoor back from a family holiday. But by the time Tharoor arrived back at his desk, Srebrenica had virtually fallen. "We were demanding explanations from Akashi; we were urging action," says Tharoor.

> After the Serbs went around the Dutch roadblock, our immediate shift of focus was to make sure there were no actions against civilians. I was assured, and there were cables from there, saying people are being properly treated, that we have people present to ensure this. We were informed that Dutchbat had negotiated successfully to place a soldier in every one of the buses. We were getting a somewhat rosy picture, and it was only well after that that we discovered the horrific truth. We had no idea, for example, that young men and boys were being dragged behind houses and shot, within earshot of Dutch soldiers. All this came out much later. They should have raised the alarm. I could have been making an enormous fuss; instead, I was telling the media that we had assurances from our people that there was no mistreatment of civilians, because that was what we were getting.

Certainly Dutchbat failed to communicate adequately that the Serbs were killing prisoners. But the danger to the captured Bosniaks was always clear and present. Tharoor and the DPKO should have acted accordingly, says a senior UN official.

"Working in the United Nations, you had to accept that any civilians falling into Serb hands, particularly in the context of military conflict, would be in grave danger of at least injury, if not death. All the evidence that we had accumulated over three or four years pointed to that, and nobody could be in any doubt about it. It was inconceivable to me that Srebrenica would fall without very substantial civilian casualties, and I don't mean civilian casualties in the context of shelling, I mean their deliberate murder."

Fearful that the reports of the massacre gathered by Peggy Hicks and her colleagues in Tuzla would languish in the UN bureaucracy, Tone Bringa, a Norwegian UNPROFOR civil affairs officer, compiled one survivor's account of a massacre at Konjević Polje and passed it to Peter Galbraith, the US ambassador to Croatia. Bringa's report of the survivor's ordeal was methodical and detailed. The evidence was the wound from a bullet that had grazed the man's temple. Galbraith hoped that this would finally persuade the Clinton administration to take action. "The United Nations had a whole collection of reports of atrocities, and this was just one more for them," recalls Galbraith.

> But we knew seven thousand people were missing, and this was proof of what happened to them, which I suspected from the start. I was sure that it would be buried by the United Nations. In Akashi's world the reaction to something like this was that the United Nations had to be careful, because it was dangerous and could lead to military action. The United Nations always needed proof, and they had strategies to ensure there was no proof. They would sit on reports or ensure the information was not highlighted, and when it was reported by the press,

it just became part of more of the same from Bosnia. But for me this was a flash message, that this massacre had happened.

On 25 July, Galbraith sent a highly classified "no distribution" cable to Washington. He reported: "A UN official has recounted to me an interview [Bringa] conducted with a Srebrenica refugee in Tuzla. The account, which she felt was highly credible, provides disturbing evidence that the Bosnian Serbs have massacred many, if not most, of the 5,000 plus military age men in their custody following the fall of Srebrenica." As the anger and shame over Srebrenica in Washington grew ever more heated, the administration felt ever more threatened.

Events suddenly moved quickly. Washington and Paris agreed to abolish the notorious dual key. NATO was given the authority to launch both close air support and strategic air strikes on its own. British Prime Minister John Major grudgingly acquiesced. UN troops were steadily withdrawn from Bosnian Serb territory, leaving no potential hostages. Mladić again attacked Bihać. This time the fight did not go his way. The Croatian army and Bosnian Croat forces attacked the Serbs from one side, while the 5th Corps broke out, smashing through the Serb lines. The Bosnian Serbs proved less efficient in fighting proper soldiers than in shelling women and children or executing elderly men. Mladić's troops were routed, the Croats met up with the 5th Corps, and the first safe area was liberated, with no thanks to either the United Nations or NATO.

At dawn on 4 August, 200,000 Croatian troops advanced on Knin, capital of Serb-occupied Croatia. The Serbs quickly fled with their families, leaving half-eaten meals on their kitchen tables. The RSK collapsed within hours. Ethnic cleansing, it seemed, was a poor basis for a state. By 10:00 A.M. the next day, the Croatian flag was flying over Knin castle. Newly armed and trained by their American advisers, the Croatian army now carried out the single biggest act of ethnic cleansing of the Yugoslav wars: in two days, between 150,000 and 200,000 Serbs fled or were expelled. Croat soldiers killed Serb civilians, burned their houses, and committed other war crimes. It was the end of a centuries-old European community that had been led to utter disaster by leaders both evil and incompetent. Having already sent signals to Croatia that he would not intervene on behalf of the RSK, Milošević duly did nothing to aid his Serb brethren—the Yugoslav army stayed in its barracks while state-controlled television showed a circus festival in Monte Carlo.

A little more than three weeks later, on 28 August, the Bosnian Serbs resumed their shelling of Sarajevo. Five mortars landed, one in Markale marketplace, site of the massacre in February 1994. Thirty-seven people were killed and more than one hundred wounded. That day General Janvier was away on personal business, leaving General Smith in command. Smith's statement to the press after the massacre was equivocal. So far, so familiar. But his ambiguity was a feint, intended to reassure Mladić until the last UN troops being pulled out of eastern Bosnia finally crossed into Serbia. Late on 28 August, General Smith turned the key authorizing strategic NATO air strikes.

Finally, NATO was going to war. It seemed only polite to let the Serbs know. The EU negotiator Carl Bildt told one of his officials to call the Bosnian Serbs. He got through to Jovan Zametica, an adviser to Radovan Karadžić in Pale. "I told him what was going to happen. He said that they had experienced air strikes before. They had shot down a British fighter over Goražde, and they were not worried. I said, 'No, you don't understand: this is a quantum leap, beyond anything that has happened before. This is really serious.'" Sensing that this was not the usual empty threat, Zametica denied that the Bosnian Serbs had carried out the marketplace bombing. "I told him that I had seen the UN report, it is clear that you did it, and the evidence is conclusive. You did it, and this is going to happen. After years of doling it out, this time they were on the receiving end. It was the most satisfying moment of my life when the bombing started."

General Smith consulted neither General Janvier nor Akashi. Even the Secretariat did not learn of Smith's decision until six hours later. Smith did speak with Admiral Leighton Smith, NATO's southern commander. Both men agreed that the air strikes should continue until the attacks on—and the threat to—Sarajevo ceased. "People say it was easy for the United States to push for air strikes as we had no troops on the ground," recalls Peter Galbraith. "But if we had stuck with Rose's position, those UN troops would still be on the ground. General Smith demonstrated there was another way."

Operation Deliberate Force began at 3:00 A.M. on 30 August. Wave after wave of aircraft took off from Aviano air base in Italy and the aircraft carrier USS *Theodore Roosevelt*, roaring over the Adriatic toward Bosnia. The skies were lit up by the flashes of the bombs and missiles as they exploded. The first wave of bombing lasted nearly three hours. At 4:45 A.M. the British and French artillery in the rapid reaction force fired six hundred shells at sixteen Bosnian Serb gun positions. When the first wave ended and the NATO guns fell silent, the city echoed to a new, unfamiliar sound: cheering. Haris Silajdžić, the Bosnian prime minister, spoke for many when he said: "I must say that I enjoyed it. I must say that because those who killed so many people, those who aimed at baby hospitals, those who aimed at children who were playing, could finally feel what it means to be targeted, defenseless, and they deserved it."[15]

Operation Deliberate Force lasted until 20 September. NATO launched 3,500 sorties to destroy Serb ammunition dumps, an arms factory, bunkers, and command posts. Targeted strikes of Tomahawk cruise missiles took out the military communication network. The Bosnian Serbs promised "massive, uncontrolled retaliation against Sarajevo." It never happened. One French plane was shot down, but there was not a single Western fatality. General Smith showed a streak of ruthlessness. He ordered repeated attacks on a military facility in the village where Mladić's parents were buried to show the Serbs that Mladić could not protect their graves, a great shame in Balkan culture. He also ensured that this news was leaked to the Bosnian press. Two months later, the American diplomat Richard Holbrooke brokered the Bosnian peace accords at an air base in Dayton, Ohio. The war in Bosnia ended. NATO's authority for the air strikes that brought the war in Bosnia to an end was based mainly on resolution 836, mandating UNPROFOR to "deter attacks" on the safe areas.[16] Resolution 836 had been passed in June 1993.

Part II

PART II

VI
Silence in the Secretariat

*Trying to alert the Department of Political Affairs in New York
about what was happening in Darfur was like speaking into a
dark well, where your words just disappeared into nothingness.*
—Mukesh Kapila, UN resident and coordinator
for humanitarian affairs in Sudan from
March 2003 to April 2004

J an Egeland gathered his maps and papers and left his
spacious corner office on the thirty-sixth floor of the Secretariat building. It was the morning of 2 April 2004, one
of the most crucial days in Egeland's twenty-five-year humanitarian career. Egeland, under–secretary general for
humanitarian affairs, had finally persuaded the members of
the Security Council to let him brief them on the yearlong dis-

aster unfolding in Darfur, a remote area of western Sudan. The
tall, blond Norwegian was something of a star in the world of
humanitarian crises, known as someone who could get things
done. A former secretary general of the Norwegian Red Cross
and chairman of Amnesty International in that country, Egeland also had helped set up the behind-the-scenes diplomacy
that led to the Oslo accords between Israel and the Palestinian
Liberation Organization. But stirring the Security Council
into action over the genocide in Sudan would prove an even
greater challenge than bringing Yitzhak Rabin and Yasser Ara-
fat together.

Egeland gave his presentation in the briefing room, next
to the Council's main chamber. The small, sparsely furnished
space quickly filled with the Council's ambassadors, their staff,
and Egeland's own officials. It was an incongruous setting for
the horrors that he was to detail. "These very important initial
briefings, which I think changed a lot of things, were the in-
formal ones," he recalls. "That was quite a strange scene, the
people crowding together, some of them standing, and my staff
stood behind me. We put up our maps which marked where
the villages had been burned, sat around the table, and I gave
my statement." The diplomats listened attentively as Egeland
described how the Sudanese government, and its proxy Arab
militia known as the Janjaweed—an Arabic word translated as
"devil on horseback," had organized a systematic campaign of
ethnic cleansing against Darfur's black African population
after rebels had launched an uprising. Egeland said that for the
past year the United Nations team in the Sudanese capital,
Khartoum, had received sustained, consistent, and credible reports of massive human rights abuses against civilians, including women and children. Pointing at the maps spotted with
the sites of destroyed villages, Egeland accused the Sudanese

government of using a "scorched-earth policy" throughout Darfur, including the destruction of schools, wells, seeds, and food supplies, making whole towns and villages uninhabitable. Thousands had been forced to flee to camps for IDPs (internally displaced persons) or over the border into Chad to escape an "organized campaign of population displacement." Even in the camps there was no safety, nor any equivalent of UNPROFOR to offer even a semblance of protection. "I told them that every day I was getting reports from my people in the field of new displacements, more civilians killed, and more villages burned out, and [that] this cannot continue."

But it did. For all Darfur's isolation, the Sudanese government's onslaught had a grim familiarity: once again the United Nations watched as villages burned, men were taken away to be executed, their homes were looted, and their women and children began a long trek to a refugee camp. Even Sudan's methodology of genocide mirrored Milošević's tactics during the Bosnian war. Milošević had emptied Serbia's prisons, filling the ranks of the paramilitary militias to commit the atrocities the JNA might balk at. Anxious that the many officers of the Sudanese army who come from Darfur might not follow orders to destroy their own society, the Sudanese government armed and trained Arab nomads—the Janjaweed—to kill, rape, and plunder with impunity. And like Milošević, Sudanese President Omar al-Bashir constantly reassured the international community that he was trying to stop the very atrocities his regime was ordering its own forces to carry out. The stream of officials flying into Khartoum to negotiate the latest "ceasefire" were reminiscent of nothing so much as the envoys trekking to Belgrade during the Bosnian war, nodding politely as Milošević assured them that he would do his best to rein in General Mladić and Radovan Karadžić. Even the number of ca-

sualties is similar: 200,000 dead and two million homeless in
the Bosnian war; more than 400,000 dead in Darfur and 2 million displaced. But the bleakest comparison is the response of the
United Nations: slow, halting, and ineffective. Why did Egeland
have to wait a year before he could brief the Security Council
about a horrific ongoing humanitarian crisis? The Secretariat,
in particular the DPA, and the Security Council, sidelined Darfur because they had given priority to peace efforts to solve a
separate conflict in the south of Sudan. The first genocide of
the twenty-first century was an inconvenience, unwelcome grit
in the machinery of international diplomacy.

Like the former Yugoslavia, Sudan is an unstable postimperial
construct: a religious and cultural mosaic with arbitrary fron-
tiers cutting through natural ethnic groupings. The largest country in Africa, Sudan borders nine states, including Egypt and
Libya to the north, Chad to the west, and Kenya to the south.
Seventy percent of Sudanese are Sunni Muslims, while the Animist minority (who believe that both living and inanimate
objects have a soul) and a substantial Christian community
are concentrated in the south. Only about 40 percent of Sudan's
population is ethnically Arab, mainly concentrated in the north,
and most of the remainder are black Africans. Darfur is the
westernmost region of Sudan, comprising three provinces, North
(Shamal) Darfur, South (Janub) Darfur, and West (Gharb) Darfur. It is spread across 125,000 square miles, the size of New
Mexico, with a population of about seven million, in which three
African groups, the Fur, Zaghawa, and Masalit predominate.

History and geography have always oriented Darfur, which
means the Land of the Fur, more toward neighboring west
Africa than toward Khartoum. Sitting astride the great trade
routes from the Atlantic coast to the Arabian Sea, until 1916

Darfur was an independent sultanate. Conquered by the British, who then ruled Sudan, it was absorbed under their rule. The British explorer and author Wilfred Thesiger served in Darfur during the 1930s. He visited its remotest areas, traveling by camel, dressed in robes, and living off the land or enjoying the traditional hospitality of Arab chieftains, such as Sheikh Hilal Musa. Thesiger enjoyed his time in Darfur, although Great Britain did little to improve the area, educating only enough locals to run the colonial administration. Fifty years later an elder named Sheikh Hilal remembered Thesiger as a crack shot, bringing down a marauding lion, the author Alex de Waal records.[1] Thesiger evokes Darfur's harsh beauty in his memoirs, *The Life of My Choice.* "We rode across endless small undulating dunes, a small group of men and camels reduced to utter insignificance by the vast emptiness all around. I was exhilarated by the sense of space, the silence, and the crisp cleanness of the sand. I felt in harmony with the past, travelling as men had travelled for untold generations across deserts, dependent for their survival on the endurance of their camels and their own inherited skills."[2] It is a world now vanished forever.

In 1989, the same year that Slobodan Milošević was elected president of Serbia, the National Islamic Front (NIF), took power in Sudan after a military coup. The NIF promptly dissolved the previous coalition government and arrested most of its ministers. The leader of the coup was General Omar al-Bashir, but real power was wielded by Hassan al-Turabi of Sudan's Muslim Brotherhood. The modus operandi of the Sudanese and Serbian regimes had much in common. Milošević manipulated the political and military elite to cement his grip on power and launched a series of wars. The NIF, like its predecessors, used Arabization and war to keep control of the country. Al-Turabi quickly set up an Islamic police state, with widespread human rights abuses, including torture, summary execution, and denials of basic freedoms. The NIF's policy of Arabization, like Milošević's "Serbianization," allowed Khartoum to fracture a multiethnic society and introduce concepts of racial and ethnic polarization that had no real roots in the community. Just as Yugoslavs were forced to define themselves as Serbs, Croats, or Bosnian Muslims, black Africans "became" Arabs because they were Muslim and spoke Arabic. Those who rejected Arabization were dismissed as mere "Africans" or worse. "Divide and rule," even when the divisions were synthetic and introduced by force, was still powerfully effective.

In fact, Darfur's ethnic lines have been blurred for centuries: Suleiman Solong, the founder of the independent sultanate, was the son of an Arab father and a Fur mother. Most of Darfur's population were Muslim and knew Arabic, and it is impossible to tell a Darfurian's ancestry from facial features alone. Most of those who are referred to as "Arabs" in Darfur are not ethnic Arabs but Africans who have adopted Islam and the Arabic language, says Haile Menkerios, head of the Africa division at the DPA. "The 'Arabization of Africans' is a process, indeed a program, that has been pursued by many Arab groups and states in north Africa and the Arabian Peninsula to convert Africans in the Sahel region to Islam and [persuade them to] adopt Arab language and culture."

Darfur was home to a complex, prosperous agricultural society that had brought wealth and security to its people for centuries. The pastoral Africans grew millet and sorghum, tomatoes, and dates. Nomadic Arabs brought their herds of camel and horses south to feed and water. Intricate family and communal relations saw the community through times of drought and hardship. Any disputes about grazing rights were

solved by a carefully evolved series of conflict resolution mechanisms mediated by tribal chiefs. The slow-burning crisis
erupted in spring 2003 when two rebel movements, the Sudan
Liberation Army (SLA) and the Justice and Equality Movement (JEM), launched an uprising against Khartoum. Their
precise demands were unclear, but they called for an equitable
share of political power and resources. The south and west
have been largely ignored and neglected for decades. There is
barely any infrastructure, paved roads, electricity, health, or
education systems in those regions.

"The 'Arab' elite are from a certain area in the riverine
center of the country, and they have controlled political and
economic power throughout Sudan's history," says Menkerios.
"The peripheries, including Darfur, have long complained of
neglect, of marginalization. For decades there has been hardly
any extension of social services or protection under the law.
Particularly in Darfur almost everyone who had even ten head
of cattle was armed to protect his property and family." At first
the Darfur rebels enjoyed some success. They attacked Al-
Fashir airport in North Darfur, seized a plane, killed many
government soldiers, burned the holding areas, and stole ammunition. They soon controlled substantial territory, including several towns and villages. Khartoum quickly launched a
systematic and brutal response to the rebellion. Over the next
few months, the army, air force, and Janjaweed destroyed hundreds of villages, killing their inhabitants. This was not an attack on the rebels, but the planned, organized destruction of
the society from which they came. It was the Milošević model,
adjusted for Africa, and it worked perfectly. A state has the right
to protect its territorial integrity, and to combat rebels who
take up arms, but Khartoum made no attempt to limit its re-

sponse to legitimate military targets or, most important, to take any measures to safeguard civilians and noncombatants. On the contrary, it targeted them.

"There were centuries of history, of intercommunal kinship networks in Darfur between the urban and other communities, of trade networks and relationships, that stretched to Libya and Chad," says John Prendergast, Africa expert at the International Crisis Group.

> There was substantial wealth in Darfur, measured not in dollars but in head of livestock and grain holdings. When you go into the destroyed villages, you can see the size of the grain silos, and these are the largest ones I have ever seen. The Sudanese government organized this very precisely, to maximize the chaos. They used the Janjaweed, drawn from a close interdependent community, to do this, which creates very significant obstacles to whatever postconflict resolution there might be. This is a classic technique. You drain the water to catch the fish, using a neighboring ethnic group.

The world's feeble response to the Bosnian war also encouraged Khartoum, says Prendergast. "There is no question of that. They have learned by watching how the world reacts to other situations, such as Yugoslavia."

It can be argued that Sudan has been disintegrating ever since it became independent in 1956. Khartoum has never enjoyed full control over its territories. The Darfur rebels were partly inspired by the Sudan People's Liberation Army (SPLA), the Christian-led guerrilla movement in the south, which controlled a large area known as New Sudan. The SPLA had fought the government since 1983, when Khartoum first attempted to impose Sharia—Islamic law—on the whole country. Led by John Garang, a former army officer who had studied at Fort Benning, Georgia, the SPLA's war with Khartoum cost more than one and a half million lives. In January 2005, after months of negotiations at the Kenyan town of Naivasha, the SPLA and the Sudanese government signed a full peace agreement, known as the Naivasha accords. Garang was sworn in as vice president and signed a power-sharing deal. It was a remarkable victory, making him head of an autonomous south Sudan, with a referendum in 2011 on possible independence. Garang died soon afterward in a helicopter crash, in circumstances that remain suspicious.

Darfur has paid the highest price for the Naivasha accords. Ironically, the end of the north-south conflict accelerated the conflict in the west. With the south all but lost, Khartoum's strategy was to concede enough that the region would choose to stay part of Sudan. But just as Milošević had given up Serb-occupied Croatia but would not compromise over Bosnia, Khartoum would concede nothing on Darfur. According to Haile Menkerios:

> When the people in Darfur saw the gains the SPLA made in sharing wealth and power, they wanted a similar deal. And then the government got scared, because Darfur is very different. The deal with the south did not touch the basic power structure in the north and was not a threat to the elite or their political power. Even if the south goes, it is like a little finger. You can cut it off, but the body remains. But Darfur is Muslim and home to many Arabized Africans. This threatened the regime much more

than the rebellion in the south. It threatened the power of the elite and their existence.

Some detected the hand of Hassan al-Turabi in the Darfur uprising. The JEM, the more Islamically oriented of the two movements, has been repeatedly linked to al-Turabi, although he denies any connection. During the 1990s al-Turabi opened the door to Islamic radicals from all over the world and offered them housing, residence permits, and even Sudanese citizenship. Al-Turabi's Popular Arab and Islamic Conference (PAIC) hosted members of the Palestine Liberation Organization, Hamas, and Al-Qaeda, including Osama bin Laden. But in 1999 al-Turabi was sacked as speaker of Parliament and the PAIC was closed down. Two years later, he was arrested after signing a memorandum of understanding with the rebels in south Sudan and held in prison for a year. In March 2004 al-Turabi was arrested again, accused of plotting a coup. The prospect that Darfur would become the crucible for regime change in Khartoum, one that would bring to power al-Turabi, President al-Bashir's greatest rival, has also driven the government's ferocious onslaught on Darfur.

Two more factors were added to this volatile mix: geography and climate. There had always been tension between the pastoral Africans and the nomadic Arabs, who brought their flocks south to graze their animals. It was a north-south divide, between settled and migratory communities, common across Africa. But in Sudan, as across the Sahel region that stretches from the Atlantic Ocean through Africa, drought and desertification had caused the arable land to erode. There was less and less land for the nomadic tribes to raise their animals, and less for the pastoral communities to grow their crops. Inevitably, the clashes intensified. As Khartoum had abolished both Darfur's local autonomy and the tribal system, traditional conflict-resolution mechanisms no longer worked. Into this vacuum stepped the Sudanese intelligence service, the Mukhabarat. Like the Serbian secret service, which had operational control over the paramilitary militias that committed the worst atrocities in Bosnia, the Mukhabarat has played a crucial role in directing and managing the onslaught on Darfur. The Mukhabarat ensured that an essentially manageable dispute over agricultural resources exploded into a casus belli for civil war between African and Arab Sudanese.

The ethnic cleansing involved usually follows a similar pattern. The first sign that an attack is impending is that the surprisingly extensive mobile telephone network goes down. This prevents news spreading, both among the United Nations and relief workers, and among the villagers themselves. Then the Sudanese air force's Antonov transport planes roar overhead. The Antonovs carry bombs that are rolled out of their open cargo bays and dropped on the villages. The Antonovs are followed by attack helicopters that strafe the villages and the fleeing inhabitants, cutting them down as they run for cover. Once the village is afire and many of its inhabitants dead, the Janjaweed ride in, torching homes, killing some more, looting, and capturing women, who are taken away and raped repeatedly. Survivors then flee into the countryside and try to make their way to a refugee camp. The Janjaweed often drop the bodies of their victims into wells, deliberately polluting the source of drinking water, and thus preventing the villagers from returning, a tactic also used by Arkan's paramilitaries in Serb-occupied Croatia during the early 1990s. Destroying clean water supplies is also "atrocity by policy."

The Janjaweed, like the Serbian paramilitaries, provide plausible deniability for the policy of genocide. Khartoum claims it does not control the militias, when in fact it provides them with arms, ammunitions, communication equipment, funds, and logistical support and coordinates their attacks with its army and air force. Initially, Khartoum denied even that the Janjaweed existed. Sudanese officials developed their own version of the "all parties are guilty" theory, which was so popular at the United Nations during the Bosnian war: Khartoum demanded that all "outlaw groups" be disarmed, but did not include the Janjaweed. Documents obtained by Human Rights Watch detail consistent evidence of the links between Khartoum and the Janjaweed. A government directive to all local "security units," dated 13 February 2004, urges them to "allow the activities of the mujahideen [Janjaweed] and volunteers under the command of Sheikh Musa Hilal to proceed in the areas of [North Darfur] and to secure their vital needs"—that is, supply them with the necessary supplies and ammunition. The document also appears to grant the paramilitaries impunity to commit atrocities against civilians: "We also highlight the importance of noninterference so as not to question their authorities and to overlook minor offences by the mujahideen against civilians who are suspected members of the rebellion."[3]

   That month, just as President al-Bashir declared that all military operations in Darfur would be ended, a "highly confidential" directive from the commissioner of Kutum Province, called for "loyalist tribes" to be mobilized and given sufficient weapons and ammunition to "secure their areas"—to ethnically cleanse the Fur and Zaghawa. In the 1930s Wilfred Thesiger had lived in Kutum. "I was immediately captivated by Kutum," he wrote. "Below my house was a broad, sandy wadi or watercourse bordered by *haraz* trees in full leaf. On the far side was a small village of thatched huts; beyond that an infinitude of bush-covered country, broken in the distance by the jagged peaks of Jabal Si."[4] The Fur and Zaghawa would never be allowed to return home. The same February 2004 memorandum calls for local officials to design a plan for "resettlement operations of nomads in places from which the outlaws withdrew."

Sheikh Musa Hilal, the most notorious Sudanese paramilitary leader, lives openly in Khartoum when not fighting in Darfur. A tall, light-skinned man in his mid-forties, with a pot belly pushing against his long white robes, he is the son of Sheikh Hilal, who had once hosted Wilfred Thesiger.[5] Like Arkan, the most notorious Serb paramilitary leader, Hilal has a certain charisma and relishes the attention of the international media. Mindful perhaps of a likely future indictment for war crimes, Hilal is charming and hospitable to Western visitors. He denies any role in war crimes. Instead, he claims he was merely taking part in a counterinsurgency operation. "When the rebels of Darfur knocked down the planes at El-Fasher, the government asked everybody to help it defeat the rebels. I have my own territory and when I was asked by the government I tried to keep my territory quiet and peaceful."[6]

In an interview with Human Rights Watch, Hilal admitted that his military operations were coordinated by central government. "All of the people in the field are led by top army commanders," Hilal said. "The highest rank is major, and officers, some sergeants, and some captains and so on. These people get their orders from the western command center and from Khartoum." He also claimed that he had no authority to disarm or demobilize his militia, which he referred to as the People's Defense Force (PDF). "It's the government's concern. They're the ones that recruited the PDF; they're the ones that pay their salaries; they give them their ID cards. They can disarm or they can leave them alone; that's the government's concern."[7]

The UN's International Commission of Inquiry (ICI) report on Darfur, published in January 2005, details the joint attack launched by the Sudanese army and the Janjaweed on the village of Surra, in South Darfur, in January 2004. More than 250 people were killed, including many women and children. Separate groups of witnesses gave UN officials a "very credible, detailed, and consistent account of the attack." It began in the early morning, when the army launched a mortar barrage. The Janjaweed rode in, firing rifles and machine guns, forced their way into the houses, and killed the men on the spot. The women were taken to the mosque. Like the mothers of Srebrenica in the base at Potočari, the women of Surra hid their young sons, wrapping them inside their *maxis*, long pieces of cloth that cover the whole body. When the Janjaweed found the boys, they shot them on the spot. The survivors fled, leaving their men unburied.[8]

As Khartoum's "counterinsurgency campaign" set Darfur ablaze in 2004, relief workers and UN officials heard increasing, consistent accounts of massacres and ethnic cleansing. The village of Kailek, also in South Darfur, mainly populated by the Fur tribe, was attacked twice, the second time in March 2004. The army and the Janjaweed advanced, backed by aircraft and military vehicles. As the villagers fled to the mountains, the Janjaweed rode in on horses and camels and hunted them down. When the survivors reached the mountains, the army began shelling the mountainsides, while soldiers opened fire with machine guns. Many of those who were captured or surrendered were immediately executed. Others were taken back to Kailek and held in a makeshift concentration camp for several weeks. As in Bosnia, local community leaders were singled out for execution, called out in front of their families, and shot on the spot. The Janjaweed's innovation was to use fire as a weapon. Children were dragged from their parents as they tried to flee the carnage and were thrown into burning houses. "There are reports of people being thrown onto fires to burn to death. There are reports that people were partially skinned or otherwise injured and left to die," the UN report notes.[9]

Nor is there safety or security in the internally displaced persons (IDP) camps. The government's February 2004 Kutum memorandum recommends that officials set up new camps for "volunteers," to "protect civilians in major cities and to conduct security missions among the citizens." The "volunteers" are Janjaweed, their "security missions" raids *inside* the refugee camps. The parallels with Bosnia, it seems, are endless: just as Bosnian troops made perilous treks through Serb territory to the enclaves of Srebrenica, Goražde, and Žepa, the refugees of Darfur have established their own "underground railway," transporting food and supplies from refugee camps in Chad back into Darfur, a journey though the desert that lasts many days. The Janjaweed have honed the techniques deployed by General Mladić. The Serb snipers that ringed Sarajevo often picked off children playing in the street, while Serb gunners precisely ranged mortars and artillery shells before firing them at schools and football fields. But Serb soldiers usually did not shoot young children down in front of their parents' eyes. The Janjaweed have no such compunction. Rashida Abbas fled Kailek after the attack in March 1994. Her husband was one of more than one hundred men to be shot, records Samantha Power. Of Rashida's six children, only four survived. When the Janjaweed rode in, she fled with a daughter in each hand, an infant on her back, and her eldest son in front of her. Her two youngest sons, Adam Muhammed and Hassan Muhammed, trailed behind her. The Janjaweed torched the roofs of the huts, and one of the

Arab militiamen grabbed the two young boys. Rashida pleaded
for their lives, but the gunman warned her to shut up or all her
children would be killed. Rashida backed away, and the Janjaweed fighter threw Adam into the fire. She heard him shouting "Mama, mama" as he disappeared into the flames. Hassan
briefly broke free and ran his to mother. The Janjaweed shot
him twice in the back. He died instantly.[10]

During the Bosnian war the Bosnian Serbs used rape as a
weapon of war, calculated to traumatize and humiliate their
victims. Even male inmates in the concentration camps were
forced to perform sexual acts upon each other. The UN special
rapporteur, Professor Cherif Bassiouni, conducted the world's
most extensive rape investigation, examining more than sixteen hundred cases of rape and sexual assault by Bosnian Serbs.
Many took place in rape camps, where women were held for
long periods. "It is very telling that in 80 per cent of the rape
cases that we investigated, the acts of rape were done with the
purpose of enhancing the element of shame and embarrassment
to the victim, of her family, and of the community, to create a
terror-inspiring effect that would cause people (*a*) to flee and
(*b*) not to return," he testified to Congress in April 1995.[11]

The Janjaweed have raised rape as a weapon of war to
new levels. This is about not sex but power and terror. Rape is
an integral part of "atrocity by policy," designed to terrorize
and humiliate both the female victim and the husbands, fathers, and brothers who were unable to protect her. Rape de-
stroys not just the bonds of society between different ethnic
groups but also internal family relationships. The profound feelings of shame and violation traumatize both the victim and
relatives. The Janjaweed even brand their victims with burning
irons. Many rape victims contract venereal disease and are abandoned by their families, stigmatized as *khasrana* (damaged).

Others are cared for, but the profound violation leaves deep and permanent mental scars. "My daughter screams at night. She is not happy as she used to be before, she cannot sit in one place; she is *mashautana* [possessed]," said one mother of a rape victim. "She is always worried and in continuous movement; I never talk to her about what happened, although she knows I know what happened to her. Of course she does: I cleaned her wounds after her return every day, but still, talking about it is very difficult. Her father became very ill since that time. He never goes out with the rest of the men and he does nothing but stay inside the room."[12]

After the joint Sudanese army–Janjaweed attack on Kailek in early 2004, up to thirty thousand people were confined there for seven weeks. The women and children at Kailek were separated from the men, confined in a walled area around the mosque, and taken away to be raped, the victims including girls as young as ten. After the rapes some victims did not have their clothes returned to them, suffering the further intentional humiliation of being forced to remain naked. One source told the UN ICI: "We also found four women with no clothes. They covered themselves with a grass mat and were imploring us not to remove it. They said that if they needed water or food, one of them had to borrow clothes from the other women to go and fetch water or food."[13] Any man who tried to protect his family was severely beaten or killed.

The Janjaweed also rape women who leave the meager protection of the refugee camps to scavenge for firewood. Venturing outside the camps demands a dark gamble: men are better able to protect themselves but are likely to be killed if they encounter the Janjaweed. Women are less likely to be killed but run a high risk of rape, even if they are very young. The UN's ICI interviewed two girls, aged twelve and fourteen, who had

left the Abu Shouk camp in November 2004 to collect firewood and were raped by government soldiers. Other victims
were forced to strip, were raped by Janjaweed, and were then
left naked on the road.[14] Mockery and shame are an important
part of this intentional humiliation. General Mladić and the
executioners at Srebrenica forced their victims to pray and
taunted them, asking, "Where is your Nasir [Oric] now, where
is your Alija [Izetbegović]?" or abused them as "Balija," a deroga-
tory term for Bosnian Muslims, before shooting them. The Sudanese soldiers and Janjaweed abuse their victims as "Abid" or
"Zurka," meaning slave or "dirty black," and tell them that the
rape will produce light-skinned babies. A particular form of
torture is the genital mutilation of rape victims. A survivor of
one attack on a Zaghawa community in North Darfur testified
to Human Rights Watch: "Some women and girls were raped,
another time, all one day, on 18 October 2004. Other women
were raped in different ways. The men didn't just rape them
but afterwards they cut their sexual parts and sewed them up.
Fifty Janjaweed committed this crime on the same day; it resulted in many people leaving for Chad."[15]

Ten years after Professor Bassiouni testified to Congress,
the UN's ICI on Darfur came to identical conclusions about
the role of rape as an integral part of ethnic cleansing. According to the ICI report, "Particularly outrageous cases of abduc-
tions, confinement and multiple rapes over protracted periods
of time have further contributed to spreading fear. Similarly,
the Commission found sufficient evidence that rape and sexual violence continued to be perpetrated against women during
their displacement, so as to perpetuate the feeling of insecurity
among them and fear of leaving the IDP sites." The ICI report
concluded that sexual violence is apparently used as "a deliberate strategy with a view to achieve certain objectives, including

terrorising the population, ensuring control of the movement of the IDP population, and perpetuating its displacement. Cases like that of Kailek demonstrate that rape was used as a means to demoralize and humiliate the population."[16]

The extent of human rights abuses in Darfur, the role of the Sudanese government, and its links of command and control with the Janjaweed were reported to the Secretariat during 2003 and 2004. Dr. Mukesh Kapila, a former medical student at Khartoum University and a humanitarian crisis expert, was seconded to the United Nations by the British government. As soon as Kapila arrived in Khartoum, in March 2003, he set up a Darfur crisis cell within the UN operation, a small team of specialists, dealing with human rights abuses and the Darfur aid operation. One official recalls: "The team held meetings with the representatives of donor countries, and he told them to tell their governments what was happening. There were efforts, very early on in this crisis, to tell the international community about Darfur, but there was a general will not to pay too much attention because people wanted to preserve the north-south agreement."

Kapila's team of human rights investigators traveled across the province, interviewing victims and refugees. This was difficult and often dangerous work, especially for those coming to testify about human rights abuses. In the summer of 2003 the sultans of all three provinces in Darfur, North, South, and West, met with UN officials. The local Walis (governors) insisted on being present, and interpreters were provided by the local authorities. "The sultans testified to us about the massacres that their tribes had been the victims of," recalls the UN aid official. "But there were oddities in the translations. I don't know Arabic, but when you hear the word *Antonov* in what the sultans are saying, and the word does not appear in your translation, you feel something awkward is happening. After they spoke to us, the sultans were arrested and held for a couple of days. We heard about this after the fact." After this the UN officials advised those wishing to testify to them not to meet them in public but to come to the UN headquarters, where hundreds of people were coming and going every day.

Day by day, Kapila and his team gathered and compiled their reports. During the summer of 2003 and throughout his year at his post, Kapila sent back a stream of detailed reports to the Secretariat, outlining the human rights abuses committed by the Janjaweed and the army. The Darfur update of 26 July 2003 reported that government forces had bombed the towns of Tinah, Kornoi, and Umm Baro, destroying a local hospital and other public buildings. The update of 14 September detailed Khartoum's support for the Janjaweed, with funds, weapons, ammunition, and "political and legal protection for the atrocities they have committed," and named a cabinet minister and air force general as their backers. The Darfur update of 30 November reported that Khartoum was trying to "normalize" the Janjaweed by incorporating them into the People's Defense Force.

Many of the reports were sent to Jan Egeland, sometimes with copies to other senior UN officials. On 18 December 2003 Kapila wrote to Egeland and to Kieran Prendergast, a veteran British diplomat who was then the under–secretary general of the DPA, a position of great power and influence: "The security situation in Greater Darfur continues to worsen. Access to both rebel and Government-held areas remains denied and/or constrained by travel permit restrictions and by militia activity in all three states, West, South, and North Darfur. An estimated 670,000 people have been newly displaced, 70,000 fled into Chad, and one million others are directly affected by the war. Our Office receives daily reports of human right violations throughout the region." Kapila concluded: "I am informed by diplomatic missions here of the growing view that the international community should press for an all-inclusive, internationally monitored ceasefire in Darfur."[17] Yet none of these reports seemed to have any impact in New York. An experienced crisis-zone worker, a veteran of Bosnia and Rwanda, Dr. Kapila was disturbed by the Secretariat's lack of response to his reports from the field. When he asked the DPA for political guidance about the framework in which he could operate, he was told that there was none, for the United Nations was not directly involved in the political process, and Darfur was seen as largely a humanitarian issue. Once again, the Secretariat gave priority to blankets and food aid, applying a palliative to the symptoms of the crisis, rather than confront its causes. "I told them this was not purely a humanitarian issue, it was a political issue as well. But beyond ritualistic noises, the DPA washed its hands of Darfur."

Back in New York, Dr. Kapila soon understood why. Senior figures in the DPA had followed the lead set by the Security Council, giving priority to the north-south accords, allowing nothing to threaten them. "The reaction in the political parts of the Secretariat was that yes, they knew Darfur was terrible, but they had to wait for the north-south conflict to be solved, and then Darfur would also be solved," Kapila recalls.

> Except in OCHA, the humanitarian affairs department, there was no appetite for understanding for the gravity of the situation, that this was a worsening trend and we needed to do something about it. There is a parallel with Bosnia here. This was more than a lack of energy or lack of will. There was a

fundamental feeling among very senior people that
this was a very inconvenient development and they
would rather not know about it. It did not fit the
United Nations' paradigm for Sudan, of a smooth
peace agreement and a new order. Real-life facts were
somewhat inconvenient.

Another senior UN official confirms this: "There was an un-
willingness to recognize the seriousness of the situation in
Darfur, and a fear that it would jeopardize the 'prize' of the
Naivasha accords." But real-life facts had to be confronted.
Egeland and Kapila planned a campaign to lobby for a robust
policy to force Khartoum to stop killing its own people.

VII
A Rwandan Reprise

I believed at that time I was doing my best. But I realized
after the genocide there was more I could have and should
have done to sound the alarm and rally support.
—Kofi Annan, on his personal responsibility over
the United Nations' failure in Rwanda

M ukesh Kapila's was not the only voice within the
United Nations raising the alarm over Darfur.
Several UN special rapporteurs on human rights
sent a series of urgent appeals to Khartoum
protesting against continuing abuses. UN humanitarian officials visited Khartoum trying to persuade the government to
stop its onslaught. But the Security Council stayed silent, and
none of these efforts stopped the scorched-earth campaign. In

early December 2003 aid workers announced that almost ten thousand new refugees had fled into Chad. The UN World Food Programme (WFP) reported that forty-six of the sixty-two villages in South Darfur had been burned to the ground, while the remaining sixteen had been looted. On 9 December 2003, one day before UN Human Rights Day, Secretary General Kofi Annan expressed, through his spokesman, his "alarm" at the continued reports of atrocities and obstruction of the relief effort. He called for a cease-fire and the resumption of peace talks. Mukesh Kapila had helped draft the statement. He and OCHA now hoped that the United Nations would finally take action on Darfur.

Annan had taken office as secretary general on 1 January 1997, after the United States delivered the coup de grâce to his former boss. Boutros Boutros-Ghali's fears had come true: his term had been forever tainted by Bosnia, the Srebrenica massacre, and the genocide in Rwanda. But Annan's repositioning of the DPKO during late 1994 and 1995, moving the department away from General Rose and Yasushi Akashi and toward the United States' stance of demanding that NATO bomb the Serbs, had boosted his standing within the Clinton administration. In summer 1995 Annan had aided the United States and NATO in steering Operation Deliberate Force through the Security Council, preventing Russia and China from becoming too troublesome. From then on, the United States supported Annan for the top job, so much so that Madeleine Albright and the State Department engineered a coup within the United Nations to ensure that he was appointed. After four years of being bullied, hectored, and left out of the loop, Boutros-Ghali's staff did not come to the aid of their beleaguered boss.

At first Annan's appointment was greeted by joy and relief by the Secretariat. There was a sense that a new era was dawning, that the United Nations could now return to its glory days, reinvigorating its founding humanitarian principles. Phone calls to the thirty-eighth floor were returned. Information was available. Staff members were consulted. Annan was hailed as a potential new Dag Hammarskjöld, secretary general from 1953 to 1961, who used the organization's moral authority to make the United Nations a powerful force in international diplomacy. But more indicative, perhaps, was Annan's term as successor to Yasushi Akashi. Annan had traveled to Belgrade in 1996, bearing a check for $1 million to pay for damage supposedly caused by French UN peacekeepers to Yugoslav army facilities. The agreement was worked out by UN lawyers, colleagues of the UN legal official who during the attack on Bihać had argued that UNPROFOR troops should not be dispatched to protect the hospital because the United Nations was not a signatory to the Geneva Conventions. These lawyers seemed to have forgotten that during its three years deployed in the former Yugoslavia, UNPROFOR had lost 167 personnel, many of them killed by the Bosnian Serbs, whose weapons and ammunition were supplied by the same Yugoslav army which Annan was now compensating.[1]

By winter 2003, with Annan well into his second term, his honeymoon was long over. Annan's call for peace in Darfur was commendable. But such demands had been issued almost daily throughout the Bosnian war without any practical effect. Sudan's NIF regime, like the Bosnian Serbs, was skilled in reading the responses of the international community: it decoded the significance of words, taking into account who was saying them and how the statements were issued. It is true that by now, behind the scenes, Annan was pushing for action on Darfur, lobbying the P5 and helping to initiate the UN's ICI. But until the end of 2003 Annan preferred quiet diplomacy to open pressure on Khartoum. His December 9 statement, almost a year into the conflict, was his first public utterance on Darfur. It was, in UN terminology, "a statement attributable to the spokesman for the secretary general." It was a statement of United Nations policy but lacked the impact of Annan himself proclaiming his anger into a microphone. On the same day, his spokesman issued another statement in Annan's name, condemning a bomb on the Moscow subway.

Khartoum understood that for all the noise and protests, Darfur was still categorized as a humanitarian issue, not a political question. What mattered was the Security Council. That is where sanctions were imposed, peacekeepers dispatched, the assets of corrupt leaders frozen. Annan's statement changed nothing. By the end of 2003 the Security Council had still not passed a resolution on Darfur. "We had tried for months to get it onto the agenda, with the support of some Council members, such as Germany, and against the resistance of others," says a UN humanitarian official. The DPA, more powerful than the humanitarian departments, wanted the Darfur crisis kept out of the Security Council and advised Kofi Annan to do the same, so as not to jeopardize the Naivasha accords. As Jan Egeland says: "To get something on the Security Council agenda is very difficult, and once you are on, it is a major thing."

Annan did not have to concede the point to the DPA. As secretary general he had considerable authority, if he chose to use it. He could have demanded a hearing from the Security Council on Darfur under article 99 of the UN Charter. But Annan failed to seize the moral high ground. "This was a classic example of both the Secretariat and the Security Council not taking the initiative and not acting in a preemptive way. If there was ever a failure, this was it," says Mukesh Kapila. "The two bodies should have prioritized the dispatch of a peacekeeping force and threatened sanctions against Sudan months earlier. The very inclusion of a crisis on the Security Council agenda is a signal to a state committing human rights abuses."

With Jan Egeland's backing, Kapila traveled to a series of capitals of Security Council members, including London, Washington, D.C., and Paris, as well as Oslo, Rome, and Brussels, to lobby them on Darfur. "Almost everywhere I went I was told not to make too much noise, because of the north-south accords. Washington said they did want to take Darfur to the Security Council, but London would not agree, and [the US] would not do anything without London's agreement." Agreement was unlikely while the British Foreign Office dusted off its Bosnia script and reworked it for Darfur.

Kapila's meetings with foreign officials were chillingly reminiscent of his compatriot Michael Williams's briefing with Foreign Office officials on Bosnia, before he took up his post at UNPROFOR. Kapila was repeatedly stonewalled. "My own government told me that in fact the situation in Darfur was far *worse* than I realized, but I shouldn't make too much noise because the north-south issue must take priority." Meanwhile, a new—or rather old—factor reappeared: the "all sides are guilty" position. Scattered reports of human rights abuses by the SLA and the JEM, minuscule in proportion to those committed by the Janjaweed and the Sudanese army, were suddenly elevated into strategic equivalence. Just as the Bosnian army had supposedly shelled its own citizens, the Darfur rebels were now said to be killing civilians. Several British members of Parliament began to press the Blair government, which had once proudly announced a new, ethical, foreign policy, on its unwillingness to take a robust stand on Darfur. In February 2005 the Conservative Member of Parliament John Bercow, a parliamentary activist on Africa and human rights, told the International Development Committee's hearing on Darfur that he was disturbed by the government's implication that there was some balance of responsibility between the government and rebels. "It does seem to me that there really is a rather important distinction, and that is [that] the rebels are starting from a very low and weak base. The rebels do not have Antonov airplanes, and they do not have helicopter gunships."

Ironically, the SPLA leadership disagreed with the West's caution on Darfur. Its leader, John Garang, had repeatedly told UN officials that the SPLA wanted Darfur to be settled at the same time as the north-south conflict. Garang understood that once he was part of the new National Unity government, he would have little leverage over the army, crucial for a solution in Darfur. The most powerful ministries, defense and interior, as well as the intelligence service, would remain in the hands of the Khartoum Arab elite. Garang understood Khartoum: with the SPLA inside the government and the north-south issue neutralized, it would have a free hand to turn on Darfur. The faster the Naivasha talks progressed, the more Khartoum stepped up its ethnic cleansing in Darfur.

Angry and frustrated, Dr. Kapila decided to go public. He traveled to Nairobi, Kenya, where most international correspondents covering Africa were based, and on 19 March 2004 he gave a live interview to BBC Radio 4's *Today* program, the favorite morning show of British politicians. "I said three things that had not been said before," Kapila recalls: "that this was the world's greatest humanitarian crisis [and] that it was a human rights catastrophe on a par with Rwanda, and I accused the Sudanese government of being behind this." The reaction was electric. The interview made headlines across the globe, and governments scrambled to respond. Kapila was cheered by his colleagues and much of the public. An anonymous Sudanese sent him a message saying, "We were voiceless and you have given us a voice. We were hopeless and you have given us hope." But the DPA and the P5 were furious. Kapila's intervention, they believed, would jeopardize the Naivasha accords. In Khartoum the Humanitarian Affairs Ministry denounced the interview as "a pack of lies."

Back in Sudan, Dr. Kapila received several death threats and was repeatedly attacked in the government-controlled media. He left for good at the beginning of April, his future career in doubt but his conscience clear. Like Diego Arria, he had spoken out and paid the price. And like Diego Arria, he could sleep at night. "Nobody could say I had not followed the proper track," he says. "I had made representations within the Secretariat and to the important countries on the Security Council. I had documented the human rights violations, and every time there was an incident I wrote to the Sudanese government. Because of my experience of Srebrenica and Rwanda, and because people in authority have a particular personal responsibility when you are dealing with extraordinary crimes against humanity, I had a duty to speak out."

Once he had gone public, Dr. Kapila decided to sidestep the bureaucracy and go straight to the top. On 22 March 2004, three days after his interview with the BBC, Kapila sent a personal memorandum to Iqbal Riza, Kofi Annan's chief of cabinet, asking him to forward it to Annan. Copies were also sent to seven senior UN officials, including Kieran Prendergast, head of the DPA, Mark Malloch-Brown, head of the UN Development Program, and Annan's deputy, Louise Fréchette. The letter detailed the involvement of the Sudanese government and the Janjaweed in ethnic cleansing and a systematic campaign of "large-scale armed violence and incidents of murder, rape, torture, and abduction." It described a "scorched-earth" policy of organized "pogroms" that showed "premeditation and planning from a higher level of a policy of extreme violence that is specifically targeted at African tribes." It outlined Khartoum's provision of air support for the Janjaweed raids, implicating government officials in war crimes. Kapila reported that the Red Cross was refused permission to operate freely, while humanitarian and relief supplies were continually obstructed by the Sudanese government's Ministry of Humanitarian Affairs.[2]

Annan never replied to the memo, but it must have been familiar reading. There were few better students of how the Bosnian Serbs committed genocide in the early 1990s with impunity than the Sudanese government a decade later. Outmaneuvered by Kapila and OCHA, the Security Council now had no choice but to listen to Egeland's presentation. The real drama came when Egeland emerged into a scrum of television cameras and reporters. He obliged his audience with strong statements about ethnic cleansing and Khartoum's scorched-earth policy, which pushed Darfur straight back onto the news agenda. Egeland's briefing to the Security Council, along with his impromptu press conference afterward, was a key turning point, says a UN humanitarian official. "The fact that Egeland took this to the Council and was able to say that ethnic cleansing was taking place, that it was systematic and supported by the Sudanese government—[it] was the first time that a senior UN official went to that level of detail and used that kind of language. It was very important." UN humanitarian officials repeatedly briefed the Security Council over the next two months. Yet it was not until 11 June that the first resolution on Darfur was passed.

Jan Egeland's Security Council briefing and Mukesh Kapila's BBC interview embarrassed the United Nations. The two men had blown open the Darfur crisis just as the organization prepared to commemorate the tenth anniversary of the genocide in Rwanda. Egeland's and Kapila's forcefulness was in stark contrast to the UN's catastrophic failure in Rwanda. Five days after Egeland's call for action, Annan addressed the UN Human Rights Commission in Geneva. The UN General Assembly had designated 7 April as an "international day of reflection" on the Rwandan genocide. Annan's audience provided no guarantee of reflection, or indeed of human rights. The Commission's fifty-three member states that year included Saudi Arabia, Zimbabwe, Cuba, and, perhaps inevitably, Sudan. Before he began speaking, Annan called for two minutes of silence. As he faced the rows of dignitaries, Annan doubtless mulled over his own role in the United Nations' catastrophic failure in Rwanda, one in which he was personally implicated.

There had been plenty of warnings of the bloodshed to come. Rwanda's two main ethnic groups, the Tutsi and the Hutu, had struggled for power since the country was awarded to Belgium by the League of Nations after the First World War. Using the old principle of divide and rule, the Belgians had groomed the Tutsis as a ruling class to enforce harsh colonial order against the Hutus. But by the time Rwanda became independent in 1962, the situation had reversed and the Hutus held power. In 1990 the Tutsi-led Rwandan Patriotic Front (RPF) invaded Rwanda from neighboring Uganda. A vicious civil war lasted until August 1993, when the RPF and the government signed a peace and power-sharing agreement called the Arusha accords. Despite this pact, the Hutu-led government set up militias, called the Interahamwe, which began attacking Tutsis and committing atrocities. Government radio stations began pumping out anti-Tutsi propaganda, even inciting murder. One week after the accords were signed, the United Nations published a report on human rights in Rwanda, compiled by Waly Bacre Ndiaye, special rapporteur on judicial, summary, and arbitrary executions. Ndiaye stated: "The victims of the attacks, Tutsis in the overwhelming majority of cases, have been targeted solely because of their membership of a certain ethnic group and for no other objective reason." Ndiaye's report, which warned of a serious risk of genocide and recommended a series of preventive steps, was largely ignored.

Instead, UNAMIR, the UN Assistance Mission to Rwanda, was dispatched at the end of 1993 to monitor the implementation of the Arusha accords. UNAMIR comprised twenty-five hundred troops, the largest contingent from Belgium, Rwanda's former colonial governing power, and the rest from Canada, Tunisia, Bangladesh, and Ghana. Its mandate was similar to that of UNPROFOR in Bosnia: to ensure security, monitor ceasefires and demilitarized zones, clear mines, and help coordinate relief supplies. The Security Council did not approve all the elements of a mandate recommended by Boutros-Ghali but authorized a watered-down version. There was no specific clause authorizing weapons collection, a lapse that would later have extremely serious consequences. By the time UNAMIR arrived in the capital, Kigali, the Arusha accords were already unraveling, and Tutsis were being targeted. UNAMIR's commander, Canadian General Roméo Dallaire, requested approval from the Secretariat for a new draft set of rules of engagement that would help prevent the kind of confusion that had so dogged UNPROFOR. Paragraph 17 of Dallaire's proposals would empower UNAMIR to use "all available means" to stop "ethnically or politically motivated crimes," such as executions or attacks on refugees. Dallaire received no formal response to his request.

The government radio station, RTLM, prepared the ground for the coming slaughter, pouring out a stream of hate against Tutsis and moderate Hutus. Lists were drawn up of those to be killed. UNAMIR was publicly warned to stay out of the way when the time came. Not every Hutu wanted to kill Tutsis. General Dallaire cultivated a high-level source in the Interahamwe, the Hutu militia, known as "Jean-Pierre." In New York, Boutros-Ghali also had his own sources. In early December, James Jonah, a senior official in the DPA, traveled to Rwanda and met President Juvénal Habyarimana. Boutros-Ghali had instructed Jonah to warn the president that the United Nations knew about plans to kill the opposition and would not tolerate it.[3]

Over the next few weeks the tension grew in Kigali until it was almost palpable. By early January 1994 Jean-Pierre had provided Dallaire with detailed information about how the mass murder would be carried out. Jean-Pierre was in charge of seventeen hundred men, scattered in groups of forty across the city. He told General Dallaire that Belgian peacekeepers would be killed to trigger a withdrawal of UNAMIR and clear the path for the slaughter. He specified the locations of weapons caches that would be used to slaughter the Tutsis and even escorted UNAMIR intelligence officers to see one for themselves. Even apart from inside information, signs of an impending massacre were ubiquitous: planeloads of arms, many supplied or sponsored by France, landed at Kigali airport, grenades and AK-47s were freely on sale, and the government was importing from China vast quantities of machetes, far more than were needed for agricultural use.[4]

Jean-Pierre became extremely anxious for his safety and that of his family. General Dallaire asked the DPKO for authorization to stop the planned genocide and offer sanctuary to Jean-Pierre and his family. On 11 January, Dallaire sent a cable to New York to the DPKO and the secretary general's military adviser, General Maurice Baril, outlining what he had learned: "Since UNAMIR mandate the informant has been ordered to register all Tutsi in Kigali. He suspects it is for their extermination. Example he gave was that in 20 minutes his personnel could kill up to 1000 Tutsis." The informant was prepared to provide the details of major weapons caches that evening if he and his family were placed under United Nations protection. Dallaire said he planned to raid the arms caches within the next thirty-six hours and asked for advice on evacuating the informant. "This HQ does not have previous UN experience in such matters and urgently requests guidance," he concluded before signing off: "Peux ce que veux. Allons-y"— Where there's a will, there's a way; let's go. According to the author Bjørn Willum, who has extensively investigated the role of the DPKO during the Rwanda genocide, UNAMIR had already begun weapons-confiscation operations. Now General Dallaire sought formal approval for the policy.[5]

But there was no will and no way. General Dallaire's cable, now known as the "genocide fax"—a clear, unambiguous warning of a planned, even announced, mass slaughter— was sidelined by the DPKO. Kofi Annan quickly replied, in a cable signed by his colleague Iqbal Riza, "We must handle this information with caution." While General Dallaire warned of extermination, Annan called for prudence. Annan told Dallaire that his request to raid the arms caches was out of the question. "No reconnaissance or other action, including response to request for protection, should be taken by UNAMIR until clear guidance is received from Headquarters." Dallaire was incredulous. The next day, his boss, Boutros-Ghali's special representative, Jacques-Roger Booh-Booh, a former foreign minister of Cameroon, replied to Annan. Booh-Booh again expressed UNAMIR's confidence in the informant's veracity and emphasized that Jean-Pierre had only twenty-four to forty-eight hours before he was due to distribute the arms. UNAMIR needed a decision, and Booh-Booh outlined General Dallaire's plan to raid the Hutu arms caches using "overwhelming force." Annan's reply, again signed by Iqbal Riza, ordered Dallaire not to proceed with his planned raid, as it went beyond UNAMIR's mandate under resolution 872.

In fact, it did not. As with Bosnia, the DPKO interpreted the mandate as it saw fit. Although there was no specific clause for weapons collection, under 872 UNAMIR was mandated "to secure the city of Kigali, inter alia, within a weapons secure area established by the parties in and around the city." This could have been judged sufficient authority. Instead, Annan ordered Dallaire to share his information with President Habyarimana. "You should assume that he is not aware of these activities, but insist he must ensure that these subversive activities are immediately discontinued," the cable continued, a move akin to General Rose asking Radovan Karadžić to inquire into reports that the Bosnian Serbs were shelling Sarajevo. Nor was Dallaire to help the informant. Instead, he should give his information to the United States, French, and Belgian embassies and request asylum from them. "The overriding consideration is the need to avoid entering into a course of action that might lead to the use of force and unanticipated repercussions," the cable concluded.

The Annan-Riza cables to Dallaire were crucial in the developing crisis. There is a powerful argument that had Annan ordered Dallaire to go ahead with his raids, the genocide might not have taken place. But bureaucracies inevitably produce stasis, as Michael Barnett, author of *Eyewitness to a Genocide,* a study of the United Nations and Rwanda, argues, and the United Nations was no exception: "UN staff came to know Rwanda as members of bureaucracies; the bureaucratic culture situated and defined their knowledge, informed their goals and desires, shaped what constituted appropriate and inappropriate behavior, distinguished acceptable from unacceptable consequences, and helped to determine right from wrong."[6] What was then judged right for the Secretariat was very wrong for Rwanda.

Worse, not only did Annan and Riza twice refuse Dallaire's requests to raid the Hutu arms caches, they then sat on his fax. They neither alerted the other departments of the Secretariat nor brought General Dallaire's warnings to the attention of the Security Council, let alone inform the substantial international press corps based at the United Nations, which could have galvanized world opinion. General Dallaire had been instructed to inform several Western embassies of what he had learned from Jean-Pierre, and the DPKO leadership judged this sufficient dissemination of the intelligence. DPKO officials apparently believed that the debacle in Somalia left little likelihood that the Security Council would authorize a robust preemptive intervention in Rwanda. Judging by the Council's subsequent behavior, they may have been right. But the DPKO's role was to provide the Security Council with information, not try to predict its policy. The Council was never given the option of acting on General Dallaire's warnings. "None of us saw Dallaire's fax, as the Secretariat never passed the information along," says David Hannay. "Annan subsequently admitted the Secretariat was at fault there."

The DPKO remained consistently cautious, and, it is now clear, extremely overcautious, throughout early 1994, even after General Dallaire's cable and warnings from Belgian UN diplo-

mats that the Hutus were preparing massacres. Dallaire continued to press the DPKO to take a more active role against the
arms caches being gathered by the Hutu extremists. But DPKO
officials argued that UNAMIR could only support the efforts
of the local authorities. These, Annan emphasized, were responsible for public security, even though plentiful information was
arriving at the Secretariat about the steady deterioration of the
security situation. Belgian Foreign Minister Willy Claes wrote
to Boutros-Ghali, warning him of the militias' activities and
calling for "a firmer stance on the part of UNAMIR with respect to security."[7] But this information, and other warnings,
were not formally submitted to the Security Council, according to Willum: "Throughout the months of January, February
and March 1994 there was no mention of militias, distribution
of weapons to these militias, or plans for subverting the peace
process whether in closed or public sessions."[8] This policy of
the DPKO's leadership caused some internal dissent, so much
so that one official even began circulating internal departmen-
tal correspondence to other UN departments in a futile bid to
inspire a reaction elsewhere in the organization.

A decade later in Geneva, Annan outlined his five-point plan
of preventive measures against genocide: preventing armed conflict; protecting civilians in armed conflict; ending impunity;
giving early and clear warnings of potential genocide; and taking "swift and decisive action" when it is clear that genocide is
happening or is about to happen. Annan also talked about
Darfur and mentioned Egeland's dramatic Security Council
briefing with its details of ethnic cleansing. "Such reports leave
me with a deep sense of foreboding. Whatever terms it uses to
describe the situation, the international community cannot stand
idle," he said. Annan demanded that aid officials and human

rights workers be given immediate access to the region. "If that is denied, the international community must be prepared to take swift and appropriate action. By 'action' in such situations I mean a continuum of steps which include military action. But the latter should always be seen as an extreme measure to be used only in extreme cases."[9] Annan also announced the appointment of a new special rapporteur to prevent genocide.

Yet Annan's speech also performed an inadvertently useful service, precisely delineating the UN's disastrous response to Darfur. Despite everything the United Nations knew about its failures in Rwanda, impressively detailed in its own 1999 report on the Rwandan genocide, in Darfur the United Nations had failed on every one of Annan's five points: the armed conflict had not been prevented; civilians had not been protected; Khartoum still acted with impunity; and in spite of a year's worth of warnings from Dr. Kapila in the field and from OCHA at the Secretariat about sustained human rights abuses, no "swift and decisive action" was taken to prevent genocide, although the United Nations' extensive humanitarian operation had saved many lives.

Perhaps even more perverse than Sudan's membership on the Human Rights Commission in 2004 was Rwanda's seat on the Security Council in 1994. It had been chosen by the African regional group in 1993. This gave Kigali the right both to vote and to take part in procedural decisions about the United Nations response to the slaughter, even while its troops were carrying it out. As Colin Keating, New Zealand's ambassador, notes, Rwanda had "a very significant capacity to block the required consensus at certain points. Rwanda was able to present significant obstacles to Council action during the time of crisis." The United Nations' failure to take decisive action on

Rwanda was also rooted in the Secretariat's failure. Not only did it fail to pass on Dallaire's "genocide fax," it failed to properly brief the Security Council at all over the reality on the ground. "It is clear with hindsight that, even in 1993, the situation in Rwanda was much more complex and dangerous than was ever indicated to members of the Council," notes Keating, reinforcing the points made by Bjørn Willum. "According to the Secretariat's reporting to the Security Council, the situation was an extension of the problem of the civil war. The deeper and more dangerous problem of a monumental threat to human life was ignored."[10]

On 30 March 1994 Boutros-Ghali presented a report to the Security Council on extending UNAMIR'S mandate. It did mention ethnic crimes but was largely optimistic, despite another warning from General Dallaire that the Hutus were preparing for massive violence. Boutros-Ghali's special representative, Jacques-Roger Booh-Booh, was still advising that Rwandan strife was essentially a civil war, and the focus of diplomacy should be on arranging a cease-fire. Meanwhile, the United States, traumatized by its humiliation in Somalia, was pushing for UNAMIR to be pulled out if both sides did not adhere to the Arusha accords. The debate in the Security Council now focused not on how to prevent new conflict in Rwanda but on the whys and wherefores of United Nations withdrawal. "The collapse of the UN mission in Somalia is absolutely crucial to understanding Rwanda," argues David Hannay. "The way in which it happened made people unwilling to put troops into a similar kind of situation. Somalia hung like a black cloud over Rwanda, which doesn't justify anything, but is very important."

Under resolution 909, passed on 5 April, UNAMIR's mandate, due to expire that day, was extended, in effect, for just six weeks, with an implied threat to close the force down if the

Arusha accords were not properly implemented. Many debates were attended by Rwanda's ambassador. The Council's lackluster approach was seen in Kigali, correctly, as a sign of the United Nations' lack of will to stop the planned slaughter. The potential withdrawal of UNAMIR fit perfectly into the planned genocide. The final lists of Tutsis were drawn up, the last weapons distributed. On 6 April the plane carrying the presidents of both Rwanda and Burundi was shot down as it approached Kigali airport. This was the signal for the slaughter to begin.

Around 8:00 A.M. the next day Prime Minister Agathe Uwilingiyimana took refuge at a UN compound in Kigali, bravely hiding in a different house from her husband and five children. General Dallaire called Iqbal Riza in New York, saying that UNAMIR might have to use force to save her. Riza replied that the mandate allowed UNAMIR to return fire only if fired on, not to open fire. Dallaire dispatched an armed escort to rescue Uwilingiyimana, but it was blocked on the way. Rwandan soldiers arrived first. They broke into the compound at 10:00 A.M., found the prime minister, and shot her dead. The Belgian UN peacekeepers guarding her were taken away and hacked to death. Brussels instantly launched an international diplomatic campaign to withdraw all of UNAMIR, in order to provide diplomatic cover for pulling out its own troops. Belgian Foreign Minister Willy Claes telephoned NATO capitals, asking for support, claiming that otherwise the Belgian government would collapse. Washington readily agreed to help, as a pullout suited its own interests. On 15 April, Madeleine Albright received her instructions from the State Department: "The United States believes that the first priority of the Security Council is to instruct the secretary general to implement an orderly withdrawal of all/all [sic] UNAMIR forces from Rwanda, taking the necessary steps to ensure that the warring parties in Rwanda respect the safety of UNAMIR and other foreign civilian and military personnel until such time as their evacuation has been completed."[11]

Albright was unhappy with her instructions and argued against them. She did not believe that UNAMIR should withdraw and called the National Security Council, hoping to speak to Tony Lake, President Clinton's national security adviser. But she reached only one of Lake's officials, who told her to calm down and said that the NSC would look into matters. Meanwhile, Colin Keating, president of the Security Council that month, was so unhappy about the quality of the information being supplied by the Secretariat that twice, sometimes three times a day, he met with the New York representatives of the International Committee of the Red Cross and Médecins Sans Frontières (Doctors Without Borders, MSF) to receive updates on the horrors unfolding. Albright, too, was dissatisfied. "There was not enough information coming up through the system. The secretary general's reports were not the kind that made you think something horrible, truly different was going on," she recalls. As the killing speeded up, Keating briefed the Council on an MSF report that detailed how Hutu militia had entered a hospital and killed all the staff, then returned the next day and killed all the patients. After hearing Keating's report on the slaughter in the hospital, Albright turned to the Rwandan ambassador and asked him to explain what was going in his country. After a "prolonged and uncomfortable silence," he said that the Tutsis were not willing to take part in peace talks. The Rwandan ambassador's continued presence on the Council, says Albright, was a disgrace. But the United States did nothing to lobby for his removal.

Meanwhile, despite General Dallaire's valiant leadership, UNAMIR was collapsing. It was underarmed, underresourced and at the epicenter of an unfolding genocide for which it was ill-prepared. The Ghanian soldiers guarding opposition politicians deserted their posts or stood by as their charges were taken away to their deaths. About two thousand civilians, including many women and children, sought refuge at a technical school in a suburb of Kigali, where Belgian UN troops were stationed, guarding Westerners. Hutu militiamen gathered outside, while the expatriates were evacuated. Once they had left, the French and Belgian troops abandoned the Rwandans. The Hutu militiamen stormed in and massacred many of those inside. As the crisis worsened, Boutros-Ghali offered the Security Council three options: an immediate and massive reinforcement of UNAMIR; a downsizing of the force from 2,500 troops to 270; or a complete withdrawal. The first, which would have stopped or at least slowed the genocide, was out of the question, for no countries were willing to contribute the necessary troops. Option three, a complete pullout, would be deeply humiliating and weaken other peacekeeping missions; furthermore, in the long term the United Nations would be needed in Rwanda to monitor any eventual peace deal.

A small group of countries supported keeping at least some UNAMIR force in place: Colin Keating knew that he could rely on the Czech Republic, Spain, Nigeria, and Djibouti to support option two, which was better than nothing. And, supporters hoped, a reduced UNAMIR could be reinforced in the future. Albright brought Washington around, while Hannay lobbied London. The Council chose option two, a decision which even today remains deeply controversial. Resolution 912, passed on 21 April, downsized UNAMIR to 270 troops. "This is always described as the Security Council reducing the force," says David Hannay. "But the Security Council did not pull out UNAMIR, as four-fifths of its soldiers had disappeared by then. The first thing we did, absent any offers of troops to replace those who had left, was to confirm those in place who were still there and give them a suitable mandate." Whatever the post-facto justifications of Western diplomats now, the downsizing of UNAMIR sent the clearest signal to the Hutu *genocidaires* that the world would not intervene to stop them.

Keating and his allies' next struggle was to get the Council to recognize, and articulate, that genocide was taking place in Rwanda under the terms of the 1948 Genocide Convention, as was clear from the reports flooding in from both UNAMIR and nongovernmental organizations. This was crucial, for such a declaration would, Keating and his allies hoped, oblige the United Nations to intervene, or at least heavily reinforce UNAMIR so that it could stop the killing. But while the United States had signed the convention in 1948, it had not ratified it until 1988, the last of the P5 to do so, and even then only with seven formal caveats about its sovereignty and jurisdiction.

The Clinton administration was determined that Rwanda would not be defined as a genocide, for fear that it would be obliged to take action to stop the killing. Asked repeatedly by reporters on 28 April whether the US government viewed the slaughter as genocide, State Department official Christine Shelley replied: "Well, I think it's—again, I was trying to get the point across that this is—in order to actually attach the genocide label to actions which are going on, that this is a process that involves looking at several categories of actions. And as I've said, certain of the actions very clearly fall into some of the categories that I've mentioned. But whether you can wrap all this up in a way that then brings you to that conclusion, I'm simply not in a position to make that judgement now."[12] Shelley's incoherence aptly symbolized the Clinton administration's political confusion and moral cowardice.

Keating and his allies failed. The Council did issue on 30 April a presidential statement on Rwanda that drew on the language of the Genocide Convention, declaring "that the killing of members of an ethnic group with the intention of destroying such a group in whole or in part constitutes a crime punishable under international law." But the word *genocide* was not included. In fact, even this statement was a compromise, issued only after Keating tabled a draft resolution threatening to force an embarrassing vote that would have revealed which countries were opposed to calling the Rwandan slaughter genocide. Washington continued to focus much energy on ensuring that the slaughter was not defined as a genocide. On 1 May a group of Pentagon experts on Africa, humanitarian affairs, and special operations, charged with monitoring Rwanda, met to discuss policy options.

The record of the meeting, since declassified, provides remarkable insight into the priorities of the Clinton administration and the US military. The second discussion point suggested that the United States should "support the UN" and others in "attempts to achieve a cease-fire." This was judged dangerous language. The next line records the group's decision: "Need to change 'attempts' to 'political efforts,' without [the word] 'political' there is a danger of signing up to troop contributions." Among the issues for consideration was whether there should be an investigation into claims of genocide. The memo notes: "Be Careful. Legal [department] at State [Department] was worried about this yesterday—Genocide finding could commit US government to actually do something."[13] There are few, if any, more succinct summaries of the Clinton administration's responses to the genocidal crises of the early and mid-1990s.

While the United States temporized, New Zealand, Secretariat officials, and the nonaligned countries drafted various options for reinforcing UNAMIR, using operational plans drawn up by General Dallaire. A new resolution was drawn up, and "put in blue"—a transition stage meaning that it could be passed by the Security Council within a day. Boutros-Ghali called on the Council to take "forceful action" to restore law and order in Rwanda.

But what little momentum had been built up steadily drained away, mainly thanks to Washington's obduracy. As the Secretariat and secretary general took one step forward in the UN's danse macabre, the United States took two steps back, dragging the Security Council in its wake. The plans to reinforce UNAMIR became bogged down in a dreamlike argument over whether the operation should be "inside-out" (reinforcements flown into Kigali and deployed across the country) or "outside-in" (reinforcements sent into Rwanda from a UN base set up in a neighboring country), which was favored by the US. "It was an almost surreal issue," records Keating. "While thousands of human beings were being slaughtered every day, ambassadors argued fitfully in New York for weeks about military tactics."

To this day Madeleine Albright regrets that she did not push as hard as she could for a reinforced UNAMIR, led by the United States, a force mandated to actually *stop* the killing. "I am still haunted by Rwanda," she says. "I didn't like my instructions and I tried to argue against them. But you have to put yourself back in time, and what we knew then is not what we know now. There were so many things going on, Somalia and Haiti, Bosnia, and there was not enough information coming up through the system. But I wish I had argued more, I really do." Compared to taking on General Mladić, confronting the Interahamwe militia would have been comparatively simple. The Hutus killed most of their victims by hand, with knives and machetes or clubs studded with nails. Neither great age nor youth brought mercy. Children were hacked to death in front of their parents, who were then killed themselves. But few Hutus had guns, and fewer still were willing to attack Westerners.

The United Nations troops who did stay under General Dallaire's command saved many thousands of lives, often simply by their presence. As the situation worsened, the Security Council again extended UNAMIR's mandate. Resolution 918, passed on 17 May, authorized the force to contribute to the safety and security of civilians at risk, through various means, including the establishment of secure humanitarian areas. This new mandate was rooted in resolution 872, which had established UNAMIR. Back in January, Kofi Annan had invoked 872 when he refused General Dallaire permission to launch raids on the Hutu arms caches and offer sanctuary to his high-level informant. Now that the Security Council wanted to retain some kind of force in the field, 872 was reinterpreted and made more robust. Just as in Bosnia, UN mandates were moveable feasts.

Had UNAMIR been reinforced, or even kept at its original force level with this kind of mandate, many hundreds of thousands of victims might still be alive. There is no question that several brigades from a NATO member state, properly armed and equipped with even light armored vehicles, would have made short work of the Interahamwe. Yet even after weeks of slaughter, the Secretariat still seemed more concerned about the United Nations' neutrality than about saving lives. In May, when Boutros-Ghali announced that a genocide was taking place and asked for troops to reinforce UNAMIR, he emphasized the United Nations' role as impartial broker: "It is not our intention to impose a certain formula on the two protagonists to the dispute. We need the agreement of the protagonists and then we will have to play the role of catalyst, of mediator."[14]

General Dallaire remained in Kigali, with just a few hundred troops under his command, emerging as one of the few heroes in the United Nations' greatest humanitarian catastrophe. In the end, all the theoretical discussions in New York over the mechanics of intervention were irrelevant. Just as happened in Bosnia, when a NATO country determined that it was in its interests to intervene in a genocide, it did so. At the end of June, France offered to send troops to Rwanda, and the Security Council accepted. Twenty-five hundred French and Senegalese soldiers rapidly set up a series of "safe humanitarian zones" in the southwest of the country, saving up to fifteen thousand lives. The killing finally stopped in late July, when the RPF, commanded by Paul Kagame, now Rwandan president, liberated Kigali. By then the Hutu militias had killed about 800,000 people, a rate of slaughter comparable to the Nazi Holocaust.

VIII

Genocide, or Maybe Not

I concluded that genocide has been committed in Darfur and that the government of Sudan and the Janjaweed bear responsibility—and that genocide may still be occurring.
—*Secretary of State Colin Powell, testimony to the Senate Foreign Relations Committee, 9 September 2004*

The United Nations has a multitude of days, weeks, years, and even decades devoted to special themes.[1] The tenth of December is annual Human Rights Day, which doubtless inspired Annan in part to issue a statement on Darfur a day before its observation in 2003. The following year was designated the International Year to Commemorate the Struggle Against Slavery and Its Abolition and the International Year of Rice; it was also part of the International Decade for Peace and Non-Violence for the Children of the World. None of which applied in Darfur, or indeed much of Africa, as the United Nations' own reports detailed. Africa's "big men"—the potentates and dictators who still ruled much of the continent—were more interested in plundering their own countries and staying in power than in pressuring Sudan to stop killing other Africans. They showed little regard for the lives of their own citizens, and hardly more for those of neighboring countries.

The United States and the Security Council were repeatedly criticized by the developing world for their failure to stop the genocide in Rwanda a decade earlier, and in Darfur now, but where were the African countries? These were, after all, African genocides. The lessons of Bosnia and Rwanda were clear: genocide is stopped by confronting and militarily engaging the perpetrators, by the robust use of airpower, and by deploying substantial numbers of armed peacekeepers on the ground. Even without military intervention many lives can be saved by a UN-backed humanitarian operation. But where were the brigades of Nigerian, Algerian, or South African UN peacekeepers protecting the refugee camps, ensuring that aid supplies got through, and securing safe routes through the conflict zone? For many African UN member states, solidarity against their former colonial masters—protecting the abusers rather than the victims—was always more important. Back in 1994, in his days at the DPKO, Annan had told the French newspaper *Le Monde* that there was a shortage of African troops for peacekeeping missions because African governments "probably need their armies to intimidate their own populations."[2]

As secretary general he took a rather more emollient line. Despite Darfur, Annan proclaimed, overall Africa was on the right track. On 25 May 2004 he spoke at a United Nations cere-

mony commemorating Africa Day. Annan praised the establishment in 1963 of the Organisation of African Unity, which in 2002
had been succeeded by the African Union (AU). He praised the
AU for its new Peace and Security Council, launched the same
day in Addis Ababa, the capital of Ethiopia. He noted "positive
signs in the Sudanese peace process" and a "renewed commitment to human rights, good governance, social and economic
reform, and development" in Africa. Annan also warned that
the international community must not close its eyes to massive
human rights violations and suffering in Darfur.

Later that day the Security Council convened. That month's
president, Munir Akram, the ambassador for Pakistan, read a
presidential statement. It expressed "grave concern over the
deteriorating human rights situation in Darfur" and called for
"immediate humanitarian access," for all sides to respect the
cease-fire, and for Khartoum to disarm the Janjaweed. This was
the first time since Jan Egeland's briefing—almost two months
earlier—that the Council had issued a public statement on Darfur. The steadily worsening crisis seemed to be a matter of little
concern. A presidential statement is far less important than a
resolution. Mountains of Security Council presidential statements on every crisis since the United Nations was founded lie
unread in libraries and databases across the world.

Two weeks later the Council passed resolution 1547, the
first to mention Darfur. Most of 1547 was about the Naivasha
accords. The resolution endorsed a recent seven-page report
by Kofi Annan on Sudan, though that report mentioned Darfur only briefly, describing the situation in that region as "catastrophic" and an impediment to the overall Sudanese peace
process. But Annan had noted prophetically: "A meaningful
agreement on Darfur will be fundamental to the success of a
future United Nations role in Sudan; to conduct a consent-
based monitoring and verification operation in one part of the

country while there is ongoing conflict in another would prove politically unsustainable inside the Sudan and internationally."[3] Resolution 1547 called on the parties to "use their influence to bring an immediate halt to the fighting" in Darfur and elsewhere. The Council agreed to send a UN advance team to Sudan to prepare to implement the Naivasha accords, asked Annan to submit new proposals for a peacekeeping force for the south, and called for a public-information campaign about the accords and the role of the United Nations.

Even this single paragraph on Darfur in 1547 was inserted only after intensive lobbying by the French ambassador. "The drafters of 1547, Britain and the United States, did not want to refer to Darfur," recalls a diplomat involved in the negotiations.

> They did not think it would help with the peace-keeping force for the north-south. They were thinking about a separate presidential statement. We supported the Naivasha accords, but we had to insist very strongly that the Council recognized the situation in Darfur. If the Security Council was to act, the most urgent priority was not to focus on future peacekeeping missions where it was quiet on the ground and there had been no fighting for two years. The priority now was to address Darfur, to maintain security there and also address the political issues. We could not separate Darfur from the rest of the country. We argued that public opinion would not understand what on earth the United Nations was doing, monitoring something that was no longer a problem, but doing nothing to help Darfur.

France's interest in Darfur was not purely humanitarian. Paris has powerful strategic and military interests in the region. The French empire in Africa had once included Chad, which borders Sudan. French oil companies had interests in Sudan. Before the genocide in Rwanda the Hutu President Juvénal Habyarimana used to dine with the late French President François Mitterrand, and his widow reportedly still maintains a flat in Paris.[4] The French press has extensively investigated the Mitterrand government's supplying arms to the Hutus. When the Tutsi Rwandan Patriotic Front (RPF) launched its attack on the Hutu regime in 1990, French troops and "military advisers" arrived in Kigali, supposedly to protect French expatriates. France's role before and even during the slaughter of the Tutsis remains murky. In his speech commemorating the tenth anniversary of the genocide, Rwandan President Paul Kagame accused France of having funded and trained the Interahamwe Hutu militia.[5] Operation Turquoise, the French safe zone in southwest Rwanda, did save thousands of lives and helped prevent the destabilization of neighboring Zaire. It also created a refuge for the Hutu killers fleeing the RPF, who, writes General Dallaire in his memoir, *Shake Hands with the Devil*, "went mad with joy at the prospect of imminent rescue by the French."[6]

Perhaps partly to atone for its murky role in Rwanda, France has strengthened its presence in its former colony Chad. French soldiers are working with the Chadian army to prevent incursions by Janjaweed raiders and to protect refugees. Chadian soldiers have already engaged the Janjaweed in several firefights. What France—and others—fear is the prospect of the Darfur conflict's spreading across its borders and destabilizing an already volatile region. Sudan is known to support Chadian rebels who work together with the Janjaweed in the border area. According to the US journalist Nicholas Kristof, who won a Pulitzer Prize for his coverage of Darfur for the *New York Times*, the Chadian rebels work hand-in-hand with Khartoum. "They are armed by the Sudanese government, they are paid by the

Sudanese government, they are protected by the Sudanese government, the Sudanese Vice-President recently consulted with
the rebels, they are entirely a pawn of the Sudanese government."[7] In April 2006 the Chadian rebels battled their way
through Chad until they reached the capital, N'Djamena, before being beaten back by government troops, an attack the
Chadian government blamed on Sudan.

Africa's arbitrary borders do not respect any ethnic lines:
Chad, too, has a substantial Christian and animist minority,
while President Idriss Déby is a Zaghawa, and that group is
very influential in Chadian politics. Sudan miscalculated by in-
volving Chad, says Abderrahim Foukara, United Nations correspondent for the independent Arab television channel Al Jazeera:
"Sudan thought they could play off the Americans against the
Europeans, but it's not always that simple. The Chad dimension
brought France into the picture, and France has been ahead of
the Americans over Darfur. The French position evolved from
'We don't want to touch this' to 'We can't let this go on.' France
is quite pleased with itself; it's leading the pack here."

The counterargument in defense of the UN's Sudan policy and resolutions such as 1547 is advanced by the DPA's Haile
Menkerios. He reasons that the Naivasha accords can provide
a template to stop the fighting in Darfur. The north-south conflict in Sudan began in 1955. Apart from a break of eleven years,
the fighting had continued until May 2004, when the Sudan
People's Liberation Movement (SPLM, the political arm of the
SPLA) and the Sudanese government signed the Naivasha accords. The war cost the lives of two million people, while four
million were forced from their homes. Sudan could now begin
to stabilize. "Stopping the war in the south was the priority, and
I think the United Nations and the international community
have done a lot to help the peace process there," says Menkerios. "Naivasha does include principles that could be used as a

basis for settling Darfur, or the conflict that may yet come in the east of Sudan."

Peace, like war, has its own dynamic. Khartoum once refused to deal with the SPLM but eventually signed a peace agreement. As of spring 2006, talks between the Darfur rebels and the government had all broken down. But the effort has to be made, says Menkerios:

> Although it has been so far impossible to stop the fighting completely in Darfur, the United Nations, the African Union, and others pushed for a cease-fire, for the government to negotiate with the rebels, to recognize them, to start a dialogue. That has not worked completely, but it has definitely led to the process of saving those IDPs [internally displaced persons] who would have been threatened with death. A million and a half people are alive now because of that cease-fire agreement and because we could rally the international community. This is an achievement of the United Nations.

With Western countries unwilling to deploy troops on the ground in Darfur, the African Union partially stepped into the breach. The new buzz-phrase along the corridors of the UN headquarters was "African solutions for African problems." Keen to show that it could bring peace to its own continent, the African Union (AU) deployed several hundred troops, known as AMIS, the African Mission in Sudan, across Darfur after the March 2004 cease-fire, which had quickly been broken. The AU soldiers, who were not under the command of the UN, were military observers mandated to monitor cease-fire violations, "contribute to a secure environment," and "protect civilians

whom it encounters under imminent threat and in the immediate vicinity, within resources and capability, it being understood that the protection of the civilian population is the responsibility of the government of Sudan." All of which made the
United Nations' resolutions on Srebrenica and UNPROFOR's
mandates seem models of clear drafting.

The truth was that AMIS was a completely inadequate response to the carnage in Darfur, but it provided a useful and
politically correct alibi for both Western and African countries.
Western diplomats had been murmuring for months that it was
not feasible to deploy white troops in black Africa, although
quite why this was so complicated was never fully explained.
Thanks to AMIS the issue was now redundant: there was no
need for Washington, London, or Paris to get involved as African countries were sending their own soldiers. Nor was African
pride bruised by having its former colonial overlords again giving orders, and Africa could now show the West what it was capable of. The Arab League especially welcomed the dispatch of
AMIS, says Al Jazeera's Foukara: "It placed the onus on the African Union rather than the League, and that must have come
as a huge relief. Individual Arab governments feeling that Darfur should be handled in a certain way is one thing, but the
League has not been able to get Arab governments to coalesce
into a common strategy for a long time."

The decision to deploy AMIS caused a rare outbreak of
smiling unanimity inside the Security Council, but anger among
many UN officials in the field. "I am demoralized, disrupted,
and upset, and I ought to be," said one UN official working on
Darfur.

> The limitations were evident to anyone with expe-
> rience of peacekeeping operations. Yet we decided

to go along with this. There is a certain logic to the
idea: the AU is a new, ambitious organization, Darfur is an African problem, it's enormously complex,
with regional, geopolitical, and Islamic dimensions,
and the AU seemed well positioned. But the more
experienced, and slightly more cynical, here won-
dered out loud whether the AU taking this on was
also less expensive for the major powers and politically far less risky than addressing it themselves.
Once a regional body takes over, there is a crippling
opacity. They have their own procedures, and it's
very difficult to track what they are doing and how
they are operating.

It was remarkable that none of the lessons of UNPROFOR
a decade earlier seem to have been learned. AMIS, too, was soon
a victim of its own contradictions. The AU soldiers were inserted
into a war zone to monitor a cease-fire that didn't exist, with a
blurred mandate and without the necessary training, weapons,
or infrastructure to protect themselves, let alone civilians. The
harsh but politically inconvenient truth was that the AU had
neither the experience nor the military capacity to make AMIS
work effectively. "This mantra of African solutions for African
issues is completely out of control," says John Prendergast of
the International Crisis Group. "Crimes against humanity are
not only African issues, and in no other region in the world is
it expected that only that region will work on its own problems. This is just naïveté and reflects our desire to subcontract
our responses to these huge problems. The AU's capacity for
logistics and command and control is so limited. The force is
not working as a deterrent."

In early July 2004 Kofi Annan went to Darfur to see the

situation for himself. Haunted by his failure in Rwanda, Annan was personally anguished by events in Sudan. The growing pressure inside Washington doubtless also encouraged him: a letter by Representative Frank R. Wolf calling on Annan to visit Darfur gained forty-five signatures in Congress. Khartoum treated Annan's visit with contempt. Together with Jan Egeland, Annan planned to visit a series of refugee camps, including one at Meshkel, a makeshift site home to three thousand people that had not yet received humanitarian aid. But when Annan and his staff arrived there, they found a muddy field that was completely empty, apart from a few soldiers. Unwilling to let Annan and the accompanying reporters witness the dismal conditions there, the Sudanese authorities had transported the refugees at Meshkel to another camp and dumped them there before Annan's arrival.[8] Sudanese officials explained, with a straight face, that they had moved the refugees to protect them from disease.

For Khartoum, aid, as much as attack helicopters, is a weapon of war. As the author Alex de Waal notes, in Sudan the verb "to starve" is transitive. One reason why Khartoum's onslaught is a genocide under the terms of the Genocide Convention is that its soldiers and the Janjaweed systematically destroy the habitat in which the people of Darfur live. Animals are stolen, crops looted and burned, wells poisoned with dead bodies. The communities are destroyed, probably forever. The victims flee into the bush and try to survive on wild foods on the long trek to Chad or a refugee camp. Many, of course, especially the young, old, and sick, die on the way. This is clearly within the definition of article 2 of the convention: "Deliberately inflicting on the group conditions of life calculated to bring about its physical destruction in whole or in part."

Like the Bosnian Serbs, Khartoum understands that it must, eventually, let some supplies through or pressure will build for international intervention. But there is plenty of room for obstructive maneuver. Basic tactics include delaying supplies at the port of entry or denying customs clearance. A more subtle refinement is making relief workers apply for a series of travel permits, each valid for a limited time, one of which always runs out before the next is granted. Once supplies are allowed through, the government demands that they be transported on Sudanese vehicles and be distributed by Sudanese relief agencies. Khartoum even requires that medicines not manufactured in Sudan, a country not known for its pharmaceutical expertise, be tested before they can be distributed. All these obstructions effectively raise the death toll in the camps. At the end of his visit, Annan and the Sudanese government issued a joint declaration, including a promise to end all restrictions on the flow of relief supplies, the end of impunity for human rights perpetrators, and disarmament of the Janjaweed. None of this happened.

Soon after Annan's return, the Security Council moved from chapter VI, operations based on consent, to chapter VII, the enforcement clause of the UN Charter. Resolution 1556, passed on 30 July, used significant diplomatic language, classifying Darfur "a threat to international peace and security." The resolution demanded that Khartoum disband and disarm the Janjaweed and bring to justice those responsible for human rights atrocities within thirty days. It echoed resolution 713 of 1991, which had imposed an arms embargo on Yugoslavia. Resolution 1556 imposed an arms embargo on the rebels and the Janjaweed, but not on the Sudanese government, freezing the military imbalance between the rebels and the government, much as the United Nations had done in Bosnia. The resolution also, for the first time, raised the possibility of sanctions, the severance of transport links and diplomatic relations, if

Khartoum did not meet the thirty-day deadline, and it formally endorsed the deployment of AMIS. In diplomatic terms, 1556 was a step forward, increasing the pressure on Khartoum. But it had little if any effect on events on the ground.

Pakistan and China abstained on resolution 1556. Speaking before the vote, China's Ambassador Zhang Yishan stated that the draft resolution still included unhelpful measures that could "complicate the situation." The "complications" included possible attention being focused on China's continuing illegal occupation of Tibet, its arms sales to Khartoum, and its extensive investment in Sudan's oil industry. China has supplied fighter aircraft, tanks, helicopters, howitzers, and ammunition to Khartoum. But more important than Beijing's lucrative trade in weapons is oil. China's "greatest oil success abroad has been in Sudan," says Human Rights Watch in its 2003 report *Sudan, Oil, and Human Rights*. In the early 1990s Beijing had projected a shortfall of fifty million tons in domestic production—30 percent of its oil needs—as its own production slowed. In 1996 the China National Petroleum Company (CNPC) took a substantial stake in Sudan's Greater Nile Petroleum Operating Company. Beijing hoped that it would produce up to ten million tons of oil a year for China by 2000. CNPC helped build a nine hundred–mile pipeline from inland Sudan to the Red Sea, built a refinery near Khartoum with a 2.5 million–ton processing capacity, and engaged in extensive oilfield surface engineering, even bringing in a team of ten thousand Chinese laborers.

China's holdings in Sudan constitute Beijing's first overseas oilfield and CNPC's largest foreign operation. By 2000 Sudan accounted for two-thirds of China's overseas oil production. Here then is global chaos theory at work: an African child is thrown into the flames in Darfur so that a commuter may drive to work in Beijing. The implied threats of sanctions in resolution 1556 had no effect. The Janjaweed were not disarmed, and the government onslaught continued throughout the summer of 2004. Despite the thirty-day deadline in 1556, passed on 30 July, it was not until 18 September that resolution 1564 was passed. It noted the Security Council's "grave concern" that Khartoum had not met its obligations, called for it to end the "climate of impunity," and authorized expansion of the AU mission and the establishment of an International Commission of Inquiry (ICI) into human rights abuses. Resolution 1564 concluded with the less-than-terrifying threat that if Sudan did not comply with both its provisions and those of 1556, the Council would "consider" additional measures, possibly against either Sudan's oil sector or government members.

"The only time the Security Council will agree on anything is the lowest common denominator of foreign policy," says a US official with extensive experience of the United Nations.

> It's a mistake to assume that the Security Council will be the leader on any issue. It doesn't work that way and the system has been broken most of the time. Each time we tried to bring up sanctions against Sudan over Darfur, even sanctions in general, China blocked it. Russia and China would not even turn up for meetings to discuss sanctions. We wanted to see oil sanctions immediately, which we think would have sent a strong message to the government to get serious. Everything gets watered down and a one-page resolution becomes seven pages. We couldn't even mention the word *sanctions,* we had to call them "measures."

In November the Security Council met in Nairobi for a special session on Sudan, chaired by the United States, that month's president. Once again the focus was on the Naivasha accords, not on Darfur. The vague commitments of 1556 and 1564 were even further watered down. The new resolution 1574 made no mention of sanctions, only "appropriate further action" against parties failing to meet their obligations. It failed to address Khartoum's refusal to disband the Janjaweed and even called on the United Nations and World Bank to provide Sudan with development aid. It was passed unanimously.

As a comparatively obscure conflict in a remote part of Africa gained unforeseen "traction" in Washington, the stresses imposed by disparate interest groups, and their differing demands, have shaped the United States' often contradictory reaction to the Darfur genocide. The four key factors are the powerful Christian lobby; human rights groups; terrorism; and, inevitably, oil. President Bush appointed Senator John Danforth as his special envoy to Sudan in 2001 to help mediate the Naivasha accords. Picking Danforth, an ordained Episcopal priest, was a signal to the Christian lobby. "The American public have been aware of Darfur and Sudan for several years, especially the conservative or religious right, which is an important constituency of the Bush administration," says a United Nations Africa expert. "They saw the conflict between north and south in caricaturist terms, as an Islamic government persecuting good Christians. And on the left there are the human rights groups and the lobby around the Congressional Black Caucus, who were active on the idea of Arab persecuting blacks, some of whom were being sold into slavery. So when Darfur came along, there were already a lot of people focused on Sudan, unlike most of the rest of Africa."

US human rights officials had long been pushing for action on Darfur. In late June 2004 Pierre-Richard Prosper, then ambassador for war crimes issues, told Congress, "We see indicators of genocide [in Darfur], and there is evidence that points in that direction," although he said that it could not be confirmed. Colin Powell, then secretary of state, asked Prosper to assemble a team to travel to Darfur to get firsthand information to determine whether a genocide was taking place. "A lot of the information that was coming in was second-, third-, or fourthhand," recalls Prosper, a former prosecutor at the UN War Crimes Tribunal for Rwanda. "These were reliable accounts, from human rights organizations, but we didn't have the context." The State Department's team spent weeks conducting an in-depth statistical survey of Darfur refugees. It interviewed 1,136 refugees in nineteen locations in Chad. "When they came back, it confirmed what we were suspecting, but it also gave a deeper picture and a full appreciation of the breadth of the atrocities," says Prosper. At the same time, Congress took a tougher stand, passing a resolution demanding that the Bush administration call the atrocities in Darfur "by its rightful name: genocide," and calling for multilateral or even unilateral action to stop the killing. Darfur became a rare bipartisan issue, says a US diplomat: "The Christian lobby is crucial, and it was watching Sudan closely. Darfur transcends the Republican-Democrat system, and the Democrats also jumped on it, as it was a freebie for them. There was no downside—it wasn't abortion, or gay marriage, or one of the other divisive issues."

Two months later the State Department released its Darfur report. Darfur, it said, was the worst human rights crisis in the world. The report showed that the Sudanese government had carried out one of the largest ethnic-cleansing operations of Muslims in modern times. More than 405 villages had been destroyed, and 123 substantially damaged. About 200,000 refugees had fled to Chad, while 1.2 million were internally displaced inside West Sudan. The report included a detailed survey of what the refugees had endured. More than 60 percent had witnessed or experienced the killing of a family member. Sixty-seven percent had witnessed the killing of someone outside the family. Eighty percent had seen their villages destroyed. There were sustained and repeated accounts of rape as a weapon of war. The Janjaweed told their victims that they would have light-skinned Arab babies, to repopulate Darfur once the Africans had been driven out. Many testimonies detailed astonishing cruelty. One woman recounted how she had been repeatedly raped by Sudanese soldiers and Janjaweed while her father was forced to watch. He was then dismembered in front of her.

As in Bosnia, the killers ensured that even the last memories of loved ones were contaminated by unbearable pain and humiliation. Another victim said that she had been held captive for a week and raped in front of her nine-month-old daughter. When the baby cried, one of the soldiers grabbed her and hit her with a rifle butt. The reports were sustained, credible, and consistent with accounts gathered by Human Rights Watch, Amnesty International, and Mukesh Kapila's team back in summer 2003. The report also included US spy satellite photographs of Darfur's burned villages. The charred foundations of the homes in Darfur were circular, rather than the square-shaped destroyed houses in Bosnia. Prosper's team found extensive evidence of the links between the Janjaweed and Khartoum. "We always believed that there was a link not only from the creation of the Janjaweed, which had its genesis in the government, but also a working relationship as far as structure," he said. "We saw there was a coordination of activity. The government would bomb areas, and the Janjaweed would ride in afterwards."

Testifying to Congress when the report was released, Secretary of State Colin Powell went further. Powell had visited Darfur in July, around the same time that Kofi Annan had gone there, and had been affected by the misery all around him. He had publicly warned Khartoum to take action to stop the Janjaweed attacks. Powell was now under intense pressure from both Christian and African-American lobby groups to declare Darfur a genocide. But was it? The week before his congressional appearance, Powell had called Prosper for advice. The two men spoke at length, while Powell leafed through a copy of the Genocide Convention, outlining his thoughts. "He is not a lawyer, but he was a lawyer on those days," recalls Prosper. "I remember feeling disadvantaged because I have the convention memorized, but he was reading it out, and dissected it. He said he thought it was genocide, and he had all the arguments, what they had been doing, point one, two, three. He looked at the nature of the atrocities, and also at the conduct of the government, and its obstructionism and why it was denying aid."

Powell's testimony that genocide was being committed in Darfur made headlines around the world. He argued that the evidence gathered by the State Department team corroborated the necessary intent of the Sudanese government and Janjaweed to "destroy a group in whole or in part" on four points—through large-scale violence, including murder, rape, and assault; the destruction of villages, foodstuffs, and other means of survival; and the obstruction of food, relief supplies, and medical supplies—while Khartoum, "despite being put on notice" several times, had failed to stop the violence. It was a turning point. Finally, the word *genocide* had been clearly articulated. But any celebration was short-lived. A decade earlier, as a member of the Clinton cabinet, Powell had outlined various military options for dealing with the Bosnian Serbs, before explaining why none was possible. Once again he marched his soldiers up the hill and then back down again. "Mr. Chairman, some seem to have been waiting for this determination of genocide to take action. In fact, however, no new action is dictated by this determination," he continued. "We have been doing everything we can to get the Sudanese government to act responsibly. So let us not be too preoccupied with this designation. These people are in desperate need and we must help them."[9]

Powell himself had demanded that Khartoum stop obstructing aid supplies to the IDP camps, and his pressure had helped the UN humanitarian operation in Darfur. But his claim that the United States was "doing everything it can" was remarkable, considering the range of options available to both the United States, the world's only superpower, and the United Nations, none of which had been implemented: serious reinforcement of the AU peacekeepers with a mandate to protect civilians; deployment of a robust force of UN troops under chapter VII, also mandated to protect civilians; creation of safe zones where refugees would be protected from the Janjaweed; imposition of a no-fly zone with enforcement measures; an arms embargo on Khartoum; meaningful targeted sanctions on Sudan's leaders and a freeze on their assets abroad; sanctions against Sudan's oil industry; even a coalition of the willing to intervene militarily.

Admittedly, organizing both a chapter VI peacekeeping mission (monitoring an already agreed cease-fire with both parties' consent) in the south and a chapter VII humanitarian intervention in the same country would be a complex undertaking. But with some of the world's most elastic minds ensconced in the State Department, the various UN missions, the DPA, DPKO, and on the thirty-eighth floor around Annan's office, this problem should not have been insurmountable, had there been the political will. There was not. Powell noted that article VIII of the Genocide Convention obliges contract-

ing parties to call on the United Nations to take the appropriate actions against genocide. This action, he said, should be a
United Nations investigation into human rights violations in
Darfur. Having just concluded one investigation which found
that genocide was occurring, Powell now called for another.

The United Nations dispatched its own team to Darfur
that winter to investigate human rights violations and determine whether a genocide was taking place, under the terms of
resolution 1564. Its 176-page *Report of the International Commission of Inquiry* was released in January 2005. It is a long, detailed, and extremely thorough report into the Darfur crisis, its
origins, its chronology, and its effects. Its grim accounting of the
loss of life and eradication of the Fur, Zaghawa, and Masalit
communities makes it one of the major works of record on
Darfur. It is depressingly familiar reading:

> The Commission established that the Government
> of the Sudan and the Janjaweed are responsible for
> serious violations of international human rights and
> humanitarian law amounting to crimes under inter-
> national law. In particular, the Commission found
> that Government forces and militias conducted in-
> discriminate attacks, including killing of civilians,
> torture, enforced disappearances, destruction of vil-
> lages, rape and other forms of sexual violence, pil-
> laging and forced displacement, throughout Darfur.
> These acts were conducted on a widespread and
> systematic basis, and therefore may amount to crimes
> against humanity.[10]

Still, the ICI reported that Khartoum had *not* pursued a policy
of genocide. Some UN insiders claimed that the ICI had concluded that Darfur was a genocide, but after sustained lobby-

ing by several P5 countries, was persuaded not to say so. "Arguably, two elements of genocide might be deduced from the gross violations of human rights perpetrated by Government forces and the militias under their control," the ICI report said—first, the *act* of killing, or causing serious bodily and mental harm, and second, the targeting of a particular group—but "the crucial element of genocidal intent appears to be missing, at least as far as the central Government authorities are concerned."

Like medieval theologians arguing over how many angels can dance on the head of a pin, the ICI's members tied themselves in knots trying to not actually state that a genocide was taking place, even though it was clear from their own report that it was. "Generally speaking the policy of attacking, killing and forcibly displacing members of some tribes does not evince a specific intent to annihilate, in whole or in part, a group distinguished on racial, ethnic, national or religious grounds," the report said.[11] In fact, the Genocide Convention does not include the word *annihilate*. Under international law genocide does not necessarily mean an extermination of a people or group. The report further confused matters by adding: "The Commission does recognise that in some instances individuals, including Government officials, may commit acts with genocidal intent," but this, it opined, would have to be decided by a court. Genocide, like the real meaning of a UN resolution, it seemed, was in the eye of the beholder. In the end it didn't really matter. Powell said Darfur was a genocide, and the killing continued. The United Nations said it was not, and the killing continued. The ICI recommended that a list of fifty-one names of Sudanese officials it said were responsible for the atrocities be passed to the new International Criminal Court for investigation.

By winter 2005 there were still no UN peacekeepers deployed, but AMIS had grown to more than sixty-two hundred troops, including battalions from Rwanda, Nigeria, and Senegal, but those troops were spread thin over an area the size of New Mexico. The parallels between AMIS and UNPROFOR are numerous. Khartoum routinely obstructs AMIS supplies and matériel—its armored personnel carriers arrived only in November 2005. General Mladić took UNPROFOR soldiers hostage; the Janjaweed—and the Darfur rebels—kidnap and target AMIS soldiers, several of whom have been killed in the line of duty. The Janjaweed are armed with heavy machine guns and armored vehicles. The Sudanese army has artillery, tanks, multiple rocket launchers, and attack helicopters. AMIS troops are equipped for self-defense, with Kalashnikov assault rifles, pistols, and rocket-propelled grenades. Like UNPROFOR's different contingents, AMIS's troops interpret their mandate as they see fit. Rwandan soldiers, mindful of their own country's history, have been among the most robust protectors of civilians. Others take a more minimal view. Language difficulties, cultural confusion, and poor command and control also hinder AMIS.

There is a highly variable level of understanding of human rights issues. Representatives from the SLA, JEM, and the Sudanese government all live on AMIS bases, which are largely unprotected. AMIS has no dedicated intelligence section. As the aid organization Refugees International records in its report *No Power to Protect: The African Union Mission in Sudan*, all the warring parties are "privy to all AMIS information, movements, and intelligence." Despite these handicaps, in some places AMIS has been able, like UNPROFOR, to "deter by presence," and AMIS troops, unlike those of NATO countries or the US Army, are actually in the field, in harm's way. AMIS troops have escorted aid convoys and taken victims of attacks to hospitals, and AMIS civilian police stationed with IDP camps have brought a sense of security. One Darfur woman told Refugees International: "I know who the AU soldiers are because they are the soldiers that don't shoot at us."[12] But AMIS, like both UNPROFOR and UNAMIR, is at best a palliative measure that in Darfur brings succor to the victims of genocide. Like the Western powers and the P5, the African Union has proved both unwilling and unable to confront its causes.

IX

A Will and a Way

To ensure the protection of civilians, including humanitarian
personnel, under imminent threat of physical violence . . .
—From the mandate of MONUC, the
United Nations Mission in Congo, as
revised in October 2004 under resolution 1565

During the Bosnian war Pakistan and the Islamic and Arab countries kept steady pressure on the United Nations to take a more robust stand against the Serbs, although the Arab states were never concerned enough to threaten an oil embargo, which might have actually affected Western policy. The Arab and Islamic bloc at the United Nations has taken a very different position on Darfur. Pakistan and Algeria, both nonpermanent members of the Security Council during the Darfur crisis, have proved powerful allies of Sudan, says one UN official working on Darfur. "Sudan was initially very successful at keeping itself off the Council agenda, with the full support of the Arab group."[1] When resolutions critical of Sudan were eventually brought before the council, Pakistan and Algeria watered them down. Even though the Fur, Zaghawa, and Masalit, the victims of the Janjaweed, were also Muslims, solidarity with Khartoum came first.

After the vote on resolution 1556, which initially seemed to herald a strong stand against Khartoum, deeming Darfur "a threat to international peace and security," Masood Khalid, the Pakistani ambassador, said that while all those suffering in Darfur were part of the Islamic *umma* (brotherhood, or community of faith), the final text lacked the "necessary balance." Instead Pakistan favored a "calibrated approach" to Darfur. Pakistan abstained on 1556, together with China. Pakistan's "calibration" was not calculated in terms of the scale of the killing in Darfur. Far more important was the opportunity to score political points against the West over Iraq, Palestine, and Afghanistan. Instead of taking a moral stand on a clear-cut human rights issue, the Muslim and Arab member states lapsed into the tired reflexes of the postcolonial era, when mutual solidarity—even with a state guilty of serial human rights abuses—was always preferable to lining up with the West. Pakistan also abstained, as did Russia, China, and Algeria, on resolution 1564, which established the UN's International Commission of Inquiry (ICI) into Darfur.

It seemed that the victims of Darfur were paying a high price for Iraq. The reports of Khartoum's human rights abuses were often discounted in the Arab and Muslim world, much of which viewed the Western media as the puppets of a sinister Jewish conspiracy, defaming Arab regimes and the Muslim countries. Many Arabs and Muslims believed that after Iraq, Sudan was next on the White House's target list. The Naivasha accords were seen as a prelude to the breakup of Sudan and establishment of a Christian satellite state, backed by the United States and the West. And still fresh in the memory of the Muslim world were Iraq's phantom weapons of mass destruction (WMDs), for which the United States had gone to war.

In February 2003 General Colin Powell, then secretary of state, had told the Security Council that Iraq had repeatedly breached UN resolutions, was still pursuing a WMD program, and was obstructing UN weapons inspectors. He showed dramatic pictures of facilities that he said held chemical weapons and ballistic missiles. He claimed that Iraq was conducting medical experiments on prisoners and that Saddam Hussein was "determined to get his hands on a nuclear bomb." Most members of the Security Council were not convinced. The United States failed to get authorization from the United Nations for military action. Nonetheless, together with its allies, it invaded Iraq, toppled the government, arrested Saddam Hussein, and occupied the country. The WMDs were never found.

Sudanese officials frequently refer to this episode when rebutting claims of atrocities in Darfur, says John Prendergast. "Their response is that it is anarchy there, it's not as bad as everyone says, people are fighting each other—remember, this is the government that said there were WMDs in Iraq, and where are they?" Prisoner abuse at Abu Ghraib prison in Baghdad, claims of torture at the US base at Guantánamo Bay, the never-ending Israeli-Palestinian conflict, chaos in Iraq—all these complaints militated against support for action against Sudan. Across the Muslim world the United States and the West were seen as hypocrites, condemning human rights abuses in Darfur while carrying them out themselves, or supporting the perpetrators. "There was a lot of skepticism about exactly what was happening in Darfur. People thought this was another type of foreign meddling, especially after the north-south conflict," says Abderrahim Foukara. "Iraq was a factor, as there was the perception that the West was now trying to divide Sudan. Arab public opinion is strongly opposed to any foreign intervention in Darfur."

The eventual achievements of the United States and NATO, which had in 1995 finally stopped the genocide in Bosnia, had bombed Serbia in 1999 to save the Kosovo Albanians, saving many thousands of Muslim lives, and had helped topple the Milošević regime in 2000, were conveniently forgotten or drowned out in the shrill chorus of accusations. The angry demonstrations across the Islamic world in early 2006 against satiric Danish cartoons of the Prophet Muhammad stand in sharp contrast with the barely noticeable reactions to the genocide in Darfur. There have been no riots, no violent public protests, no attacks on Western or any other embassies, no flag-burnings, no threats against the perpetrators, and no economic boycotts in protest at the deaths of more than 400,000 Muslims and the displacement of two million more in Sudan.

A cynic might argue that Bosnia never really ignited the anger of the Muslim world because Bosnian Muslims were white Europeans. A more straightforward kind of racism seems to shape policy towards the black Africans displaced from Darfur, at least in Egypt. For months up to three thousand refugees— whom UN officials said could safely return home in the wake of the Naivasha accords, even though most did not come from South Sudan—lived in squalor in a squatters' camp in Cairo, protesting the refusal of the UNHCR to give them refugee status. In December 2005 Egyptian riot police attacked the camp. They first used water cannon, but the refugees refused to move. In the early hours of New Year's Eve, thousands of riot police stormed in, wielding clubs and truncheons, killing and injuring adults, children, and babies in scenes of chaos and brutality. The official death toll was twenty-six, but many observers placed the number of casualties much higher. The police raid caused a flicker of interest and then faded from the headlines. Egyptian President Hosni Mubarak later expressed regret for the deaths. Ironically, several dozen of the refugees fled into the Sinai Desert and crossed the border into Israel, where human rights workers pressed for them to be given asylum.

Iraq, meanwhile, has stayed in the news, as invasion has given way to occupation and continuing strife threatening civil war. Iraq worked on several levels for Khartoum. It united the Muslim world against possible further Western intervention or even "interference." Its grim realities were also a powerful counterweight for the more radical voices prepared to countenance direct action in Darfur. With so many soldiers mired in the fallout of Saddam's regime, there was simply no appetite in Washington, London, or any Western capital for dispatching troops into another Muslim country. Khartoum threatened another Iraq if Western troops were sent in. "You would need to go in, kill some bad guys, have the Sudanese government realize that in fact this was in their interest, and then secure the whole zone," says a UN official working on Darfur. "It's a fantasy. That wasn't going to happen." The Security Council would not authorize a military invasion, John Danforth, former US envoy to Sudan and US ambassador to the United Nations, told the BBC, and not only because China would veto it.

> Did the world want to invade another Muslim country? Did the United States? Again, we have done that recently once, what kind of support would we

have gotten within the United States, from any other country in the world for such an invasion? If we had such an invasion, where would it stop and on whose behalf would we be acting? ... One of the rebel groups in Darfur was associated with al-Turabi, the very hard-line former President of Sudan, very Islamic. Were we going to weigh in militarily on his behalf? Is there going to be an alliance with him?[2]

In May 2004 the Arab League dispatched a fact-finding mission to Darfur. The press release issued afterward was surprisingly robust, referring to "gross human rights violations" and calling for greater security to protect victims. Sudanese Foreign Minister Mustafa Osman Ismail reacted with fury, decrying the release as typically "Western" and full of inaccuracies. Under pressure from Khartoum, the League's brief flirtation with the reality of Darfur soon ended. A new press release was circulated, outlining the "errors" in the first, and Sudan soon had all the public support it wanted from its Arab neighbors. On 9 August the Arab League met in emergency session in Cairo to discuss the Darfur crisis. The twenty-two member states rejected both sanctions and intervention against Sudan. Instead, they supported Khartoum's "promises" to disband the Janjaweed and punish human rights violators. What Sudan needed, according to the Arab League, was more time. Khartoum was not to blame for the carnage in Darfur, the League announced. It was all Israel's doing, as Tel Aviv was supplying the SLA and the JEM with weapons—a charge both groups denied. Faced with a catastrophic loss of human life, the systematic destruction of an ancient Muslim society, and a massive public relations disaster, this was the Arab League's best defense: blame the Jews.

The Arab League's pusillanimity sparked anger in the more forward-thinking Arab capitals. "If the Arab League has a purpose, and the idea of collective Arab action has any legitimacy, then surely the situation in Darfur in western Sudan is the kind that begs for active Arab intervention," thundered the English-language *Daily Star* newspaper in Beirut, which demanded that the League's secretary general, Amr Moussa, travel to Darfur. "The Arab League is an imperfect institution, we know—but rarely has imperfection been taken to such extremes of negligence and irresponsibility. . . . Darfur is an ideal opportunity for the contemporary Arab world to snap out of its trajectory of political complacency and moral lassitude."[3]

Like the Milošević regime, the Sudanese government has mastered the art of manipulating and playing off different parts of the international community, says Pierre-Richard Prosper, the former US ambassador at large for war crimes:

> The Arab world has been very vocal on other issues, and here is a situation where they should have been equally as vocal but were not. We saw this in the north-south conflict, when Sudan launched all kinds of initiatives, and now they have turned around on terrorism. They are very skilled at giving the international community something in one place, and then taking it away somewhere else. The Arab and Muslim countries could pressurize Sudan very effectively, isolate it to the extent that it would have to curb these activities. But Sudan knows it does not have to worry about the Security Council because of China and their Arab and Muslim brothers.

Sudan's sophisticated diplomacy has bought the government valuable time, says a UN official working on Darfur. Khartoum understands how to manipulate the African and Islamic countries at the United Nations. "They have a regional constituency and an international one. There are different groups that they call on to buy space to maneuver. And if you examine things closely, they have disagreed with international proposals, but they have not engaged in naked obstruction. It's always case-based or disagreement with a particular argument. For example, they will send a message out that, OK, we can have an international force, but only African troops."

More important than the fact that Iraq and Darfur are both Muslim regions is the fact that the debate over multilateral action during international crises has been inconclusive, argues Prosper.

> The Arab and Muslim world, much of Europe, and the developing countries all condemn the United States for leading the invasion of Iraq but are unable to organize a coherent international response to stop the genocide in Darfur. These countries say that the way to deal with these issues is by working through international and multilateral organizations such as the United Nations. We are still waiting for that to happen. The United Nations passed a series of resolutions on Darfur, but we are not getting the necessary action. The response of the African Union is insufficient. The United States cannot carry these burdens alone. Other countries need to step up here.

As Darfur burned during 2005, the United Nations remained focused on the Naivasha accords. DPA officials say that Naivasha helped ensure that Darfur also received attention. One official argues: "The United Nations was already engaged in Sudan, had been engaged, so when Darfur began the focus was already there." But the focus was not translated into meaningful action. Resolution 1590, passed on 24 March, authorized, under chapter VII, the deployment of ten thousand UN peacekeepers to Sudan. But UNMIS, as the new force was known, was mandated only to monitor the north-south accords. France pushed for UNMIS to aid the African Union force to deploy their troops on the ground in Darfur, or at least help with transport and logistics. After pressure from France, an extra paragraph was inserted, requesting UNMIS to "closely and continuously liaise with the African Union Mission in Sudan (AMIS)." But this was only a request, not a mandate, a crucial difference. "If the AU was not willing to be placed under the authority of the United Nations, then we thought the United Nations and UNMIS could help in other ways, such as with logistics, as the United Nations has the means to do that, and with the deployment of civilian police units in Darfur," says a diplomat involved in the negotiations. "But the United States, Britain, and the Secretariat all took the view that the troops deployed to the south could not be distracted from their main purpose, and the same was true for their logistics budget, so, sadly, it did not happen. We think UNMIS is disproportionate in size, and a lot of resources could have been used to help Darfur."

Five days later, the Security Council passed resolution 1591, which ordered a freeze on assets and a travel ban for human rights violators, but, because China had threatened to use its veto, did not include sanctions on Sudan's oil industry. Resolution 1591 demanded that Sudan stop using its air force for military flights over Darfur (as it had already twice agreed to do) but had no enforcement mechanism for a no-fly zone. It praised the AU for the work of AMIS but offered no new troops or funds. It also urged the establishment of a sanctions committee to iden-

tify the Sudanese officials to be targeted. Sanctions that hit officials in their pockets can be very effective. Milošević's support
began to melt away when his associates could no longer travel
abroad and had their bank accounts frozen. Jan Egeland, the
UN's humanitarian chief, notes: "I know that is something they
really talk about now in Khartoum. You know, even people who
never travel really hate the prospect of not having the opportunity to travel, and even people who have no foreign assets
really fear a freeze on foreign assets." But Khartoum's elite
could sleep easily—by spring 2006 the committee had still not
drawn up its list.

The United Nations has learned some lessons from Rwanda and
Srebrenica, and in several cases has even applied them. In spring
2000 Kofi Annan appointed Lakhdar Brahimi, Algerian ambassador to the United Nations, to head a panel of peacekeeping
experts examining the United Nations' future role in conflict
zones. The Brahimi report, as it was known, was released in August 2000 and recommended a series of revolutionary innovations in the DPKO, from strategy and planning to logistics and
public information. For example, according to the report, the
Security Council should leave all resolutions authorizing missions with sizable troop levels in draft form until the secretary
general receives firm commitments of troops and necessary
support from member states. The whole peacekeeping operation needs to be speeded up, with traditional consent-based
peacekeeping operations dispatched within thirty days, more
complex ones within ninety days. The report called for the relationship between the Secretariat and the Security Council to
be strengthened and clarified: "The Secretariat must tell the
Security Council what it needs to know, not what it wants to
hear, when formulating or changing mission mandates."[4]

Probably the Brahimi report's most important recommendation was a crucial psychological shift: UN troops must no
longer stand by while civilians were massacred around them, if
they can intervene. "United Nations peacekeepers—troops or
police—who witness violence against civilians should be presumed to be authorized to stop it, within their means, in support of basic United Nations principles."[5] The report argued
that while consent of the local parties, impartiality, and the
use of force only in self-defense must remain the three pillars
of peacekeeping operations, these concepts are open to interpretation. The report's analysis of "impartiality" seemed far removed, for example, from Yasushi Akashi's understanding of
the term. The report noted: "Impartiality for United Nations
operations must therefore mean adherence to the principles of
the Charter: where one party to a peace agreement clearly and
incontrovertibly is violating its terms, continued equal treatment of all parties by the United Nations can in the best case result in ineffectiveness and in the worst may amount to complicity with evil. No failure did more to damage the standing
and credibility of United Nations peacekeeping in the 1990s
than its reluctance to distinguish victim from aggressor."[6] The
report called for UN troops to be able to defend themselves
and their mission mandate with robust rules of engagement,
not ceding the initiative to attackers. The report was implicitly
critical of the Secretariat and the DPKO, recommending that
"the Secretariat must not apply best-case scenarios where local
actors have historically exhibited worst-case behaviour."

The Brahimi doctrine was soon put to the test in the Democratic Republic of Congo, then torn apart by civil war, starvation, disease, and multiple foreign interventions. The roots
of the chaos stretch over the border to the Rwandan genocide
of 1994. Congo, too, was once a Belgian colony. With an area of

900,000 square miles, the country is two-thirds the size of western Europe and is rich in diamonds, gold, and timber, as well
as several rare minerals, including coltan, vital for mobile tele-
phones. Under the rule of Mobutu Sese Seko, a kleptomaniac
despot who had taken power in 1965, Congo (then named Zaire)
fell apart. For decades Mobutu and his cronies plundered its
plentiful resources, salting away hundreds of millions of dollars in numbered bank accounts. Mobutu's own fortune was
estimated at $4 billion. With the support of France, the Franco-
phone Mobutu, like many African dictators, believed he would
stay in power forever.

 As the Hutu *genocidaires* fled vengeful Tutsis in the summer of 1994, Mobutu allowed them to settle in refugee camps
in eastern Congo. Many Hutus kept their weapons, and soon
they took control of the camps. Fed and cared for by the international community—a policy decision some compared to
providing succor to the SS after the Second World War—the
Hutus regrouped and began attacking the Tutsi minority in
Congo. In response Paul Kagame, the Tutsi president of Rwanda
who took power after the genocide, boosted his support for a
rebel group led by Laurent Kabila. Kabila's movement steadily
grew in power and influence, and in May 1997 it toppled Mobutu
in a coup, supported by troops from Rwanda and Uganda. For
a short while it seemed Congo might yet stabilize and normalize. But Kabila's grandiose plans for rebuilding the country faded,
and the country slid back into war, encouraged by several
meddling neighbors casting greedy eyes on its riches. Rwanda
and Uganda turned against Kabila and backed a new rebel movement, which then advanced on the capital, Kinshasa. Namibia,
Zimbabwe, and Angola sent troops to support Kabila.

 It was a familiar African story, and the conflict soon
threatened to engulf the whole region. Congo's economy col-

lapsed, and the people went hungry. The country was being stripped clean by the invading armies as they fought over their booty. The war dragged on until 1999, when all six countries involved and the rebels signed a cease-fire, known as the Lusaka accords. Later that year the Security Council deployed a peace-keeping mission, known by its French acronym MONUC. By then Congo was one of the world's biggest humanitarian disasters. The United Nations later estimated that since 1998 an estimated 3.5 million people had died in Congo, mostly as indirect casualties of the war, through hunger and disease. There were 3.4 million internally displaced persons, including one million children, as well as hundreds of thousands of refugees in the neighboring countries. Half the population was under the age of eighteen, and one out of five did not reach the age of five. In most of the country there was no infrastructure or health or education system. Congo was less a failed state than a nonexistent one. MONUC was just fifty-five hundred strong.

The force's involvement seemed doomed from the start. Despite the Lusaka accords, Congo's neighbors continued to plunder the country. In April 2001 a United Nations investigative panel accused military commanders in Rwanda, Uganda, and Burundi of systematically exploiting Congo's resources, together with various international criminal cartels, and of prolonging the conflict to further loot the country. In January of that year President Kabila was shot dead by a bodyguard and replaced by his son Joseph. But MONUC and the United Nations continued working steadily to stabilize the country. In July 2002 Uganda and Rwanda signed a peace deal under which Rwanda pulled out its troops and Congo agreed to arrest and disarm Hutu militiamen accused of committing genocide in Rwanda in 1994. That autumn Uganda agreed to withdraw its troops, and power-sharing talks, brokered by the United Nations, began in South Africa. Zimbabwe and Angola also began pulling out their forces.

At the end of 2002 the government and rebel groups signed a peace deal on power sharing. President Kabila set up an interim government, to rule until elections in 2005. Buoyed by Kofi Annan's optimistic reports of the improving situation in Congo, the Security Council in December 2002 passed resolution 1445, which boosted MONUC to 8,700 military personnel; resolution 1493 in July 2003 reinforced the force to 10,800. Annan had not received the 24,000 personnel he requested, but by October 2004, with the passage of resolution 1565, MONUC had expanded to 16,700 personnel, one of the largest UN peacekeeping missions ever. As important as the numbers was MONUC's mandate. Among the force's tasks were to "ensure the protection of civilians, including humanitarian personnel under imminent threat of physical violence," to "assist in the promotion and protection of human rights with particular attention to women, children and vulnerable persons, investigate human rights violations to put an end to impunity," and to "seize or collect" illegal arms. UN peacekeepers in Congo were no longer required to wait for human rights abuses to occur. They could go into action to protect those under "imminent threat." After nine Bangladeshi peacekeepers were killed in March 2005, MONUC launched a retaliatory raid, together with the Congolese army, on the rebel base. Bangladeshi, Pakistani, Moroccan, and Nepalese UN troops deployed attack helicopters and heavy machine guns to, in the words of a MONUC press release, "neutralise" the "armed elements." Press accounts reported that fifty rebels had been killed. MONUC troops launched "cordon and search" operations to seize the rebels' weapons and cut off their weapons and financial supply lines. When rebels opened fire, MONUC troops fired back, and not over the attackers' heads. How many more Bosniaks and Rwandans might still be alive had UNPROFOR and UNAMIR been tasked with "putting an end to impunity"?

At the end of December 2005 Congo held an election on a new draft constitution, the first free vote in more than forty years. With a turnout of more than 50 percent, more than 80 percent voted in favor of the draft. Such was the enthusiasm that election material was carried to the people through the country by helicopter, by canoe, and balanced on carriers' heads. Massive problems remained. There was no rule of law nor any infrastructure to speak of, and much of the country's wealth was sitting in inaccessible secret banks accounts. Thousands of heavily armed militiamen and rebels roamed the country, unwilling to be disarmed by MONUC, despite its robust mandate. Rwanda and Uganda continued their meddling, and perhaps ten thousand Hutu *genocidaires* remained in the country. Skirmishes continued between rebel groups and MONUC and the government army. But international election observers judged the balloting as essentially free and fair, the first step on the long path toward a functioning state.[7]

MONUC was not the only robust UN force in Africa. UNMIL, the UN mission to Liberia, was deployed in October 2003. Liberia was also a failed state, torn apart by civil war for more than a decade. Teenage militiamen high on alcohol and drugs controlled most of the country, stretching human intestines across the road at their checkpoints. Refugees poured over the borders into Sierra Leone and the Ivory Coast, while inhabitants of the capital, Monrovia, survived by eating dogs and garden snails.[8] UNMIL's fifteen thousand peacekeepers received an extensive mandate to establish peace and security, help establish the rule of law, safeguard human rights, and prepare for national elections in October 2005. UNMIL was also clearly mandated to "protect civilians under imminent threat of physical violence." Soon after Jacques Klein, UNMIL'S head of mission, arrived, he paraded his UN troops through the streets of Monrovia. Klein, an American diplomat, had formerly served as Kofi Annan's special representative in Bosnia after Dayton.

Klein aimed to tell the Liberian warlords, in his own words, "'Don't screw with us. We have more firepower than you do.'" When UNMIL troops were stopped at roadblocks, they swiveled their machine guns toward the militiamen. The threat worked: the militiamen moved aside and handed over their weapons. The authority of the United Nations was no longer being flouted, and a country that had existed in name only was slowly becoming a functioning state. UN-supervised democratic elections took place on schedule. When Klein ended his mission in autumn 2005, his main regret, he told the BBC, was that he did not have an even tougher mandate that would have let the United Nations run the country. Despite being marred by reports of sexual abuse by peacekeepers, MONUC and UNMIL were judged successes overall. Back in January 1994 General Roméo Dallaire had written on his fax to the DPKO: "Peux ce que veux"—Where there's a will there's a way. In Congo and Liberia at least, it seemed there were both.

If the United Nations cannot prevent genocide, its legal organs have at least clarified for the modern world what genocide is. Srebrenica, Rwanda, and Darfur are now linked by a steadily evolving corpus of humanitarian law that transcends national boundaries. Pierre-Richard Prosper served as a UN prosecutor at the international war crimes tribunal for Rwanda (ICTR). There Prosper won the first case of genocide under the 1948 Genocide Convention and persuaded the tribunal to recognize

rape in war as an act of genocide and a crime against humanity, setting new precedents in international law. "We have now
got out of the theoretical debate about genocide," Prosper declared. "When we were doing research for the trial, the only
writings that existed were from professors, academics discussing
hypothetical situations. In the past people thought genocide
was only extermination, like the Holocaust. But it's much wider
and includes acts that fall short of death but contribute to the
destruction of a group."

Prosper was disappointed that the UN's ICI failed to describe Darfur as a genocide:

> I think it is, and there were some things that were
> missed in that report. They looked at the camps in
> the autumn and said conditions were bad, but not
> that bad. They should have looked at what those
> camps were like in April, May, or June, because not
> only were they in awful condition, but there was a
> concerted effort by the Sudanese government not
> to allow humanitarian assistance in. We had to de-
> ploy at the highest levels, including sending Secre-
> tary Powell to get Khartoum to open up the hu-
> manitarian corridors. When a government is put
> on notice that a genocide is being committed and
> fails to act, you have to ask why.

In April 2005 the Security Council passed resolution 1593, which,
following the recommendations of the UN's ICI, referred the
situation in Darfur to the new International Criminal Court
(ICC), also located in The Hague. The ICI forwarded names of
fifty-one Sudanese officials for investigation, causing fury in
Khartoum. President al-Bashir publicly pledged on a copy of

the Koran that no Sudanese officials would ever be extradited, a promise reminiscent of President Milošević's mocking reaction to his first indictment for war crimes in Kosovo in May 1999. The ICC is already investigating human rights abuses in Uganda, the Democratic Republic of Congo, and the Central African Republic, but Darfur is the first ongoing humanitarian crisis to be referred to the court and is a crucial test case for the court's credibility. African dictators also slept a little less easily after the former Liberian president Charles Taylor was arrested as he attempted to flee Nigeria in April 2006. Taylor initially appeared in custody at the Special Court for Sierra Leone, set up by the government of that country and the United Nations, but was then transferred to The Hague to be tried at the facilities of the ICC after a request from Sierra Leone. He faces eleven counts of war crimes, including murder, rape, enslavement and the conscription of child soldiers.

Unlike the international criminal tribunal for the former Yugoslavia, the ICC is not part of the UN. It was established in 2002 by the Rome Statute, which has been ratified by ninety-nine countries, including most of the world's democracies, but not the United States. Washington has consistently opposed the ICC, partly as a sop to the conservative lobby, which opposes any loss of sovereignty to an international body, and partly because of irrational fears that US citizens would be arrested if they had served in conflict zones that were later referred to the court. This is extremely unlikely, because the ICC is responsible for prosecuting only the most egregious war crimes, crimes against humanity, and genocide, and then only if the suspect's home country refuses to prosecute. John Bolton, the new US ambassador to the UN, was strongly opposed to 1593, which referred Darfur to the ICC. He agreed not to use the US veto only after intense negotiations with France and

Great Britain that produced an exemption for US citizens from investigation or prosecution. After a flurry of high-level diplomacy, the United States, together with China, Algeria, and Brazil, abstained. Resolution 1593 highlighted how empty was the perpetual Chinese threat of veto, says John Prendergast: "We were telling the administration that this was just posturing; the Chinese always do this and they do not want to be isolated. They do not want to be the country that actually stands up and actually uses the veto. Condoleezza Rice decided that because of the pressure from Congress, she would test the Chinese on this, and they abstained like we said they would." Resolution 1593 was "an achievement and not a small achievement," says one UN official dealing with Darfur, but, as he notes dryly, "it's a little sad that we are at the stage where we have to be so pleased by getting a referral to the ICC."

The United States' zigzags over the ICC and Darfur were indicative of a wider struggle and uncertainty within the Bush administration over how to react to the crisis. John Danforth, the US envoy to Sudan, had been appointed UN ambassador in June 2004 but resigned in December. Danforth had not been consulted before Colin Powell's declaration that genocide was taking place in Darfur, nor did he agree with it. The word was used for "internal consumption within the United States" he told Feargal Keane of the BBC, to appeal to the Christian right, and he "didn't think it would do any good."[9] And as Powell argued before the Senate Foreign Relations Committee, the use of the word did not predicate a duty to take any "new action." "The Genocide Convention says that states have a duty to prevent and punish," says Pierre-Richard Prosper,

> but the meaning of prevention here has never been defined. People define it the way they want. It is a

silent question; I would define *prevent* at a minimum, as diplomatic engagement and maximum as
military. I always argue that a signatory state must do
whatever is appropriate. The scope of that varies. It
depends on proximity to the genocide, the depth of
engagement—there is a whole litany of criteria.
Sudan has the first duty to prevent and punish. The
United States has clearly carried the lion's share of
the burden in Sudan but could do more. There are
times when we could have been more aggressive.

An old mutual friend has proved most useful to Khartoum
in preventing any more aggressive response by the United States.
Osama bin Laden moved to Khartoum in 1991, and his con-
struction company was soon thriving. He built a road linking
Khartoum with Port Sudan and a modern international airport nearby, according to declassified CIA documents. With
the help of senior government officials, bin Laden's import-
export firm, Wadi al-Aqiq, secured a near-monopoly on Sudan's
main exports of corn, sunflowers, sesame seeds, and gum arabic, a vital ingredient in many medicines, glue, and candies.

Bin Laden brought in several hundred Afghan war veterans from Pakistan and by 1994 had set up at least three terrorist training camps in northern Sudan. Islamic militants from
Asia and the Middle East poured into Sudan. But under intense pressure from the US, Sudan expelled bin Laden in 1996,
and he returned to Afghanistan. After 9/11 bin Laden's links to
Sudan assumed new importance. Fearful that it might be next
to be invaded after Afghanistan, Sudan was only too happy
to cooperate with the United States. Khartoum wants good relations with the United States, says John Danforth: "The government of Sudan was intensely interested in the United States,

and in our government and what the response of our government would be to whatever they did."[10]

Perhaps the only surprise is that it took Khartoum so
long to grasp the principle of linkage between Darfur and the
war on terrorism. It is difficult to threaten Sudanese intelligence officials and military and political leaders coordinating
the onslaught against Darfur with arrest for war crimes when
their assistance is required to fight Al-Qaeda. The ever prag-
matic Sudanese ruling elite quickly remodeled itself. No longer
the launching pad for the new Caliphate, the world Islamic
state, Sudan was now a strategic partner in the fight against
terror. The US intelligence community quickly welcomed the
Sudanese intelligence service, the Mukhabarat, into its embrace.
The CIA reopened its Khartoum station, while the Mukhabarat
handed over bin Laden's former colleagues to the FBI to be
questioned, together with his bank accounts, according to an
investigation by Ken Silverstein of the *Los Angeles Times.*

The Mukhabarat also raided terrorist suspects' homes,
seizing documents and passports and handing the evidence to
US officials, and expelled Islamic extremists to Arab countries
whose intelligence services work closely with the United States.
Silverstein spoke to several senior figures in the Mukhabarat,
including its chief, General Salah Abdallah Gosh. Gosh was included on a list issued by Congress of Sudanese officials con-
trolling Janjaweed operations, yet in 2005 Gosh was flown to
the US in a CIA private jet to meet intelligence officials. Like
Slobodan Milošević a decade earlier, Gosh had somehow become a part of the solution, not the problem. He told Silverstein: "We have a very strong partnership with the CIA. The information we have provided has been very useful to the United
States."[11]

The Sudanese government closed the office of Hamas, the Palestinian Islamic movement, in Khartoum. It hosted a UN-sponsored workshop on counterterrorism and the fight against organized crime. It pledged to implement the twelve international conventions and protocols against terrorism. Even so, Sudan as of spring 2006 remained classified as a sponsor of terrorism by the State Department.

After terrorism, nothing focuses minds in Washington as much as oil. Once it was clear that the Naivasha accords were going to work, all sorts of unusual "businessmen" began arriving in Khartoum, asking UN officials for surprisingly detailed briefings on the political and military situation. US oil interests in Sudan date back to the early 1970s, when the senior George Bush was US ambassador to the United Nations. Bush reportedly aided US companies in investing in Sudan and alerted Khartoum, then a US ally, that US satellite imagery indicated the presence of oil.[12] Chevron discovered three major oil sites, and together with a subsidiary of Royal Dutch Shell spent $1 billion drilling fifty-two new wells and carrying out seismic testing. But the exploration did not go well. Where oil was found, the Sudanese government displaced the local population. Khartoum deployed roving bands of Arab raiders to clear out the African tribes, many of whom subsequently died of disease or malnutrition. Others were killed, and their children sold into slavery.[13] Ongoing civil war with the Sudan People's Liberation Army and other rebel movements, as well as the military coup in 1985, persuaded Chevron to pull out. Eventually, Chevron sold its entire concession. If and when Sudan is finally open for business, the US oil industry is waiting to go in. As Representative Donald Payne, who has been very active on Darfur, argues: "There are still a lot of untapped oil resources in Sudan. And that's a part of this agenda of trying to normal-ize relations with Sudan, so that US oil companies can go in and start exploring oil."[14]

The most bizarre example of the contradictions shaping US policy on Darfur came in October 2005, when US Ambas-sador John Bolton blocked Juan Méndez, the UN special rap-porteur on genocide, from briefing the Security Council on Darfur. Méndez had to submit a written report instead. Bolton said that Washington wanted the Security Council to take more robust action on Sudan instead of just talking. It was true that the United States had played a leading role in highlighting the genocide in Darfur. But more cynical observers suggested that Bolton's rationale for stopping Méndez from briefing the Coun-cil was based more on fears that his revelations would increase the pressure for the United States to intervene. Few doubted that if the United States, the world's only superpower, really wanted to save Darfur, it would be doing much more. Once again, the United States lined up with Sudan's defenders, China, Russia, and Algeria. France's ambassador, Jean-Marc de la Sablière, protested in unusually undiplomatic language that he regret-ted and deplored the decision.

Blocked from addressing the Security Council, Méndez held a press conference. He told the assembled reporters that the situation had deteriorated into a "great state of lawlessness." With no villages left to burn, no animals left to steal, and no crops left to destroy, the Janjaweed were now launching "con-certed, massive" attacks into the IDP camps, deploying waves of horseback riders reinforced by truckloads of Sudanese sol-diers. Khartoum had taken no steps at all to disarm and disband the Janjaweed. The Arab militias were now so coordinated with the Sudanese army that the distinction was meaningless. "No one talks about the Janjaweed any more and whether they can be called something or other," Méndez said. "I don't have any doubt in my mind that a fighting force that constitutes a militia that's very highly organized and that has ties to the government of Sudan is still very much in operation."[15]

Kofi Annan, too, warned that Darfur was spinning out of control. Aid workers and AMIS troops were being kidnapped and held prisoner, and roads were no longer safe. "The looming threat of complete lawlessness and anarchy draws nearer, particularly in western Darfur, as warlords, bandits, and militia groups grow more aggressive," Annan said in his monthly report to the Security Council in November. Just as Milošević had created a Frankenstein's monster in General Mladić, Khartoum has given free rein to the Janjaweed. Janjaweed militiamen occupied Geneina, in West Darfur, for four days after a firefight with government policemen. Even if Khartoum wanted to, it could no longer bring the Janjaweed to heel. Janjaweed militiamen set up checkpoints on roads, charging drivers less than the government did for a security detail. Not only was there no peace in Darfur, the first signs of a bandit para-state were emerging.

The United States had declared that a genocide was taking place, the United Nations that Darfur was the world's greatest humanitarian crisis. And still the conflict continued. "People compare Darfur to Rwanda, but in Rwanda the world left with its tail between its legs," says Jan Egeland, the UN humanitarian chief. "The West took out its soldiers and said we cannot do anything about this. In Darfur we, the United Nations, are running one of the biggest relief operations in the world at the moment, with thousands of courageous relief workers." But the victims were not even safe inside a refugee camp, Egeland acknowledged. "I feel as a humanitarian very strongly that the world keeps these people alive, we feed them, we clothe them, we give them shelter, we give them health care, but we don't protect them. And here is from my humanitarian perspective the big sort of challenge repeatedly missing, that you must have some force there, that can really robustly protect the people and disarm all of these militias, and it's not there."

By summer 2006, more than three years after the crisis began, Egeland's force was still not there, despite increasing talk of turning AMIS into a full-fledged UN mission with a chapter VII mandate. The Security Council had passed resolutions 1547, 1556, 1564, 1574, 1590, 1591, and 1593, not one of which prevented Sudan, a UN member state, from continuing to commit genocide against its own citizens.

X

A Meager Reckoning

Welcome, President Milošević
—Greeting spelled out in flashing lights at the
US air base in Dayton, Ohio, October 1995

The video shows the Scorpions ushering the prisoners forward one by one, as though they were about to enter a room or climb on a bus. Azmir Alispahić, the sixteen-year-old boy who wanted to be a doctor, trembles as he watches the men line up. The prisoners walk ahead, stop, stand still; the Serbs shoot each in the back. The men lurch forward as the bullets hit them, then crumple into the long grass. One man twitches several times before he lies still. After the Serbs have shot four of the men, they untie Azmir and another prisoner and order them to pick up the corpses. The cameraman urges the others to hurry up, as the battery on the camera is dying. The camera pans around the execution-ers. They are pleased with their morning's work, the smoke drift-ing from the muzzles of their guns. Azmir's turn soon comes. In his last moments he turns and looks at the camera.

In October 1995 the United States flew Serbian President Slobodan Milošević, Croatian President Franjo Tudjman, and Bosnian President Alija Izetbegović to Dayton to negotiate a peace settlement. Under intense pressure from Richard Hol-brooke, President Clinton's envoy to Yugoslavia, the three lead-ers signed the Dayton accords, and the war ended. "Holbrooke was a breath of fresh air," recalls Douglas Hurd, the former British foreign secretary. "He didn't moralize at our expense. He did a powerfully good job of sorting it out." As US ambas-sador to the United Nations, Holbrooke had brokered a deli-cate deal over the United States' unpaid dues, which eventually led Congress to release almost $1 billion. Dayton, too, was a diplomatic triumph, but critics argued that the Bosnian Serbs were well rewarded for their ethnic cleansing. The accords di-vided Bosnia into two halves: the Bosniak-Croat Federation, with 51 percent of the territory, and Republika Srpska, the Serb Republic, with 49 percent. There were ten cantons and a three-member presidency—a Serb, a Croat, and a Bosniak—and three separate armies.

The Federation began a stuttering recovery. Republika Srpska remained a wasteland, with no functioning economy, where the executioners spent their days in smoky cafes boast-ing of their prowess in the killing fields. Radovan Karadžić and General Mladić were not invited to Dayton, as the international criminal tribunal for the former Yugoslavia (ICTY) had indicted them for genocide in July 1995. In a sense they were irrelevant anyway. Everyone understood that the only man who counted was Milošević, even though Serbia had technically never been at war. The Serb president treated the Bosnian Serbs with contempt at Dayton, refusing to let them use his fax machine and throwing their letters to him in the dustbin. Milošević was interested only in dealing with Holbrooke, who was technically one of three chairmen but in reality rammed the peace deal together.

In later years Holbrooke remained sensitive about charges that by focusing on Milošević, he legitimized, even strengthened in power, a man who was later put on trial himself for war crimes and genocide. But he stood firm that it was at the time the right thing to do: "We brought Milošević to Dayton, and we were correct about the importance of putting him on American soil. Yitzhak Rabin said to Clinton, and Clinton quoted this to everyone, that you don't negotiate peace with your friends, you negotiate with your adversaries. Unlike a lot of other well-intentioned negotiators, including a lot of Americans, I never mixed it up with Milošević. I never drank with him, although he was in my mind a thug, but he was not then a war criminal, otherwise we would not have negotiated with him."

It is true that Milošević was not formally indicted until May 1999, but the United States was well aware in 1995 of his central role directing the wars in Croatia and Bosnia. That was why he was invited to Dayton. Once the Dayton accords were signed, the United States and the West even had a vested interest in keeping him in power. But it was correct to focus on Milošević, argues Hurd. Hurd highlights the crucial difficulty of trying to stop genocide being committed by states that are part of the international community:

> Milošević was rightly the center of those diplomatic
> efforts precisely because he had the power, despite
> his protestations, to change course. The relationship

between justice and diplomacy is a huge question, which comes up over and over again when bad men are in control and you are trying to alter the way they behave. But you do try, and you must try. You cannot say, "You are a bad man and I will have nothing to do with you." That leaves you no options between doing nothing and bringing him down and killing him. You try and persuade people that their best interests lie in behaving better, and that seems to me to be entirely legitimate.

The United Nations now faces a similar dilemma in Darfur. Interventionists argue that sustained pressure on Khartoum—targeted sanctions, assets seizure, and indictments for crimes against humanity—will help force the Sudanese regime to stop the atrocities. The ICC's sealed list of fifty-one names quickly had an effect on the government's stability. The Khartoum rumor mill began working overtime. Who was on the list? Who was willing to talk? How to stay off it? The prospect, however distant it may seem, of one day being called to account for human rights abuses focuses the mind wonderfully. Despite all the bluster in Belgrade in 1995 and Khartoum in 2005, once the legal wheels start rolling, many of those who know they are likely to be indicted begin to think about cutting a deal in exchange for a lesser sentence or even immunity.

Before John Prendergast was expelled from Sudan in 2003, Sudanese officials repeatedly questioned him about the new ICC. "One of them was asking me millions of questions about the implication of the tribunal, how will it work, what are the mechanisms for apprehension, the effect of the ICC," Prendergast recalls. "There was no punitive action taken against them during the first two years of this crisis, and I think they thought there never would be." A threatened regime becomes unstable, even paranoid, as former allies prepare to turn on each other to save themselves. In January 2000 the Belgrade rumor mill whispered that Arkan, the most notorious Serb paramilitary leader, was sending out feelers to the ICTY. One day a gunman walked up to him in the lobby of the Intercontinental Hotel in Belgrade and shot him several times in the head. By then the Milošević regime was a virtual police state, but the killer was never caught.

The "realist" counterargument, advanced by some diplomats trying to stop the Darfur crisis, is that the United Nations should court the more moderate wing of the NIF, which they believe does want a negotiated settlement in Darfur. Suitably encouraged, the moderates would then strengthen their position and gain influence to wind down the conflict. But why would the Sudanese leadership be interested if once the conflict is over, its members will be soon in the dock at the ICC? Haile Menkerios, Africa chief at the DPA, argues, like Douglas Hurd, that "bad men" have to be persuaded. "There is conflict all around," Menkerios says. "So many leaders of these conflicts have committed abuses, crimes, and the killing and the suffering of innocent civilians continues as long as the conflict continues. So you have two choices. You can consider them criminals, bring them to face justice and get them out of the way, or invite them to negotiate for a peaceful settlement. When there is neither the internal capacity nor the external will to do the first, then there is no other choice but to invite them to negotiate, often for power sharing in a transitional arrangement to stop the wars." Considerations of peace come before those of justice, argues Menkerios. "You have to act in the interests of the victims, and they first and foremost want peace to survive and justice to be pursued in a way that will not hurt peace. Of course, ultimately there can be no peace without justice, but in the short run, in these circumstances, you don't have much of a choice, do you?"

But persuasion in diplomacy, as in many other areas, requires a stick as well as a carrot. Dayton happened because the United States helped break the arms embargo, a newly armed Croatia attacked the Serbs, and NATO bombed. The attack on Srebrenica would also have collapsed if the West had shown more resolve, says Holbrooke:

> I argued then that we should intervene with massive bombing. I believed then, and I am certain now, that had we bombed, the whole thing would have stopped immediately. The Bosnian Serb army were street bullies, thugs, an absolute rabble. But the British, the French, and the Dutch cut some kind of private deal, the details of which are not recorded, but which must have happened, that they would use their position within NATO to veto any air strikes until the Dutch troops were safely out of Srebrenica. Somehow, the greatest democracies, with the most powerful arsenal in the world, were scared of Mladić, whose idea of military combat was to slit a pig's throat in front of a Dutch colonel.

A former UNPROFOR official agrees: "My impression was that the Serbs would back off, when there was a serious demonstration that they had crossed a red line. A wide scale use of air attacks on 6 July, once they crossed into the enclave, would have given them a severe fright and they would have stopped."

But without a credible threat of force, negotiations and their often erroneous assumption of a common interest in reaching an equitable solution assume a dynamic of their own. Instead of solving conflicts, the endless rounds of discussions stabilize the positions of the perpetrators. With the United Nations apparently ready to talk forever, there was no incentive for the Serbs to stop the war in Bosnia and none for Khartoum to stop the massacres in Darfur. War helped keep them in power and was the most effective means for the ruling elites to preserve their privileges.

The human factor is also important. The attention of the world's diplomats is both seductive and addictive. Courted by the United Nations, provincial thugs and warlords become important international statesmen. When Marrack Goulding traveled to Knin in 1991 to meet with rebel Serb leader Milan Babić, his very presence granted a kind of legitimacy to an outlaw regime. Radovan Karadžić relished the attention of the world's media when he was repeatedly flown to five-star hotels in Geneva, to be presented for his approval a series of maps dismembering Bosnia along ethnic lines, just as he had demanded. Robert Zoellick, the United States envoy to Sudan, said that he had been to Khartoum more often than New York. The ultimate logic of this is that the United Nations eventually seeks to keep in power the very people organizing the atrocities, as evinced by Yasushi Akashi's cable of May 1995, in which he expressed concern that air strikes against the Bosnian Serbs would "weaken Milošević."

After he left the Foreign Office in the summer of 1995, Douglas Hurd, it seemed, had few difficulties in dealing with "bad men." Hurd was appointed deputy chairman of NatWest Markets, a subsidiary of the British bank National Westminster. In the summer of 1996 Hurd traveled to Belgrade with Pauline Neville-Jones, a former political director of the Foreign Office, who had been head of the British delegation to

Dayton. After Dayton, some sanctions were lifted and Serbia was open for business. NatWest Markets agreed to partly privatize the state-owned Serbian Telecom and was reportedly paid at least £10 million in commission.

With hindsight, Hurd regrets his visit to Belgrade, which, he says, he wanted to see for himself after so long dealing with the former Yugoslavia. "It was a mistake for me to go, as the deal was done anyway. The visit wasn't absolutely necessary for the deal, but because I had spent so much time thinking about Bosnia, I was curious." The deal itself was not a mistake, Hurd says. "It was legitimate, and at that stage, after Dayton, it was perfectly reasonable to help Serbia down that route and to dismantle the apparatus of the state. It was not for us to enquire what Milošević did with the money." Perhaps someone should have. Many in Belgrade argue that the privatization of Serb Telecom bankrolled Milošević's next war: the Serb assault on the Albanian-dominated Serb province of Kosovo in 1998.

Some among the Bosnian Serb military leadership were haunted by Srebrenica, not because of its human cost but because they understood that eventually there might be a reckoning. That may have seemed unlikely initially, judging by the international community's feeble response to previous atrocities. But over the next few months the more perceptive Bosnian Serb officers realized that Srebrenica was a massacre too far. "On one level the Serbs' assessments were correct, because NATO did not want to intervene in Bosnia," says a former UNPROFOR official. "But they got overconfident, and killed all those people. What they got massively wrong was that although the international community is fickle and basically does not want to engage, that does not go on forever. There are some lines, and they crossed one."

In late December 1995 US General Bill Nash met with General Radislav Krstić, commander of the Drina corps, whose troops had carried out much of the killing. General Nash was commander of Task Force Eagle, the US-led component of the NATO force in Bosnia to implement the Dayton accords. As a military courtesy, Nash wanted to inform Krstić how he would deploy his troops. "I knew Krstić was implicated in Srebrenica, but he was not then indicted," recalls Nash. The two men had lunch together in Zvornik. When the meal was almost over, Krstić asked Nash, "Have you ever heard of a town called Srebrenica?" Nash paused, then replied that he had. Krstić asked whether Nash knew about the battle for Srebrenica in 1992. "For the next twenty minutes or so he told me about all the atrocities that the Bosniaks had committed in the early days of the war, and he went on and on," Nash recalls. "I just listened and said that was interesting, but had heard that there had been other actions there more recently. It was clear to me at the time that he was rehearsing his defense. I never saw him again."

In 1995 Krstić was indicted by the ICTY on six counts of genocide and crimes against humanity for his role at Srebrenica. Krstić was arrested by NATO-led stabilization force troops in December 1998 and arrived in The Hague the next day.

The ICTY had its genesis in the UN's Commission of Experts investigation into the Yugoslav wars, led by Professor Cherif Bassiouni, but few UN officials ever believed that it would ever hear a case. Cynics dismissed the tribunal when it was set up in 1993 as a sop for the human rights lobby, easing the pressure over Bosnia in the United Nations with no political cost. At first the skepticism seemed well founded. The United Nations had authorized Bassiouni to investigate war crimes but provided him with no resources. The commission had one full-time staff member, four part-timers, no investigators, and no

money with which to hire them. Bassiouni started work using
resources provided by DePaul University, where he taught law.
A team of volunteers eventually compiled more than thirty-five
hundred pages of reports, with support from the MacArthur
and Soros Foundations. UN member states eventually contributed $1.3 million, a minuscule sum for the work involved.[1]

Yet slowly and steadily the ICTY took on a life of its own.
When President Clinton took office, Washington's interest re-
vived. Madeleine Albright was one of the tribunal's strongest
advocates. "At first people did not take the idea seriously," recalls Jim O'Brien, a former State Department lawyer involved
in setting up the tribunal. "But we took it through the law, one
step at a time, and nobody could say no to any of them. Is it
good to gather the information? Who could say no? Is it good
to publish it? Who could be against that? Is it good to evaluate
it and have some experts take a look at it? Who could say no?
Then you are faced with the choice, because it certainly appears
that there are individuals who did this as a conscious act. How
can you be against punishing them? People had been hiding
behind the supposed complexities, and suddenly it wasn't so
complex after all."

Based in the headquarters of a former insurance company, the ICTY has indicted 162 people, of whom 76 were in
custody as of May 2006, either on trial, awaiting trial, or serving sentences. Detainees are initially held at the UN's nearby
detention center, where they enjoy comfortable living conditions. Cells have cable television, a coffee machine, and a shower.
Detainees have the use of a gym, a kitchen to prepare their own
food, even a conjugal room for visits from their wives. They can
learn foreign languages or take classes in ceramics, where they
make ashtrays or decorative plates. There is little ethnic tension between the different groups, who, after all, once lived in

the same country. Serbian inmates greeted Slobodan Milošević as "Mr. President." An inmate who is found guilty is transferred abroad to serve his sentence.

Twenty-one people have been indicted over Srebrenica, including Radovan Karadžić; General Ratko Mladić; Slobodan Milošević; General Momčilo Perišić, the former chief of staff of the Yugoslav army; Dražen Erdemović, the former member of the 10th sabotage unit; and several senior officers in the Bosnian Serb army, including security chief Colonel Ljubisa Beara and General Radislav Krstić. These were a tiny fraction of those involved in organizing the massacre, executing the victims, and burying their bodies. By May 2006 the ICTY had delivered a total of just forty-three guilty verdicts for the three wars in the former Yugoslavia. Cases usually focus on senior figures involved in the most egregious war crimes. Few who actually pulled the triggers at Srebrenica will ever be called to account. At his trial Dražen Erdemović named men who still live freely in Serbia or Bosnia as commanders and members of his unit who had also massacred Bosniak prisoners.

Some of the perpetrators may yet find themselves in the dock at the Bosnian War Crimes Chamber in Sarajevo. The trial of eleven Bosnian Serbs charged with genocide in connection with the Srebrenica massacre began in May 2006, and the chamber will continue its work after the ICTY closes down, theoretically in 2008. Yet if the ICTY has failed to bring real justice to the victims of Srebrenica, it has brought a kind of historical closure. The tribunal's investigations and trials have established an invaluable and extraordinarily detailed record, both historical and legal, of how the massacre was planned and implemented. During Krstić's trial in 2001 the court heard grim details of a request by Colonel Beara, the Bosnian Serb army's security chief, to Krstić for help in distributing thousands of "packets" or "parcels"—code for men being taken to their execution. The tribunal has also established that the Srebrenica massacre was a genocide under international law and has accelerated the development of international jurisprudence on war crimes. These are noteworthy achievements. There were muted cheers in Tuzla and Sarajevo in August 2001 when Krstić was found guilty of genocide and sentenced to forty-six years' imprisonment. The sentence was later reduced to thirty-five years when the appeals chamber found Krstić guilty of the lesser charge of aiding and abetting genocide.

The tribunal's greatest setback was the death of Slobodan Milošević in his cell in March 2006. There was much talk that Milošević had "cheated justice" and won a final victory. It is true that his trial, which began in summer 2001, had become bogged down in technicalities and difficulties over his failing health. But Milošević's passing was not any kind of victory, nor did he cheat justice. The man once courted by the world's statesmen and diplomats passed the last years of his life locked each night into a prison cell, deprived of his freedom, and separated from his family, charged with sixty-six counts of war crimes, crimes against humanity, and genocide. Among his fellow prisoners was his onetime bodyguard Nasir Oric, the former commander of Srebrenica. Oric was initially charged with six counts of war crimes, including the beating and killing of Serb prisoners by soldiers under his command. Oric's trial was dogged by controversy, with some analysts arguing that he had been indicted to show that the tribunal was not biased against the Serbs. Counts four and six of Oric's indictment, charging him with plunder, were later dropped. The judge noted that although there was evidence that a bed and television set had indeed been looted, this was not serious enough for the ICTY's jurisdiction.[2] Oric was found guilty in June 2006 and sentenced to two years in prison.

That same month Radovan Karadžić and Ratko Mladić, the ICTY's two most wanted, still remained at large after more than a decade in hiding, probably somewhere in the former Yugoslavia. Justice for the dead of Srebrenica was low on the West's list of priorities after Dayton, and its leaders made a deliberate decision not to try to apprehend Karadžić and Mladić, for fear that the effort would destabilize Bosnia and plunge the country back into war. Repeated intelligence reports located Mladić at his old headquarters, near Han Pijesak, north of Sarajevo, but the order was never given to arrest him. General Bill Nash recalls: "The United States could have said get him, while he was in our sector. We could have attacked the bunker at Han Pijesak. . . . It would have been an attack with artillery, tanks, attack helicopters, and there would have been a fight, and once it was over he might have escaped, been captured, or have been skilled. But most important, Dayton as a peace process would have been over."

Both Mladić and Karadžić know that the NATO troops in Bosnia have no jurisdiction outside the borders, so any arrest would have to be carried out by the police and armed forces of Serbia or Montenegro, if that is where they are hiding. This would be politically difficult, but as both countries hope to join the European Union, the prospect of eventual membership, or other political and economic levers, could be used to persuade their governments to arrest the fugitives, if the political will existed. But it does not. Karadžić and Mladić remain at large, says General Nash, because "nobody with the capacity to give the order to get them has done so." The ICTY's two most wanted remain heroes to many Serbs, and shops in Belgrade and Banja

Luka still sell T-shirts and key rings emblazoned with their images. Karadžić has continued his writing career on the run,
smuggling his works out from the mountains through a chain
of helpers. In spring 2002 his supporters even staged his new
play, *Situation,* a drama mocking the international community, in a Belgrade theater.

But if complete justice remains elusive, a line now runs from
The Hague to Kigali to Khartoum. Somehow, whatever the interests of the superpowers, international criminal justice has
assumed a relentless, unstoppable dynamic of its own. The
ICI's report on Darfur specifically refers to the ICTY's first
trial, which was the first international trial for war crimes since
the Nuremberg trials of senior Nazis. Duško Tadić, a Bosnian
Serb, had engaged in acts of great cruelty at Omarska concentration camp, including severe beatings and attacking a prisoner with a knife. He was also present while prisoners were
forced to sexually mutilate another prisoner. In May 1997 Tadić
was found guilty of war crimes and crimes against humanity
and subsequently sentenced to twenty years. In July 1999 Tadić
was convicted of nine additional counts and sentenced to a
further five years. (The total sentence was later reduced on appeal to twenty years.)

Judges ruled in July 1999 that militias or paramilitary units
are under state control when they are financed and equipped by
the state and the state also participates in the "planning and
supervision of military operations." However, the state does
not need to issue specific orders or instructions for single military operations.[3] Drawing on the Tadić case, which itself drew
on the proceedings of the UN's International Criminal Tribunal in Rwanda (ICTR), the ICI argued in relation to Darfur
that "When militias attack jointly with the armed forces, it can

be held that they act under the effective control of the Government," and thus are "acting as *de facto* State officials of the Government of Sudan."[4] In layman's terms, this means Sudanese government officials could be held responsible for Janjaweed atrocities under the principles of "command responsibility" even if they did not specifically order specific attacks to be carried out.

The corpus of law governing "command responsibility" further evolved in March 2006, when the ICTY convicted the first of its indictees for crimes solely committed by their subordinates. Ironically, considering the reasons for the tribunal's genesis, both were officers in the Bosnian government army. Enver Hadžihasanović, commander of the Third Corps, was sentenced to five years in prison for murder of and cruelty to Bosnian Croat and Serb civilians and soldiers held by foreign fighters under his control. Judges argued that Hadžihasanović knew that the foreign troops, known as the El Mujahed detachment, were extremely brutal and violent with no regard for humanitarian law, and he should have used force to prevent the crimes the foreign fighters committed against their captives. Amir Kubara, who commanded the Third Corps' Seventh Mountain Brigade, was sentenced to two and a half years for plunder by troops under his control. Crucially, as Helen Warrell of the Institute of War and Peace Reporting, a London-based media charity, noted, "At no point did the prosecution allege that either of the Bosnian army leaders had planned or ordered any of the crimes themselves."[5]

John Prendergast of the International Crisis Group recalled that Sudanese officials closely follow developments at the international tribunals, so these verdicts should be of great concern to those organizing the genocide in Darfur. But the UN tribunals have also taught Khartoum lessons, says a UN human rights official. "These people are not stupid enough to repeat

what happened in Rwanda or Srebrenica," the official says. "I
don't think anyone will make that kind of mistake again. They
are like Milošević; they don't put things in writing. It is public
knowledge now, what you do and what you don't do if you wish
to get rid of a certain group among the population." Khartoum
has more subtle weapons, albeit just as deadly, he explains:

> They use Sudan's climate and geography. Eighty to
> 90 percent of the villages are destroyed, and people
> are living in the refugee and IDP camps for the sec-
> ond or third season. It takes months, if not years, to
> recultivate, and there is already a problem of deser-
> tification. Then they block supplies to the camps, and
> you can read the World Health Organization reports
> on how many people die because of that, thousands
> every week. The worst thing is that the victims know
> that nothing will happen to the perpetrators, and
> the international community doesn't care.

In the West, the politicians' whispering campaign continues, counseling inaction on Darfur. Bosnia could not be saved
because it was small and mountainous. Darfur cannot be saved
because it is large and flat. "Everyone says Darfur is the size of
France, which is true, but it is not the same because it is not in-
habited like France," the UN human rights official says. "The
actual conflict zones are small, with very limited means of warfare from the Janjaweed. I cannot believe that in 2005, nations
who can send men to the moon, who have laser weapons and
God knows what, cannot do something against 150 people on
camels with Second World War rifles. I cannot believe it." The
same arguments against intervention are used now as were
used during the Bosnian war. In the summer of 1993 Douglas

Hurd gave a speech at the Travellers' Club in London, saying that "most of those who report for the BBC, the *Times*, the *Independent*, the *Guardian* have all been in different ways enthusiasts for pushing military intervention in Bosnia. They are founder members of the 'something must be done' school." The speech caused widespread anger and for many encapsulated the poverty of Britain's response to the war in Bosnia. But more than a decade later Hurd stands by his words:

> It's permanent, this school—you see it in Darfur now—and they don't usually think it is their job to go beyond that statement; that is not a huge help. There is a right and even on occasion a duty to intervene, but in practice it will be a matter of practice; it will not be absolute. Rwanda is the prime example where the world is overwhelmingly blamed for that. Clinton and Annan apologized for that, but the same thing happens again in Darfur—why, because the practicalities are baffling. The only practicality, it seems to me, is the one that is being tried and seems to be faltering, to try to get African troops in.

The practicalities are indeed difficult, but not baffling. Hurd's argument is part of the latest tactic to defuse pressure over Darfur: presenting one extreme option—Western military intervention—as the only alternative and then explaining that it would not be feasible because it would bring down the wrath of the Arab world, especially after Iraq. It is true that putting Western troops on the ground would risk opening a new front in the clash between Islam and the West. Khartoum would quickly "play the Jihadi card," says a senior UN official, and present itself as the latest victim of the Western "crusaders." Osama bin Laden himself has called for Muslims to resist any Western intervention in Darfur. But while NATO troops on the ground would be the most effective means of stopping the killing and protecting the refugees, they are not the only option. There is no need for white European soldiers to engage the Sudanese army. There is already a force of international soldiers in Darfur, deployed with the consent of the UN, the African Union, and the Arab League: the African Union AMIS peacekeepers.

The answer is simple: transform AMIS into a viable UN peacekeeping force under a chapter VII enforcement mandate, with sufficient troops and materiel, while NATO supplies the necessary logistical and intelligence support to protect the IDP camps and stop the Janjaweed. If this strategy were combined with targeted sanctions on key Sudanese political leaders, freezing their assets abroad—a surprisingly effective means of destabilizing and dividing criminal regimes—and sanctions on Sudan's oil industry, the conflict in Darfur could be ended quickly and Sudan forced to sign a peace agreement. As Mukesh Kapila told the British Parliament: "This war costs money and it is bankrolled by the oil wealth and other resources, and it is bankrolled through the pockets of a few individuals at the very top, and these people should be hurt where it matters most, their pockets. This would have a salutary effect on the conflict more than anything else."[6]

Nor is it certain that China and Russia would actually wield their veto. For all their threats, Beijing and Moscow are reluctant actually to take such a step. Vetoes are threatened, or hinted at, far more than they are used. A statement from a Chinese or Russian diplomat that the wording of a paragraph is "unacceptable" is usually enough for it to be removed before the resolution is presented. There is a powerful dynamic for consensus on the Security Council, which is why resolutions often reflect the "lowest common denominator," as one US official said. Russia and China only abstained on resolution 1593, which referred Darfur to the ICC. A Chinese or Russian veto over Darfur would blow apart all sorts of useful consensuses, both stated and tacit. It would set a dangerous precedent for future Security Council discussions of Beijing's interests in Tibet and Taiwan, and Moscow's own scorched-earth campaign in Chechnya. The United States should have called Sudan's bluff far more often in the Security Council, says John Prendergast. "The threat of the veto by the Chinese or Russians is a fig-leaf for the US administration," he argues. "They said for months, for a year, that they could not get anything through on Darfur because they couldn't get it past the Chinese veto. The Chinese strategy worked: they knew nobody cared enough, so every time the United States proposed targeted sanctions, they said they would veto it. The United States backed down because they needed their vote on things like Iraq, Iran, North Korea, et cetera, et cetera. The United States preserved that relationship, and Sudan burned and burned."

With skillful diplomacy and political will, the Security Council's drive for consensus could be turned on its head to produce a robust policy instead of a watered-down one, especially if the United Nations learned from its debacle in Bosnia. "The United Nations was never equipped to do the job properly in Bosnia," argues Colin Keating, New Zealand's ambassador to the UN in the mid-1990s.

> The most important lesson is that, whether you're intervening as the United Nations, or as a multi-national coalition, or whatever, you've got to be con-

figured in a way that enables you to use force to accomplish your mission, if necessary. There has been a history of using forces as symbols, rather than as serious operations units. The United Nations was never equipped to do the job properly in Bosnia, not because they were stupid or didn't know what forces or equipment were needed. At key points along the way decisions were taken either for financial or strategic political reasons to deprive them of the resources and capacities of what needed to be done, if it needed to be done.

The UN did not bring adequate force to bear in Bosnia or Rwanda to stop the killing, nor is it doing so in Darfur. This is partly because once again the US administration is paralyzed by the prospect of potential American casualties and the fear of "mission creep," even if the US Army were confined to logistics and transport, rather than deploying combat troops. Somalia still casts a long shadow over the Pentagon. Dispatching a single US C-130 transport plane would require presidential approval, says Richard Holbrooke:

This would still be an American military engagement with potential for combat. The Pentagon argues if you send one, they will ask for three, which is often true, and they will need jeeps, and you will have to secure the runway, which could get ambushed, and a dirt runway is an easy place to hide a landmine, and American lives are at stake, and do you want to take that risk, Mr. President? I have sat in on meetings in the White House and heard the Pentagon argue against the smallest things based

on this mission creep argument. They have a valid
point, but it has to be dealt with, because sometimes we have to take these risks.

One reason the risks must be taken at some point is that
doing nothing to stop genocide also carries a risk, perhaps an
even greater one in the long term. Any serious consideration of
United States and Western interests—the question of moral
courage aside—must also take this into account. In a global
world isolationism is no longer a practical policy. The genocides in Bosnia and Darfur may seem remote, but their consequences reverberate across the world. As Madeleine Albright
argues: "We are in a different world now. I would say to the average person, who is focused on their own family, that if you
don't take care of these issues early enough, they will come
back around. These are the hotbeds that create the terrorists,
and in this day and age, when we have the ability to be informed about what is going on across the world, nobody can
say anymore they didn't know what was happening."

The Bosnian war was an opportunity lost. A rich European Muslim culture that could have forged a new relationship
between Islam and the West vanished forever under a rain of
Serb artillery shells. Only now it is becoming clear how high a
price the West will have to pay. A small group of Arab students
enrolled at Hamburg technical university certainly knew what
was happening to their Muslim brothers and sisters during the
1990s. The students spent much time watching gruesome footage
of the wars in Bosnia and Chechnya, called "Jihadi" videos.
The graphic scenes of Serb atrocities and the failure of the
West—and the Arab world—to stop the slaughter helped radi-
calize these students. They frequently discussed Bosnia on their
visits to the Al-Quds mosque, in downtown Hamburg, where

preachers would detail the reality of Serb ethnic cleansing and the destruction of Muslim culture and society. In 2001 the students, who made up the Hamburg cell of Al-Qaeda, traveled to the United States. On 11 September, cell members piloted three of the four hijacked planes: Mohamed Atta flew American Airlines flight 11 into the first tower of the World Trade Center, Marwan al-Shehhi flew United Airlines flight 175 into the second tower, and Ziad Jarrah crashed United Airlines flight 93 into a field in Pennsylvania.

During the Bosnian conflict bearded Arab fighters known as mujahideen began to appear on the front lines, fighting with the government army against the Serbs. They were hard men, many of them veterans of the Afghan war against the Russians, courageous on the battlefield, hostile to Westerners and intolerant of the women soldiers in the Bosnian army. Their Saudi traditions were at odds with Bosnia's more relaxed Ottoman Islam. The Bosnians had considered themselves to be Europeans, but after their rejection by the West, they turned east. Saudi Arabia and Iran stepped into the gap, supplying weapons, money, and manpower. Despite the culture clash, the mujahideen were initially made welcome. "Some of them might be motivated by the possibility of fighting a jihad, but I only wish there were more of them. Their presence shames Europe," one army commander said.

The foreign fighters soon formed their own "El-Mujahed" detachment. But many Bosniaks were deeply ambivalent about their hard-line allies. The mujahideen repeatedly violated the Geneva Conventions and were often brutal to Serb and Croat prisoners of war and captured civilians. The ICTY judges sentencing Enver Hadžihasanović, commander of the Bosnian army Third Corps, noted that mujahideen soldiers under his command had beheaded a Serb prisoner, Dragan Popović, with an axe and then forced other prisoners to kiss his severed head while singing and chanting.

It is now known that some of the mujahideen were connected to Al-Qaeda. James Baker, the US secretary of state who had dismissed Bosnia with the words "the United States doesn't have a dog in this fight," was more wrong than he ever imagined. The Bosnian government issued more than a thousand passports to the mujahideen, many of whom have since disappeared. Radical Islam has taken root not just in Bosnia but across the Balkans. Saudi relief organizations provide aid to victims of the war, Saudi funds pay for mosques to be rebuilt, and Saudi publications propagate a harsh, intolerant Islam. The vast majority of Bosnians are not sympathetic to the radicals, but the bitter legacy of the war has made some ready to listen. One of the darkest ironies of the conflict is that Bosniaks believe that they were abandoned because the West did not want a Muslim state in Europe. But as one young Bosniak soldier predicted a decade ago, his voice grim and resigned, "Europe will bring about here the very thing it fears."[7]

Saving lives brings a warm glow and welcome plaudits, but when states finally intervene, it is primarily to preserve their own interests. President Clinton bombed the Bosnian Serbs to keep NATO from splitting in two and to defuse the growing pressure from Congress to intervene. France invaded Rwanda at the end of the genocide to prevent all its former colonies in central Africa from collapsing into bloodshed. NATO attacked Serbia in 1999 because the Kosovo conflict threatened to set the southern Balkans ablaze and drag in Albania and Macedonia. Genuine leadership demands a kind of moral courage, which Clinton and the West found very belatedly, if at all. "The post of leadership of the free world is vacant," sneered French President Jacques Chirac after a visit to Washington in June 1995. NATO did send troops to Bosnia and Kosovo, but only after the real fighting was over. "To be fair to the United Nations, and with the benefit of ten years' hindsight, it is curious that during the worst conflict in Europe since 1945, the troops on the ground in Bosnia were UN peacekeepers, not NATO soldiers," says Michael Williams, former spokesman for UNPROFOR. "It is bizarre that after Dayton, we have had hardly a life lost, but we have NATO peacekeepers deployed in Bosnia, with all the equipment and weaponry that the United Nations never possessed. In that regard very heavy responsibility for the Bosnian catastrophe falls on NATO and the Western alliance."

The NATO bombing of Belgrade in spring 1999 was a spectacular demonstration of the West's military capability, but it came too late for Srebrenica. Cruise missiles precisely targeted not just certain buildings in the defense ministry complex but specific rooms. Had the West acted with similar resolve when the Bosnian war first started, history might have taken a very different course, argues David Owen: "It was an amazing experience for me, returning to Belgrade and seeing the fantastic accuracy of those cruise missiles. I thought, if only we had done something like that, a proper demonstration of sophisticated Western power, in 1992 or 1993, when their attitude was particularly outrageous. What a difference it would have made." After Kosovo, the West wearied of Milošević. He was finally toppled in October 2000 after a one-day uprising covertly organized by the American and British intelligence services from their office in a side street behind the Budapest Opera House, in neighboring Hungary. When the protestors took to the street and Milošević ordered the army and state security service into action, they stayed in their barracks, thanks to a series of prearranged deals with the West, allowing them to preserve their power and influence in a post-Milošević Serbia. This is known as "blocking the response mechanism." Perhaps even now General Salah Abdallah Gosh, the head of the Sudanese Mukhabarat, is considering similar offers from the CIA or Great Britain's MI6. He was certainly made welcome when he was given a British visa and visited London in early 2006 for medical treatment. Should the United States finally decide that regime change is also necessary in Khartoum, securing new oil supplies and more dusty files about Osama bin Laden's sesame seed business will be quite as vital as saving Darfur.

XI

Command Responsibility

After Rwanda and Srebrenica, the Secretariat cannot
still lean back and say we are waiting for the Security
Council to tell us how far they want to go on Darfur,
which, to a great extent, is what is happening now.
—UN human rights official

I f there is a sense of shame among Secretariat officials for
the United Nations' failures in Srebrenica and Rwanda, it is
not a career hindrance. Those implicated have been neither
penalized nor demoted. The most conspicuous example
is Kofi Annan, head of the DPKO during both the Bosnian war
and the Rwandan genocide, who was afterward promoted to
secretary general. Once Annan took office, on 1 January 1997,
he quickly found new posts for his protégés. Shashi Tharoor,

the DPKO team leader on Yugoslavia, was appointed Annan's director of communications and special projects. In 2001 Tharoor was promoted to under–secretary general for communications and public information, responsible for the UN's overall communications strategy. Tharoor certainly excelled at communicating his literary interests. Between 1989 and 2005, in addition to carrying out his UN duties, Tharoor published three novels, a collection of short stories, and four works of nonfiction. In June 2006 India nominated Tharoor as its candidate for secretary general.

Iqbal Riza, Annan's deputy in the DPKO, who signed off on the two cables in January 1994 ordering General Roméo Dallaire not to raid the Hutu arms caches in Kigali, was promoted to be Annan's chief of cabinet, one of the most influential behind-the-scenes positions in the United Nations. The DPKO's instructions to General Dallaire were not a mistake, especially after Somalia, Riza argued later. Dallaire's cable was alarming, but needed clarification. "Dallaire was asking to take such risks going outside his mandate. And we said no. . . . We are given a specific mandate by the Security Council. These troops are not our troops. We have to borrow them from governments, who give them in the context of that mandate, for the tasks to be performed in that mandate."[1] Peter Schmitz, the DPKO's Yugoslavia desk officer, soon followed Riza to the thirty-eighth floor, as a political adviser to Annan.

After his return to New York, Yasushi Akashi was appointed under–secretary general for humanitarian affairs, but he left the United Nations in 1997. Nine years later, Akashi still strongly defends the United Nations operation in Bosnia. In an e-mail to the author, he wrote: "It is easy to criticise some aspect or segment of UNPROFOR's performance or decisions when you do not take into account the overall situation, man-

dates, constraints and the shortage of resources." Any evalua-
tion of the United Nations' work should be done with the "correct historical and political perspectives," and robust responses
had been used, and had worked, in both Sarajevo after the February 1994 marketplace massacre and in Goražde. Akashi claimed
that UNPROFOR did not know the Serbs' intentions in Srebrenica until after the city was occupied, and even then the information available was "incredibly limited." He wrote: "I received reports on debriefings of Dutch troops in Zagreb. These
reports were partial and the soldiers were obviously still under
great shock. As a result there was underreporting to us by the
soldiers involved."[2]

As to whether the United Nations should be, in Madeleine
Albright's words, "excessively neutral," he argued: "You will
lose your usefulness as an intermediary in conflict situations
and humanitarian emergencies when you lose your impartiality." Nor had the United Nations focused too much on Milošević
to bring the Bosnian war to an end: "The question of the use
of Milošević was simply due to his greater intelligence and
understanding of the overall picture than some of his less intelligent lieutenants and partners. One has to be tactical in some
situations and also aware that greater intelligence might mean
greater cunning."

David Hannay, the British ambassador to the United Nations during the Bosnian war and the Rwanda genocide, was
elevated to the peerage and appointed Britain's special representative for Cyprus. Douglas Hurd, the British foreign secretary, soon joined Hannay in the House of Lords. Hurd remains
troubled by Bosnia. "Bosnia was the only issue which really
worried me," he recalls.

> The first Gulf war and dealing with Saddam Hus-
> sein were intellectually straightforward. Bosnia was

not; it was new ground. This business of intervening where we had no British interests, commercial or strategic, simply on humanitarian grounds, working with the Americans, it was all relatively new. There were no guidelines, no precedents. We put all the emphasis on trying to stop the war, not on sending in troops to impose a solution. I think it was right, but the war dragged on, and one has to reflect on that. We should have been bolder in the use of the dual key, overriding United Nations' objections, and using bombing earlier and in greater force. It is possible, although not certain, that the war might have been brought to an end earlier.

David Owen, the EC's special envoy to Yugoslavia, also had Bosnia on his conscience. Owen was designated a Companion of Honour in 1993 but turned it down. "I didn't see how anyone could have any pride in this whole thing. I said there was no honor. I felt a sense of shame," he recalls, although he accepted the distinction the following year. In December 1999, on the release of the United Nations' report on Rwanda, Kofi Annan did speak of his "bitter regret" over the failure to stop the genocide: "On behalf of the United Nations, I acknowledge this failure and express my deep remorse."[3] Only one senior UN official publicly stepped down after Srebrenica: Tadeusz Mazowiecki, the special rapporteur on human rights. After meeting survivors of Srebrenica in Tuzla, Mazowiecki handed in his resignation letter in late July 1995, saying that he could no longer participate in "the pretence of human rights."

The pretence continues, and nowhere more so than in the annual meeting of the UN Commission on Human Rights (CHR). The six-week-long session is held at the United Nations complex in Geneva, usually in March and April. The truly diligent may also attend the annual three-week Sub-Commission on the Promotion and Protection of Human Rights, also held in Geneva, during the summer. The days are taken up with plenary sessions, speeches, statements, and working groups. Those states that are human rights abusers skillfully play the system to prevent discussion of anything of substance.

Filibustering until the six weeks end is often rewarding. In 2004 a surprisingly critical resolution on Darfur was proposed. The Commission proposed sending a team to Darfur to investigate, but Sudan refused to grant the team visas. It went instead to Chad, where it gathered much detailed testimony. The team returned and wrote a report highly critical of Khartoum. A new draft resolution was proposed, which probably would have passed once the team's report was released. Sudan quickly began negotiating, offering to let in a second UN team if the release of the first report were postponed. The UN officials agreed, feeling that they could not pass up the opportunity to get firsthand information. Sudan then used the presence of the second UN team to delay the vote until the very end of the session, by which time its diplomats had managed to weaken the text until it was virtually meaningless.

Over the past few years, governments hostile to human rights have formed a powerful block at the CHR, dubbed "the abusers club" by Human Rights Watch. Libya, Sudan, and Algeria have found natural allies in China, Cuba, and Russia, while South Africa has worked hard to ease pressure on Sudan and Zimbabwe. In 2003 Najjat Al-Hajjaji, ambassador of Libya, had chaired the commission. It was, for her, a most successful session: draft resolutions critical of Sudan and Zimbabwe were defeated, the post of UN investigator of human rights in Sudan was abolished, and a resolution on human rights in Palestine was passed "recalling particularly" General Assembly resolution 37/43 passed in December 1982, which sanctioned the use of "all available means, including armed struggle," for peoples faced with "colonial and foreign domination and foreign occupation." This was read as support for Palestinian suicide bombers.[4]

A draft resolution on sexuality, proposed by Brazil, highlighted the probably unbridgeable gulf between the West and the Middle East on some aspects of human rights. "The draft was very straightforward. It simply said that people who have a different sexual orientation from straights should not be persecuted. It was nothing revolutionary, but the Arab countries went ballistic," recalls Joanna Weschler, of Security Council Report, an independent UN think tank, who attended the 2003 session for Human Rights Watch. The resolution was repeatedly delayed by procedural maneuvers. "The Arab countries said that they needed to go to prayer, because it was a Friday. They spent half the day talking about that, and then they broke to pray. The vote was put off until next year, and by then the Arab countries had put enough economic pressure on Brazil that it never happened. It is incredibly frustrating to watch this, and it makes you very angry."

Zimbabwe, like Sudan, remained a member of the Human Rights Commission throughout 2005, despite its atrocious human rights record. In May 2005 President Mugabe ordered Operation Murambatsvina, meaning "drive out trash." The army and police launched a lightning demolition campaign across the country, razing homes and businesses and leaving 700,000 people with nowhere to work, eat, or sleep. The single biggest act of social destruction in Africa for years passed uncondemned by the Commission on Human Rights and the General Assembly, although Annan himself called it a "catastrophic in-

justice." Sudan's friends at the United Nations are not confined
to Africa and the Arab world. In November 2005, when Great
Britain introduced a draft resolution to the General Assembly's
third committee on human rights in North Korea, Sudan's
representative opposed it. He told the assembled diplomats
that Sudan was "following with great interest" North Korea's
efforts to "protect human rights." Sudan, he explained, would
vote against the draft resolution, as "the very fact of submitting
draft resolutions which target a specific country is politiciza-
tion, selectivity and double standards."[5]

The United Nations General Assembly and its satellite
organs have long proved reluctant to criticize human rights
abuses in the developing world. The leaders of the postcolonial
nations, while happy to help themselves to the Western aid that
keeps their citizens alive, can always be relied on to attack the
West's allies. Between 2003 and 2005, the country most criticized by various UN bodies was not Sudan, Iran, or Zimbabwe,
but Israel. According to statistics compiled by "Eye on the UN,"
a Web site reporting on the United Nations, in 2005 alone, 107
resolutions, decisions, draft resolutions, reports, and other measures were taken against the Jewish state, an average of more
than two a week. The United Nations is obsessed with Israel.
Israel was criticized by the General Assembly, the Economic
and Social Council, the Commission on Human Rights, the
International Labour Organization, the World Health Organization, the World Food Programme, the UN Scientific, Edu-
cational and Cultural Organization (UNESCO), the Security
Council, the Committee on the Exercise of the Inalienable Rights
of the Palestinian People, the Commission on the Status of
Women, and the Special Committee to Investigate Israeli Practices Affecting the Human Rights of the Palestinian People and
the Other Arabs of the Occupied Territories. Although Sudan

was the second-most-criticized country, with seventy mentions, there is no United Nations "Special Committee to Investigate Sudanese Practices Regarding the Ongoing Genocide in
Darfur." The Democratic Republic of Congo was third, with
forty-one mentions. The United States was tied for eighth.[6]
There are legitimate human rights issues in both Israel and the
Palestinian Territories (and in the United States), and scope,
too, for considered criticism of some of the Jewish state's actions and policies. But not to the extent of 107 censures a year,
nearly as many as were issued to Sudan and Congo combined.
For the one-party states and dictatorships that make up much
of the UN's membership, though, criticizing Israel is a useful,
if not essential, diversion from their own human rights records.

There are occasional reality checks. The best work on
human rights is done by the special rapporteurs, who chronicle
in detail, sometimes under dangerous conditions, the abuses
carried out by UN member states. Tadeusz Mazowiecki's reports are an invaluable contemporary record of the horrors of
the Bosnian war. Juan Méndez, the special rapporteur for the
prevention of genocide, has taken a strong and principled stand
on Darfur. But as long as the absurd spectacle of countries like
Libya and Sudan setting human rights policies continues, the
rapporteurs' investigations will simply be set aside. In one way
the Commission on Human Rights performs a valuable service for those pondering the long-term viability of the United
Nations in its current form. It highlights the profound contra-
diction of the United Nations' adjudicating on, or intervening
in, human rights issues when the abusers are its own members.
It also raises a wider issue: why are these states permitted to
join or remain members of the United Nations at all? Every
member state agrees to abide by the UN Charter and the Universal Declaration of Human Rights. Some UN human rights

officials argue that universal membership at least gives a basis for discussions. Governments that abuse human rights can be reminded of their obligations. But with no enforcement mechanism, these noble sentiments, and the United Nations itself, become ever more debased. The words that make up the United Nations founding documents become empty, depleted of all meaning. And as they wither, so do the very concepts they articulate.

When UN officials visited Sudan to discuss Darfur, they were treated with near-contempt, recalls a member of one delegation: "The Sudanese were in denial to a level that was almost insulting. Government ministers lied, or claimed they had published a report when no such report exists, or quoted documents that don't exist. They do not care. The only thing they care about is sanctions, because the government would collapse, as there is nothing to hold it together. But they know they will not be touched because they have oil contracts and the Security Council is blocked, and if I was that government, I would not care either." In April 2006 Khartoum even initially refused to allow Jan Egeland, the UN humanitarian chief, to enter the country, doubtless fearful of what he would discover in Darfur. The stated reason was that he might be in danger because a Norwegian newspaper had published some of the controversial cartoons of the Prophet Muhammad.

As long there is no linkage between membership in the United Nations and observance of human rights, Sudan has no reason to reform. Membership in the European Union (EU) provides a useful analogy. Before an applicant state is allowed to join, it must satisfy Brussels that it has met the necessary standards in a comprehensive range of issues, including human rights, the rule of law, a free press, an independent judiciary, democratic elections, and so on—in short, the basics of a modern, civilized society. This usually necessitates rewriting a myriad of laws, and only after Brussels is satisfied that its criteria have indeed been met is the applicant state allowed to join, and only then do the grants and loans start arriving.

For all its own faults, the EU has been *the* primary motor of change in postcommunist Europe, helping engineer the transition from dictatorship to democracy and functioning civil societies. Its rules must be adhered to, and in theory an EU member state that repeatedly flouts them can be expelled. Membership in the United Nations does not bring member states the same financial benefits as joining the EU. But it does bring several others. It confers legitimacy and prestige on those perpetrating human rights abuses, providing them with psychological and political succor and the plentiful company of kindred spirits. Inside the UN complex in New York, the world's tyrants are suddenly worthy interlocutors, their opinions sought by the superpowers, their egos massaged, their meetings with world leaders broadcast on their state-controlled television at home, their domestic political standing boosted, their opponents weakened.

Nor should personal factors be neglected. How more enjoyable is time spent in New York, with its shops and luxury hotels, than in Khartoum or Harare. The threat of losing all these privileges of membership could prove a useful weapon for human rights. But transferring the standards of the EU to the United Nations is rejected out of hand on the thirty-eighth floor. "You can follow this discussion in universities, but you have to be practical," scoffs one official close to Annan. "A United Nations where every country or state on the planet is more useful than one with different tiers of membership. Membership is membership, and you have to use this body here as a forum to deal with issues. If you exclude someone from the club, then you cannot expect them to discuss with you or follow the club rules. One should not oversimplify that issue."

When we chronicle the United Nations' failures in Rwanda, Bosnia, and Darfur, it is almost tempting to fall back on essentialist or theological explanations about the enduring power of evil, a force even more dangerous and resilient in a world of high-velocity weapons, mass transportation, and global communications. Evil does endure, as evinced by any cursory viewing of the night's television news, but there are those with the power, ability, and responsibility to prevent its triumph. The human factor is crucial. The United Nations failed to stop genocide in Rwanda, Bosnia, and Darfur not because of forces beyond its control but because both diplomats and Secretariat officials took specific decisions at certain times.

During the Bosnian war many sneered at Madeleine Albright behind the scenes, as she sometimes showed emotion over what was happening. As a refugee herself, Albright understood better than most the reality of ethnic cleansing. Yet somehow her human empathy was seen as a liability. There is a taboo at the United Nations against "getting emotional" about death and tragedy, says Ed Joseph, the former UNPROFOR official who urged that UN troops protect Bihać hospital. "From the time I first found myself in the war zone of Sarajevo in the summer of 1992," he wrote in the *Washington Post*, "I was stunned by the bland demurral that headquarters reflexively issued when we sought action from the peacekeepers: 'It's not in our mandate.'" But while there is some risk from rushing to judgment, there is a greater risk from exaggerated clinical objectivity. "Without a sense of guided outrage, of empathy for the victims of abuse," Joseph wrote, "organization staff, even human rights workers, are prone to 'move on' and accept it when bureaucracies shrug their shoulders." The interests of the UN, not the victims, all too often come first: "Unfortunately, senior UN officials still peddle the line that the Secretariat was merely the servant of a divided Security Council that failed to provide the UN with enough resources in Bosnia. In fact, the Secretariat independently resisted any use of force in Bosnia, including NATO airpower that could have more than compensated for shortfalls on the ground."[7]

Despite the three failures discussed in this book, arguably the world is more, not less, in need of the United Nations—a United Nations, and a Secretariat, dedicated to the organization's original aims: to resolve conflicts peacefully and prevent further genocides after the Second World War, its first priority a commitment to defend human rights, not its own interests. That will demand a massive shift in mentality. "The United Nations is not just a workplace. It is a mindset," says a US diplomat formerly stationed there. "It is not like NATO, an organization with a means to accomplish a specific end. Many of the people working there believe in the United Nations as something to make the world a better place. But what I saw during Bosnia was that the United Nations would rather be true to its principles of neutrality than get anything done. Its job was to apply Band-Aids rather than deal aggressively with the roots of the issue."

Yet the Secretariat takes its cues from the P5, including the United States. US diplomats may decry the DPKO's jealous guarding of the United Nations' neutrality—for example, Akashi's refusal to authorize air strikes against the Serbs—but US troops were deployed on the ground in Bosnia only once the fighting was over. Had President Clinton showed more steadfastness and confronted the Bosnian Serbs before late summer

1995, the Srebrenica massacre might never have happened. Great Britain and France at least put their soldiers in harm's way in Bosnia. The United States did not. It is easy to blame unelected UN officials when political leaders such as President Clinton lack the courage to take risks, their eyes always focused on domestic opinion polls. "Akashi does have to bear some responsibility for the debacle in Bosnia and the tragedy in Srebrenica," argues a former UNPFOFOR official. "But the governments of the time have a much greater responsibility than that which falls on his shoulders. He was acutely aware of the limitations of what he could do. Srebrenica did not occur in an obscure part of Africa, but in Europe in 1995, while twenty thousand troops were deployed there."

What the United Nations must do is revert to, and enforce, its founding principles. Even with its manifest failures, the United Nations is worth saving. Some sectors work very well. Its humanitarian and relief agencies have saved, and continue to save, millions of lives. The UN peacekeeping missions in Congo and Liberia, for example, stabilized and helped put those countries on the road to recovery. The Electoral Assistance Division and the UN Development Programme do valuable work building democracy in countries such as Afghanistan and Iraq. UN human rights investigators provide accounts of record of abuses, gathering evidence that can later be used to prosecute perpetrators. The UN tribunals for the former Yugoslavia and Rwanda have led to the establishment of the International Criminal Court and accelerated international criminal justice. Despots and dictators now presumably sleep a little less easily. Across the world, the blue United Nations flag still represents for many the ideals of its founding Charter. The United Nations' most important asset is what remains of its moral authority, but lack of any credible mechanism to ensure that its members respect human rights is steadily corroding that asset's worth.

The solution is that UN member states that fail to live up to the requirements of the UN Charter and the Universal Declaration on Human Rights should be sanctioned, suspended, and, in extreme cases, expelled. The threat of such actions would have an effect. Human rights abusers know that as long as they are accepted as part of the international community, they have little to fear. They are courted, flattered, asked to consider changing their ways. But why should they, as long as they remain UN member states in good standing? Realists will argue that it is unrealistic to expect the United Nations to ensure that every country observe every paragraph of international human rights law. Perhaps. But it is realistic to demand that the United Nations take action against member states that commit genocide, the most egregious crime against humanity. If it cannot, or will not, do this, then ultimately what is the point of the organization?

And member states should also understand that with the rights of UN membership come responsibilities, says Michael Williams, the former UNPROFOR spokesman who returned to the United Nations in 2004 as director of the Asia and Pacific division in the DPA. "Look at Darfur," he says. "India, Brazil, and Japan all want to be on the Security Council, but they are not playing a serious role here. Where are their peacekeepers in Darfur? Where is the Brazilian or the Indian brigade? You can castigate the Bush administration and western Europe, but at least they have a half-hearted commitment to enforcing international humanitarian law. With a large number of the other powers there is no commitment at all."

The lessons of Srebrenica and Rwanda a decade ago, of Darfur now, are that a crucial issue in reforming the United

Nations is to radically alter the relationship between the Secretariat, led by the secretary general, and the Security Council. The kinds of mistakes made by UN officials in New York and Zagreb during the final attack on Srebrenica and its aftermath, the excessive caution shown by Kofi Annan and Iqbal Riza over Rwanda, must never be repeated. It is true that the DPKO's job was not to function as UNPROFOR's command center but to serve the Security Council, so that it could respond with adequate information. But on those crucial days in early July 1995 the DPKO failed, says a senior former UNPROFOR official:

> Mission headquarters does not sit over the peacekeepers' shoulders and say they should do this or that. That is largely delegated to the field. But when the Secretariat was dealing with the Security Council, it did the wrong thing. The Americans on the Thursday, once OP Foxtrot had fallen, asked for a briefing to answer three questions: are the Serbs continuing to advance; are they continuing to fire; have there been requests for air strikes? The Secretariat answered on Monday. They fudged the first two and did not answer the last question of whether there had been requests, whereas in fact there had been five.

The United Nations is led from the top. The secretary general can, and should, draw on the organization's moral authority, its founding principles of international law, and its vast institutional memory of dealing with wars and crisis zones to proactively drive its response to genocide, instead of waiting for the Security Council to make its decisions. This exact power is granted by article 99 of the UN Charter, which specifies that the secretary general "may bring to the attention of the Security Council any matter which in his opinion may threaten the maintenance of international peace and security."

The three crises examined in this book show that an issue's being on the Council's agenda is no guarantee that the United Nations will take meaningful action. But a United Nations led by a secretary general who sets the agenda, who does not pander to the interests of the P5, and who returns the Secretariat to the United Nations' founding humanitarian principles, could reinvent the organization as a force for much greater good. Annan's spokesman, Stéphane Dujarric, says that this is already happening and rejects criticisms that Annan had not been robust enough on Darfur. In an e-mail to the author he argued that Annan had repeatedly tried to raise public awareness and had pushed for stronger action both in the Security Council and in the international community. Annan had been involved in deploying the AU force in Darfur, the planning for a transition to a UN peacekeeping force, and the UN's ICI on Darfur.[8] All this is true, but Annan did not make his first public statement on Darfur until December 2003, nine months into the crisis.

And for human rights activists Annan and the Secretariat have not been proactive enough. "If the Security Council members are not going to change their calculations much, then the one variable is how dynamic and confrontational the Secretariat will be in making the case for more aggressive action," says John Prendergast of the International Crisis Group. "I think Annan really cares about Darfur, but is that going to get us anything? No. He should be using the moral high ground, generating ideas, saying, 'Look, this is what we can do, what needs to be done by the Security Council, NATO, the EU, the AU,' to get them together and say how are we going to build a relevant force. Of course if he was really radical, he would be a one-term secretary general, so it is a question of personal courage, of taking a stand."

All politics is about the room for maneuver, says David Harland, head of the DPKO's Best Practices Unit, which synthesizes the lessons learned from each mission for future deployments. This principle is perhaps especially true in the United Nations, where so many vested interests compete for power and influence, from rival departments of the Secretariat to the P5. "As soon as you have that space, do you move toward confrontation, force it onto the agenda, and push the pace?" Harland asks. "Or do you stay passive and say it will all be better if the problems went away? At Srebrenica we may have erred on that side." When faced with a human rights crisis, the United Nations needs to draw a line in the sand, which, if crossed, will trigger consequences, Harland argues. Without clear guidance on how to respond to the Serb assault, Dutchbat resembled a lobster getting boiled one degree at a time. "There was no trip wire at Srebrenica for air attacks on the Serbs. But there are moral imperatives to take action when something bad is happening, and we have got to say we are going to do this. We should have forced a crisis."

Among the disastrous confluence of events around Srebrenica, from the Bosnian battlefield to the capitals of the great powers, there is also a clear United Nations chain of responsibility, argues a former UNPROFOR official: "From Captain Groen on the ground, to Colonel Karremans and Major Franken at Potočari, to Colonel Brantz at Tuzla, to General Janvier and Akashi in Zagreb, to Shashi Tharoor and Kofi Annan in New York and the members of the Security Council, if at any point, somebody had said, 'This doesn't make sense at all,' and if at any point they had sent the order down, from any one of those levels, that you will hold your ground and we will bring maximum resources to bear, it is quite likely that seventy-seven hundred people would still be alive."

There is no red line, no trip wire, but there is a set routine at the United Nations after each failure to stop genocide. Once the platitudes have faded away, a report is commissioned to find out what went wrong, or what is still going wrong. The United Nations inquiries into Rwanda, Srebrenica, and Darfur are thorough and comprehensive works of record, full of invaluable detail. They comprehensively highlight the organization's failures of policy, process, and response. But despite these catastrophic failures, no one is ever held accountable for mistakes.

Instead, as we have seen, those responsible are frequently promoted. "It is a much debated question here whether officials should be called to account in some judicial or at least administrative process," says David Harland.

> Opponents say no, because then nobody will contribute to peacekeeping missions if we get into the blame game. But the lack of accountability is convenient. There is this endless Ping-Pong game between the Secretariat and the member states. The states blame the Secretariat for making mistakes, and they blame the member states for a lack of political will. Are those people from the Dutchbat officers on the ground up the chain of command to the Security Council responsible for what happened at Srebrenica? Responsible in the sense of a causal link, that the victims might be alive if they had taken

other decisions, then the answer is yes. I think that
a degree of accountability would strengthen the
system rather than weaken it.

Mukesh Kapila argues the case even more strongly: "Why has
nobody in the Secretariat or the foreign ministries of the
world's most powerful nations lost their jobs because of the
failure in Darfur? It is only when individuals are held accountable for what they fail to do—despite good knowledge of what
they have to do—that we will really be able to say 'never again'
to genocide."

Battered over human rights and growing calls for radical
reform—especially by the United States, which pays 22 percent
of the United Nations' budget—Annan had high hopes for the
UN summit in September 2005. But the world's attention was
distracted by the scandal over the UN's Oil-for-Food Programme. After Iraq invaded Kuwait in 1990, it was subject to
severe sanctions, but in 1996 it was allowed to sell oil to buy
food and medicines. The UN oversaw the scheme, which eventually reached $64 billion in oil sales and $37 billion in pur-
chases for Iraq.[9] The combination of vast sums of money, a
Middle Eastern dictator, lax oversight, and international oil interests had predictable results. The program head, Benon Sevan,
resigned after being accused of taking kickbacks, while Kojo
Annan, son of Kofi, concealed the length and depth of his relationship with an inspection company that had won a UN
contract worth $10 million. Sevan denied any wrongdoing. Ac-
cording to Kojo's lawyer, Kojo acknowledged that he had not
been completely candid with his father.

Kofi Annan himself was accused not of corruption but

of lax oversight. On 22 April 2004, the day after the Security Council authorized its investigation into Oil-for-Food, Iqbal Riza, Annan's chief of staff, ordered that three years' worth of files on the program be shredded. Riza said that the files were duplicates. Other international figures named in the report included Jean-Bernard Mérimée, the French ambassador to the UN who had worked with David Hannay to draft the UN resolutions on the safe areas. Mérimée was accused of receiving more than $160,000 in commissions from oil allocations granted to him by the Iraqi regime.

The September 2005 United Nations summit brought together 170 leaders. Annan presented a series of reform proposals, addressing the crucial issues facing the UN: expansion of the membership of the Security Council; a definition of terrorism; creation of a Peacebuilding Commission to stop post-conflict states from collapsing into war again; various management reforms; the halt of weapons proliferation; and the formation of a new human rights council, to replace the deeply discredited Commission on Human Rights. The most complicated and important issue was humanitarian intervention. Scarred by his experiences at the DPKO during Bosnia and Rwanda, Annan thought hard about how to balance the UN Charter's commitment to states' sovereignty against protection of human rights. He had convened a high-level panel to consider this dilemma. The panel acknowledged that the United Nations had failed to prevent crimes against humanity. It drew on the Brahimi report and proposed a new and potentially extremely significant interpretation of the United Nations' role: that it *was* mandated to safeguard civilian populations, despite nations' sovereignty. Annan proposed that the UN adopt a new principle, the "responsibility to protect," as a basis for collective action against genocide, war crimes, and crimes against humanity. In the last resort, this might include military action, under chapter VII.

Overall, the summit was not a success. It highlighted the impossibility of getting 191 states to agree on anything except the most anodyne proposals. Annan put a brave face on the fudges and compromises that finally emerged. No plans could be agreed on to reform the Security Council after the African Union blocked proposals from India, Brazil, Japan, and Germany. Terrorism was "strongly condemned" but remained undefined after the developing world and the Arab bloc pushed for an exemption for "the legitimate right of peoples under foreign occupation to struggle for their independence"— a coded expression of support for the insurgents in Iraq and Palestinian suicide bombers. There was no agreement on whether the new Peacebuilding Commission should be managed by the Security Council or the General Assembly, no agreement on weapons proliferation. A proposal to transfer some of the General Assembly's authority to the Secretariat also failed. The Summit did agree on "responsibility to protect."[10] The principle was now established, but that was no guarantee of implementation, says David Hannay, who sat on Annan's high-level panel: "I am a strong supporter of this, but can we make it work? The most likely place for this to happen is Africa, which means the Africans have to get better at preventing these situations, and outsiders have to provide more assistance. Not just the EU but countries like India. If the government of Sudan had believed this might happen, the Janjaweed might never have been unleashed."

The push for reform of the Commission on Human Rights, did eventually bear some fruit. In March 2006 the General Assembly voted to replace the commission with a new Human Rights Council (HRC). Candidates for membership will have to make commitments to human rights and persuade a majority of the 191 member states to vote for them in a secret ballot. Once elected, HRC members will have to cooperate with the Council's investigations and will be scrutinized by their peers. States that commit human rights violations can be suspended. But critics pointed out that the only criteria for candidacy for the HRC are geographical, with a certain number of seats allocated to different regions. There is no enforcement mechanism to ensure that a stated "commitment" to human rights will be respected. The results of the first elections to the council in May 2006 received a cautious welcome from human rights organizations as the "abusers club" was significantly diminished, although Cuba, China, Saudi Arabia, Pakistan, and Russia all won seats. Iran did not. Libya, Sudan, Syria, and Zimbabwe did not stand for election.

As for peacekeeping, despite the Brahimi report and "responsibility to protect," little has changed in practice, argues one UN human rights official: "Every peacekeeping mission now has a standard paragraph in its mandate, saying the peacekeepers are obliged to protect civilians at risk and not only themselves when they are at risk. This is the institutional lesson, but it remains on a formal level. Member states do not yet understand and have not internalized what it actually means to go into a country and claim responsibility for that situation." In Darfur the discussions about new mandates promising robust peacekeeping and protection of civilians mean nothing until UN troops are actually deployed with a robust mandate, the official argues, one still denied AMIS. "The AU troops monitor cease-fires and violations and write reports, exactly as

UNPROFOR did. They have a paragraph they should protect civilians, but it does not go so far to say they should intervene directly if they see something is happening."

Far from the UN complex in New York, far from the Secretariat's nuanced deliberations, survivors of genocide now endure a kind of living death themselves, seeking the strength to carry on under the weight of unbearable grief. A protected witness identified only as DD, who lost her husband and two of her three sons at Srebrenica, testified at the trial of General Krstić in July 2000. She told the court that every morning when she wakes up she covers her eyes so as not to see the neighbors' children going to school. The memories of her own lost family are too painful. "As a mother, I still have hope," she said. "I still can't believe that this is true. How is it possible that a human being could do something like this, could destroy everything, could kill so many people? Just imagine this youngest boy I had, those little hands of his. How could they be dead? I imagine those hands picking strawberries, reading books, going to school, going on excursions." Her voice cracked as she spoke, and she broke down in tears.[11]

A torn family photograph in the fields of eastern Bosnia, bones bleached white in the dust of Darfur—these remnants of lives lost sumbolize the human cost of the United Nations' failures to stop genocide. The pattern seems set and unbreakable. If and when the United Nations commissions an inquiry into its failure in Darfur, whole paragraphs of its report on Srebrenica could be pasted in: "Nor was the provision of humanitarian aid a sufficient response to 'ethnic cleansing' and to an attempted genocide. The provision of food and shelter to people who have neither is wholly admirable, and we must all recognise the extraordinary work done by UNHCR and its partners in conditions of extreme adversity, but the provision of humanitarian assistance could never have been a solution to the problem in that country."[12] The words of Tadeusz Mazowiecki, former UN special rapporteur on human rights, who resigned after the Srebrenica massacre, are as true now as when he wrote them in August 1995: "One cannot speak about the protection of human rights with credibility when one is confronted with the lack of consistency and courage displayed by the international community and its leaders. The reality of the human rights situation today is illustrated by the people of Srebrenica and Zepa."[13]

Not far from the White House and the seats of the US government is the United States Holocaust Museum. The visitor is given a card with a photograph and brief biography of a Holocaust victim to read as he or she progresses through the museum, the better to grasp the human story of one of the six million. The museum is now an almost compulsory stop for visiting international politicians. But even those not cynical by nature may suspect that remembering the dead of the Holocaust can prove a most useful alibi for not stopping more deaths in Darfur.

The vanished Jewish communities of eastern Europe are memorialized in sepia photographs, faded journals, and scratchy black-and-white newsreels. These aged media bring an almost reassuring distance to the horrors they record. That was then, but this is now. But now is also Srebrenica, Rwanda, and Darfur. The information age brings us live, real-time genocide. Part of the video of the Scorpions executing their prisoners can be seen on the Internet.[14] Television brought the news of Azmir Alispahić's death to his mother, Nura, in June 2005. Copies had been made of the video recording of the Scorpions executing the men and boys. All but one had been recalled. It was tracked down by Nataša Kandić, a Serbian human rights activist, who released it to the media and the ICTY. Extracts were shown on Bosnian television. That evening Nura Alispahić witnessed what no mother should ever have to see: a broadcast of her son's murder: "I turned on the television to watch the news and at that very moment this video was shown. I thought some mother will now recognize her son and some sister her brother. And then I realized it was my own son on the video. My son and another man were told to remove four men who had been executed first. I saw him briefly looking to the left, like he was asking for help. And at that moment he was shot."[15]

Nobody who wants to know what happened at Srebrenica, in Rwanda, or in Darfur can now say that they do not. Perhaps one day, not far from the US Holocaust Museum, there will be a museum commemorating the Darfur genocide. The visitor may be handed a small card with a photograph and brief biography of someone who once lived in Darfur and may have the opportunity to trace the victim's great trek from her destroyed home village to a refugee camp in Chad. The museum's display cases might contain crumpled boxes of UN relief aid; a scale for weighing starving babies; maps of the old trade routes that crisscrossed the province; a burned-down grain silo; framed Security Council resolutions; transcripts of speeches by Kofi Annan and George Bush; the provisions of the Naivasha accords; an AK-47; a recording of Mukesh Kapila's interview with the BBC *Today* program; the wing of an Antonov transport plane; even a Janjaweed uniform.

In April 2006 the Security Council passed resolution 1672, which finally imposed sanctions on Sudanese leaders accused of war crimes in Darfur, more than a year after resolution 1591 had ordered an assets freeze and travel ban for human rights violators. Resolution 1672 barely covered one side of a sheet of paper. It named just four people, only two of whom were government officials or proxy allies: the military commander for western Sudan and the notorious Janjaweed leader Sheikh Musa Hilal. The other two were rebel commanders. Once again, it seems, "all sides are guilty." Great Britain and the US had pushed for a much longer list but could get agreement only for these four. China, Russia, and Qatar abstained. This resolution, and the referral of fifty-one names to the ICC, was the sum total of direct punitive action authorized by the Security Council against Sudanese officials and their allies responsible for the genocide in Darfur.

By early summer 2006, more than three years after the Janjaweed launched their first raids, discussions of Darfur still continued in the DPKO, the DPA, and the Security Council, in Washington, London, and Paris and at NATO headquarters. It seemed inevitable that AMIS would be brought under the command of the United Nations, and the AU's mission would be transformed into a UN peacekeeping force. Spurred by large demonstrations—and a well-publicized trip to Darfur by the actor George Clooney—the Bush administration again found its voice. There was talk of deploying twenty thousand UN troops, supported by NATO. But with so much to discuss about the practicalities of this, and the complicated political and diplomatic realities, Khartoum has nothing to fear for a long time yet.

Appendix

The following are the texts of three UN documents, one concerning each of the three crises I have examined in the book. Document 1 is Yasushi Akashi's cable to Kofi Annan, dated 8 May 1995, outlining his reasons for refusing to authorize air strikes against the Bosnian Serbs after Sarajevo was shelled. Document 2 is General Roméo Dallaire's cable to the DPKO, dated 11 January 1994, asking for permission to raid Hutu arms caches and for protection for his informant inside the Hutu militia. Document 3 is Dr. Mukesh Kapila's special note to Iqbal Riza, dated 22 March 2004, for the attention of Kofi Annan, outlining the extent of human rights abuses and calling for the UN to take firmer action on Darfur. Spelling and punctuation of the originals have been preserved; capitalization has been regularized for the Dallaire cable, which was transmitted in all uppercase letters.

Document 1

1. At approximately 13:30 local time yesterday (07 May) afternoon, several mortar or artillery rounds fell in the vicinity of the entrance to the tunnel running under the Sarajevo airport

on the Butmir (south) side of the runway. Reports vary, but we believe that 10 people were killed and between 10 and 15 injured, a mixture of military personnel and civilians. No UN personnel were injured or killed. The firing is attributable to the Bosnian Serb army. UNPROFOR is prevented from conducting a proper investigation of yesterday's incident due to BSA threats to target any U.N. vehicle that approaches the area where the shells landed. As a result of this attack, General Smith has recommended that NATO carry-out an air-strike; the attack is considered, *inter alia,* a violation of SCR 836 (1993) and the NAC Sarajevo decision of 9 February 1994. At this point, based on the recommendation of the Force Commander, the Deputy Force Commander, and others, I have decided that we should not at present proceed with the request for an air-strike. My decision is subject to constant review.

2. In a meeting this morning with my senior military and civilian staff, the negative ramifications of responding to the attack by an air-strike were discussed at length. In addition to the normal concerns raised in such circumstances (U.N. hostages, blockage of convoys, supply problems to the enclaves . . .), a number of other considerations relevant to the present situation were considered. Our greatest concern was the possibility that an air-strike now would de-rail the stabilization process begun in Croatia, undermine the moderates in the Knin leadership. encourage adventurism on the part of Martic and Karadzic, and weaken Milosevic, rendering the possibility of the FRY recognizing Bosnia and/or Croatia more remote. We assumed that an air-strike would also force a break in negotiations with the Bosnian Serbs on the Sarajevo airport, and would likely bring about an indefinite rupture in UNPROFOR's relations with them. Were the United Nations to request an air-strike in

response to the entirely unacceptable though relatively limited shelling of Sarajevo, just days after the Croatian army overran Sector West without physical resistance by UNCRO, our credibility as an impartial force with the Serbs in Bosnia and Croatia could suffer irreparable harm, notwithstanding the different U.N. roles in the two situations. The fact that the Bosnian government refused to accept the proposed extension of the COHA [cessation of hostilities agreement] was also raised at the meeting. Lastly, from a purely technical perspective, the actual firing piece has so far not been identified, though we recognize that our inability to do so does not preclude the possibility of requesting an air-strike on other targets violating the exclusion zone.

3. In favor of air strikes, we noted that the BSA could be engaged in a deliberate game of provocation against the United Nations that will only get worse until we take action in response; however, this approach requires that we be prepared for the possibility of BSA escalation if we are to respond to their provocations. An air-strike could also perhaps assist Milosevic in showing the folly of Karadzic's chosen path of confrontation with the international community. Lastly, with the airport at minimum operations already, its closure subsequent to an air-strike would not make a substantial difference to our already degraded operations in Sarajevo.

4. Weighing carefully the above considerations, I have decided not to proceed further at this time. It should be noted that, as no U.N. personnel were injured or put at close risk by the attack, there was no consideration of using Close Air Support. Since the attack, however, there has been continued intermittent shelling of Sarajevo, with a particularly heavy round of

shelling from about midnight to 02:00 and then some more rounds later in the morning (local time). There are no reports on casualties yet. The Force Commander is in close touch with General Smith in Sarajevo, and the situation will be closely monitored and continually re-assessed. I will keep you fully informed, and consult with you as and when necessary.

5. I have attached a two page message sent to me by General Smith on the subject. [Attachment not included here.]

Document 2

1. Force commander put in contact with informant by very very important government politician. Informant is a top level trainer in the cadre of Interhamwe-armed militia of MRND.

2. He informed us he was in charge of last Saturdays demonstrations which aims were to target deputies of opposition parties coming to ceremonies and Belgian soldiers. They hoped to provoke the RPF BN to engage (being fired upon) the demonstrators and provoke a civil war. Deputies were to be assassinated upon entry or exit from Parliament. Belgian troops were to be provoked and if Belgians soldiers resorted to force a number of them were to be killed and thus guarantee Belgian withdrawal from Rwanda.

3. Informant confirmed 48 RGF PARA CDO and a few members of the gendarmerie participated in demonstrations in plain clothes. Also at least one minister of the MRND and the sous-prefect of Kigali were in the demonstration. RGF and Interhamwe provided radio communications.

4. Informant is a former security member of the president. He also stated he is paid RF150,000 per month by the MRND party

to train Interhamwe. Direct link is to chief of staff RGF and president of the MRND for financial and material support.

5. Interhamwe has trained 1700 men in RGF military camps outside the capital. The 1700 are scattered in groups of 40 throughout Kigali. Since UNAMIR deployed he has trained 300 personnel in three week training sessions at RGF camps. Training focus was discipline, weapons, explosives, close combat and tactics.

6. Principal aim of Interhamwe in the past was to protect Kigali from RPF. Since UNAMIR mandate he has been ordered to register all Tutsi in Kigali. He suspects it is for their extermination. Example he gave was that in 20 minutes his personnel could kill up to 1000 Tutsis.

7. Informant states he disagrees with anti-Tutsi extermination. He supports opposition to RPF but cannot support killing of innocent persons. He also stated that he believes the president does not have full control over all elements of his old party/faction.

8. Informant is prepared to provide location of major weapons cache with at least 135 weapons. He already has distributed 110 weapons including 35 with ammunition and can give us details of their location. Type of weapons are G3 and AK47 provided by RGF. He was ready to go to the arms cache tonight—if we gave him the following guarantee. He requests that he and his family (his wife and four children) be placed under our protection.

9. It is our intention to take action within the next 36 hours with a possible H hr of Wednesday at dawn (local). Informant states that hostilities may commence again if political dead-

lock ends. Violence could take place day of the ceremonies or the day after. Therefore Wednesday will give greatest chance of success and also be most timely to provide significant input to on-going political negotiations.

10. It is recommended the informant be granted protection and evacuated out of Rwanda. This HQ does not have previous UN experience in such matters and urgently requests guidance. No contact has as yet been made to any embassy in order to inquire if they are prepared to protect him for a period of time by granting diplomatic immunity in their embassy in Kigali before moving him and his family out of the country.

11. Force commander will be meeting with the very very important political person tomorrow morning in order to ensure that this individual is conscious of all parameters of his involvement. Force commander does have certain reservations on the suddenness of the change of heart of the informant to come clean with this information. Recce of armed cache and detailed planning of raid to go on late tomorrow. Possibility of a trap not fully excluded, as this may be a set-up against the very very important political person. Force commander to inform SRSG first thing in morning to ensure his support.

13. Peux ce que veux. Allons-y.

Document 3

1. I would be grateful if you could please draw this Note to the personal attention of the Secretary-General.

2. It is my sad duty to advise the Secretary-General of my considered view that the crisis in the Greater Darfur Region contin-

ues to deteriorate to the point that it may now be characterized as "ethnic cleansing". This conclusion is based on information from UN staff and other credible humanitarian observers in the field as well as eye witness testimonies of local people drawn to our attention (some of the latter have been detained or otherwise seriously harassed by the authorities after talking to us).

3. Salient relevant observations are as follows:
- There appears to be a systematic campaign of oppression including large scale armed violence and incidents of murder, rape, torture and abduction directed specifically against populations of black African tribal origin directed by the Arab militia known as the Jinjaweed.
- This is accompanied by the systemic forced displacement of populations of black African tribal origin manifested through the organized burning and destruction of their villages and homes, and akin to a deliberate "scorched earth" policy.
- The organization of the above programs appears to display features of a command-and-control structure demonstrating pre-meditation and planning from a higher level of a policy of extreme violence that is specifically targeted at African tribes. The term "zurka-free areas" (derogatively translated by locals as "nigger free") has been applied by interlocutors in the Darfur Region as the explicitly stated objective of those responsible for the violence.

4. Other contextual information is as follows. Overall, we estimate that at least one million of the six million population in the Darfur Region are directly affected by the violence (including 110,000 refugees and some 600,000–700,000 IDPs), with wider consequences touching almost everyone in Greater Darfur and increasingly other parts of the Sudan. For example,

violent relocation of Darfurian IDPs in Khartoum as well as forced conscription of civilians into the Armed Forces is reported from many places. The Jinjaweed are reported to receive military assistance and direction from sympathetic elements within the structures of the Government of Sudan (GoS), with indications that GoS military campaigns (including air assets) have taken place in joint orchestration. Individuals in responsible positions of authority have been named to us as being implicated and are therefore open to charges of war crimes. The ICRC has been refused consent to operate freely in the region. UN-Sudan humanitarian programmes in Greater Darfur are only able to inch forward with very modest improvements because they continue to be obstructed by the GoS Ministry of Humanitarian Affairs. This is done in various ways including lengthy delays in granting clearances for essential equipment and staff, severely limiting our capacity to function on the ground in accordance with our Minimum Operating Security Standards. This has a direct bearing on the international community's ability to provide humanitarian assistance in a consistent and meaningful manner. We have brought these concerns to the attention of the GoS on numerous occasions, to little avail.

5. There is considerable backing for the above observations from the international community including key concerned Member States, NGOs and civil society organizations. There is concern—which I have echoed publicly—that the situation in Darfur is reminiscent of the earlier period of the crisis in Rwanda, which ultimately progressed to genocide because of lack of timely recognition of the problem and action by the international community.

6. *Recommendations* for the Secretary-General include more urgent efforts to bring the conflicting parties together to agree

on an internationally monitored ceasefire, a UN OHCHR mandate to include protection of civilians in the Sudan, advocacy for unobstructed humanitarian access for the UN and our implementing partners, and the offer of a humanitarian briefing to the Security Council. The UN may also like to develop a position as and when there are calls made by others in the international community for the perpetrators of the ethnic cleansing policy to be brought to justice—in line with similar recent accountability efforts in other situations.

Notes

Each direct quotation not otherwise cited is drawn from the author's interview with the quoted source.

INTRODUCTION

1. Maass, *Love Thy Neighbor*, 170. See also Maass, "UN Keepers of the Siege."

2. Amended Indictment, 2 December 1997, against Mile Mrkšić, Miroslav Radić, Veselin Šljivančanin, and Slavko Dokmanović. ICTY.

3. Coalition for International Justice, "New Analysis Claims Darfur Deaths Near 400,000," press release, 21 April 2005.

4. Rafael Lemkin, *Axis Rule in Occupied Europe: Laws of Occupation, Analysis of Government, Proposals for Redress* (Washington, D.C., 1944), 79–95. This chapter can be found at http://www.preventgenocide.org/lemkin/AxisRule1944-1.htm

5. Goulding, *Peacemonger*, 121.

6. "UK 'Spied on UN's Kofi Annan,'" BBC News online, 26 February 2004, http://news.bbc.co.uk/2/hi/uk_news/politics/3488548.stm

CHAPTER 1. A SAFE AREA

Epigraph. Interview with Slobodan Milošević, *Death of Yugoslavia* television series transcripts 3/54, Liddell Hart Centre for Military Archives, Kings College, London.

1. Goulding, *Peacemonger*, 308. Asked about his memories of Milan Babić, Sir Marrack replied: "I stand by what I said then. I *did* like him and admire his qualities *at that time*. Subsequent events and revelations showed that my judgement of him had been wrong. But the sentence you quote describes what I thought about him at that first encounter; please don't ask me to re-write history." E-mail to author, 19 April 2006.

2. Ajami, "Mark of Bosnia."

3. Tom Gjelten, "Siege," n.d., www.crimesofwar.org/thebook/siege.html

4. Gjelten, "Professionalism in War Reporting."

5. Cited in Sudetic, *Blood and Vengeance*, 242.

CHAPTER 2. MASTER DRAFTERS

Epigraph. Author interview.

1. Interview with Warren Christopher, *Face the Nation*, CBS-TV, 28 March 1993.

2. Lewis Mackenzie, e-mail to author, 9 February 2006.

3. Leonard Doyle, "Muslims 'Slaughter Their Own People,'" *Independent*, 22 August 1992.

4. General Mackenzie recalls: "I was skeptical due to the circumstances reported to us by our duty officers in Sarajevo during my short hiatus back in Belgrade. Probably the most compelling factor is the fact that there is not a mortar crew in the world that could fire a single bomb from an area weapon—not a pinpoint weapon—and hit a specific street in a built up area. At the time the criminal elements on all sides were making a killing and perpetuating the conflict was high on their priority list—they too could have been involved. The side with most to lose from such an attack were the Serbs but nevertheless my comment was—'We will never know.'" E-mail to author, 9 February 2006.

5. Shawcross, *Deliver Us from Evil*, 42.

6. Rose, *Fighting for Peace*, 26.

7. Quoted ibid., 152.

CHAPTER 3. COUNTDOWN

Epigraph. Shashi Tharoor, confidential memo to Kofi Annan and Yasushi Akashi on the future of UNPROFOR, 6 December 1994. David Rohde collection. OSA archive, Budapest. HU OSA 337.

1. Netherlands Institute for War Documentation (NIOD), *Srebrenica*, part II, chapter 8, "Dutchbat in the Enclave," /www.srebrenica.nl/en/

2. Ibid.

3. Honig and Both, *Srebrenica*, 119.

4. Suljagic, *Postcards from the Grave*, 50.

5. UN Civil Affairs Srebrenica Trip Report, September 1994, unsigned. David Rohde collection. OSA archive, Budapest. HU OSA 337.

6. Quoted in NIOD, *Srebrenica*.

7. UN Civil Affairs Srebrenica Trip Report.

8. See also Vulliamy, "How the CIA Intercepted SAS Signals."

9. General Rose, e-mail to author, 10 February 2006.

10. Ibid.

11. Yasushi Akashi, e-mail to author, 14 April 2006.

12. Tharoor memo to Annan and Akashi.

13. Quoted in Simms, *Unfinest Hour*, 326.

14. Shelling in Sarajevo; Possible Use of Air-Strikes, cable, Akashi to Annan, 8 May 1995. David Rohde collection. OSA archive, Budapest. HU OSA 337.

15. Letter from Kofi Annan to Yasushi Akashi, 9 May 1995, with copy of 8 May letter from Muhamed Sacirbey. David Rohde collection. OSA archive, Budapest. HU OSA 337.

CHAPTER 4. THE FALL

Epigraph. Cable sent at 4:06 P.M. Monday, 10 July 1995, from UNHCR Srebrenica to UNHCR offices. David Rohde collection. OSA archive, Budapest. HU OSA 337.

1. I have drawn on *The Fall of Srebrenica*, the United Nations' 1999 report, for many of the details of the final assault included in this chapter.

2. Rohde, *Safe Area*, 28.

3. United Nations, "Fall of Srebrenica," 64, ¶282.

4. Cable from Akashi to Annan, Z-1130, 11 July 1995. David Rohde collection. OSA archive, Budapest. HU OSA 337.

5. Rohde, *Safe Area*, 193.

6. Gutman and Bruce, "How Troop-Hostage Talks Led to the Slaughter of Srebrenica." The authors quote an aide to General Janvier: "We were the supplicants. Janvier proposed the meeting, Janvier proposed the deal."

7. Roy Gutman and Cabell Bruce, *Srebrenica: A Bosnian Betrayal*, documentary telecast on Great Britain's Channel 4, May 1996.

8. Record of 9 June meeting between Yasushi Akashi, General Smith and General Janvier. David Rohde collection. OSA archive, Budapest. HU OSA 337.

9. Current Situation in BiH, cable from Annan to Akashi No. 1981, 15 June 1995. David Rohde collection. OSA archive, Budapest. HU OSA 337.

10. Cable from Akashi to New York, Z-1141, 12 July 1995. David Rohde collection. OSA archive, Budapest. HU OSA 337.

11. Gutman, "Big Atrocity."

CHAPTER 5. RECENTLY DISTURBED EARTH

Epigraph. Quoted in Rohde, *Safe Area*, 334.

1. Albright presentation to UN Security Council, 10 August 1995. David Rohde archive, OSA, Budapest. HU OSA 337. For further reading on what the United States knew of the massacres in Bosnia, and when, see Lane and Shanker, "Bosnia," and Wiebes, *Intelligence and the War in Bosnia*, 313–48.

2. Human Rights Watch, *Fall of Srebrenica*, 20.

3. United Nations, "Fall of Srebrenica," 78, ¶349.

4. Trial of General Radislav Krstić, ICTY, 31 March 2000, testimony of Colonel Joseph Kingori, http://www.un.org/icty/transe33/000331it.htm

5. Roy Gutman and Cabell Bruce, *Srebrenica: A Bosnian Betrayal*, documentary telecast on Great Britain's Channel 4, May 1996.

6. "Bosnia: A Criminal's Confession," *Le Figaro*, 8 March 1996.

7. Dražen Erdemović, testimony to the ICTY, Friday, 5 July 1996. http://www.un.org/icty/transe5&18/960705it.htm

8. Transcript of Erdemović trial, 5 July 1996, ibid.

9. Suzana Šašic, "Mladić's Monster Finally Talks," *Slobodan Bosna*, 1 September 2005, based on an interview with an unnamed former member of the 10th Sabotage Unit. English translation provided by the London-based Bosnian Institute, www.bosnia.org.uk

10. Browning, *Ordinary Men*.

11. Confidential cable from US UN Mission to US embassies, State Department, etc., 15 July 1995 (declassified).

12. Confidential cable from US Embassy Zagreb to State Department, US embassies, etc., 14 July 1995 (declassified).

13. United Nations, "Fall of Srebrenica," 82, ¶375.

14. Ibid., 85, ¶390.

15. "Pax Americana," *The Death of Yugoslavia* television series, episode six. Liddell Hart Centre for Military Archives, Kings College, London.

16. Operation Deliberate Force was also authorized by the North Atlantic Council decisions of 25 July and 1 August 1995, which were endorsed by Boutros-Ghali.

CHAPTER 6. SILENCE IN THE SECRETARIAT

Epigraph. Author interview.

1. De Waal, "Counter-Insurgency on the Cheap."

2. Thesiger, *Life of My Choice*, 212.

3. Human Rights Watch, *Darfur Documents Confirm*.

4. Thesiger, *Life of My Choice*, 186.

5. McDoom, "Accused Darfur Militia Leader."

6. Quoted in Karl, "Darfur Disaster."

7. Human Rights Watch, "Exclusive Video Interview."

8. United Nations, "Report of the International Commission of Inquiry on Darfur," 74, ¶272.

9. Ibid., 75, ¶274.

10. Power, "Dying in Darfur."

11. Testimony at "Genocide in Bosnia-Herzegovina," a hearing before the Commission on Security and Cooperation in Europe, Washington, D.C., 4 April 1995.

12. Quoted in Human Rights Watch, "Sexual Violence and Its Consequences," 10–11.

13. United Nations, "Report of the International Commission of Inquiry on Darfur," 90, ¶344.

14. Ibid., 92, ¶348.

15. Human Rights Watch, "Sexual Violence and Its Consequences," 6.

16. United Nations, "Report of the International Commission of Inquiry on Darfur," 94, ¶353.

17. Mukesh Kapila, Note to Mr. Egeland and Mr. Prendergast: Political and Security Update on Darfur, Sudan, 18 December 2003.

CHAPTER 7. A RWANDAN REPRISE

Epigraph. "UN Chief's Rwanda Genocide Regret," BBC News online, 26 March 2004, http://news.bbc.co.uk/2/hi/africa/3573229.stm

1. Shawcross, *Deliver Us From Evil*, 191.

2. Mukesh Kapila, Note to Mr. Riza: Sudan: Ethnic Cleansing in Darfur, 22 March 2004.

3. I have drawn on the introduction to the UN report on the Rwandan genocide.

4. Gourevitch, *We Wish to Inform You*, 104.

5. Willum, "Legitimizing Inaction," 8.

6. Barnett, *Eyewitness to Genocide*, 7.

7. Quoted in Willum, "Legitimizing Inaction," 7.

8. Ibid., 10.

9. Kofi Annan, "Action Plan to Prevent Genocide," speech to UN Commission on Human Rights, 7 April 2004.

10. Colin Keating, "An Insider's Account," in Malone, *UN Security Council*, 501.

11. Confidential cable from US Department of State to US UN Mission, "Talking Points on UNAMIR Withdrawal," 15 April 1994 (declassified 4 May 2000), http://www.gwu.edu/~nsarchiv/NSAEBB/NSAEBB53/

12. Quoted in Power, *Problem from Hell*, 360.

13. Pentagon officials' Rwanda discussion paper, 1 May 1994 (declassified 18 November 1998), http://www.gwu.edu/~nsarchiv/NSAEBB/NSAEBB53/

14. Willum, "Legitimizing Inaction," 13.

CHAPTER 8. GENOCIDE, OR MAYBE NOT

Epigraph. Colin Powell, testimony to the Senate Foreign Relations Committee, 9 September 2004. http://www.state.gov/secretary/former/powell/remarks/36042.htm

1. I confess a modest personal interest here. In 1985 I worked for the British committee convened to commemorate International Youth Year.

2. Quoted in Shawcross, *Deliver Us From Evil*, 195.

3. Report of the Secretary General on the Sudan, Security Council, 3 June 2004, S/2004/453.

4. Harding, "Short Cuts."

5. President Kagame also said: "In 1992, I was invited to go to France, I was told this was in efforts to find a peaceful resolution to the problems here in Rwanda.

"And officials that I met were senior officials, who told me very clearly, very openly, that if the RPF (Rwandan Patriotic Front) did not stop fighting, if we continue making advances into Rwanda, that we should bear in mind that we shall find none of our relatives alive." "Excerpts: Kagame Marks Genocide," BBC News online, 7 April 2004, http://news.bbc.co.uk/1/hi/world/africa/3609001.stm

6. Roméo A. Dallaire with Brent Beardsley, *Shake Hands with the Devil: The Failure of Humanity in Rwanda* (Toronto: Random House Canada, 2003), 426.

7. US Holocaust Memorial Museum, "Bearing Witness for Darfur: Can We Prevent Genocide in Sudan?" report from the Chad-Darfur border, 21 March 2006, http://www.ushmm.org/conscience/analysis/details.php?content=2006-03-21

8. Wax, "Refugees Moved Before Annan Visit."

9. Powell testimony before Senate Foreign Relations Committee.

10. United Nations, "Report of the International Commission of Inquiry on Darfur," 3.

11. Ibid., 4.

12. Refugees International, "No Power to Protect: The African Union Mission in Sudan," November 2005, 19.

CHAPTER 9. A WILL AND A WAY

Epigraph. Mandate of MONUC, the United Nations Mission in Congo, as revised in October 2004 under resolution 1565. http://www.un.org/Depts/dpko/missions/monuc/mandate.html

1. I was unable, in spite of extensive efforts, to include the voices of the Arab and Islamic officials in this book. The Sudanese and Algerian missions to the United Nations failed to respond to repeated requests for interviews, by telephone, e-mail, and fax. The ambassador of the Arab League, Yahya Mahmassani, agreed to an interview, then canceled it at the last moment and refused to reschedule.

2. John Danforth, edited transcript of interview with Feargal Keane for BBC Panorama, broadcast 3 July 2005, http://news.bbc.co.uk/1/hi/programmes/panorama/4647211.stm

3. "Go to Darfur, Amr Moussa, and Reclaim Arab Decency," *Daily Star,* Beirut, 27 April 2004.

4. Report of the Panel on UN Peace Operations, August 2000, 12.

5. Ibid., x.

6. Ibid. ix.

7. "A Giant Leap Forward," *Economist,* 5 January 2006.

8. "Rebuilding Failed States."

9. Danforth, BBC interview transcript.

10. Ibid.

11. Silverstein, "Official Pariah Sudan."

12. Human Rights Watch, *Sudan, Oil, and Human Rights*, 95.

13. Ibid., 107.

14. "Bush Administration Allied with Sudan Despite Role in Darfur Genocide," Democracy Now, 3 May 2005, www.democracynow.org/article .pl?sid=05/05/03/1357228&mode=thread&tid=25

15. Heinlein, "UN Security Council Refuses."

CHAPTER 10. A MEAGER RECKONING

Epigraph. *Death of Yugoslavia* television series, episode five. Liddell Hart Centre for Military Archives, Kings College, London.

1. Congressional Hearings on Genocide in Bosnia, 4 April 1995.

2. Merdijana Sadovic, "Tribunal Update 410," Institute for War and Peace Reporting, 10 June 2005.

3. "Judgement," 15 July 1999, *The Prosecutor v. Dusko Tadic*, Case no. IT-94-1-A, www.un.org/icty/Supplement/supp6-e/tadic.htm

4. United Nations, "Report of the International Commission of Inquiry on Darfur," 36, ¶123. The passage reads in full: "When militias attack jointly with the armed forces, it can be held that they act under the effective control of the Government, consistently with the notion of control set out in 1999 in *Tadić (Appeal)*, at §§98-145. Thus they are acting as *de facto* State officials of the Government of Sudan. It follows that, if it may be proved that all the requisite elements of effective control were fulfilled in each individual case, responsibility for their crimes is incurred not only by the individual perpetrators but also by the relevant officials of the army for ordering or planning, those crimes, or for failing to prevent or repress them, under the notion of superior responsibility."

5. Warrell, "Command Responsibility Convictions."

6. Mukesh Kapila, testimony before the United Kingdom Parliament, Select Committee on International Development, 22 February 2005, questions 179–99.

7. LeBor, "How Omarska Drove Bosnians."

CHAPTER 11. COMMAND RESPONSIBILITY

Epigraph. Author interview.

1. Interview, Iqbal Riza, "The Triumph of Evil: How the West Ignored the Warnings of the 1994 Rwanda Genocide and Turned Its Back on the Vic-

tims," *Frontline*, PBS, January 1999, http://www.pbs.org/wgbh/pages/front-line/shows/evil/interviews/riza.html

2. Yasushi Akashi, e-mail to author, 14 April 2006.

3. "Statement on Receiving the Report of the Independent Inquiry into the Actions of the United Nations During the 1994 Genocide in Rwanda," 16 December 1999, http://www.un.org/News/ossg/sgsm_rwanda.htm

4. UN Commission on Human Rights, Question of the Violation of Human Rights in the Occupied Arab Territories, Including Palestine, 2003–6, Report on the 59th Session, 2003.

5. Quoted in Anne Bayefsky, "Country-Specific Criticism at the UN: A No-No," *Eye on the UN*, 28 November 2005, www.eyeontheun.org/editor.asp?p=140

6. See "Straight UN Facts," *Eye on the UN*, www.eyeontheun.org/facts.asp

7. Joseph, "Bystanders to a Massacre."

8. Stéphane Dujarric, e-mail to author, 30 March 2006.

9. "Fair-Minded Report."

10. See "Hardly Radical."

11. Video footage of trial of Radislav Krstić (IT-98-33), witness DD, 26 July 2000, on ICTY CD *Bridging the Gap Between the ICTY and Communities in Bosnia and Herzegovina: Srebrenica.*

12. United Nations, "Fall of Srebrenica," 105–6, ¶491.

13. Tadeusz Mazowiecki, letter to the chairman of the UN Commission on Human Rights, 27 July 1995.

14. See Stephen Talbot, "Srebrenica: The Video of a Wartime Atrocity," *Frontline*, PBS, 13 July 2005, http://www.pbs.org/frontlineworld/blog/2005/07/srebrenica_the_1.html

15. Quoted in Hamilton, "Atrocity Film May Prepare Ground."

Select Bibliography

Books and Articles

Ajami, Fuad. "The Mark of Bosnia: Boutros-Ghali's Reign of Indifference." *Foreign Affairs*, May–June 1996.

Albright, Madeleine. *Madam Secretary: A Memoir*. London: Pan, 2004.

Arendt, Hannah. *Eichmann in Jerusalem: A Report on the Banality of Evil*. London: Penguin, 1994.

Babbin, Jed. *Inside the Asylum: Why the United Nations and Old Europe Are Worse Than You Think*. Washington, D.C.: Regnery, 2004.

Barnett, Michael. *Eyewitness to Genocide: The United Nations and Rwanda*. Ithaca, N.Y.: Cornell University Press, 2002.

Bennett, Christopher. *Yugoslavia's Bloody Collapse: Causes, Course, and Consequences*. London: C. Hurst, 1995.

Browning, Christopher R. *Ordinary Men: Reserve Battalion 101 and the Final Solution in Poland*. New York: HarperPerennial, 1998.

Burns, John. "A Siege by Any Other Name Would Be as Painful." *New York Times*, 17 August 1993.

Clark, Wesley K. *Waging Modern War*. Oxford: Public Affairs, 2001.

"Daddy Wore a Blue Helmet." *Economist*, 21 April 2005.

Danner, Mark. "Clinton, the UN, and the Bosnian Disaster." *New York Review of Books*, 18 December 1997.

De Waal, Alex. "Counter-Insurgency on the Cheap." *London Review of Books*, 5 August 2004.

Dorril, Stephen. *MI6*. London: Simon and Schuster, 2000.

"A Fair-Minded Report at a Crucial Time." *Economist*, 7 September 2005.

Fasulo, Linda. *An Insider's Guide to the UN*. New Haven: Yale University Press, 2005.

Flint, Julie, and Alex de Waal. *Darfur: A Short History of a Long War*. London: Zed, 2005.

Gjelten, Tom. "Professionalism in War Reporting: A Correspondent's View." Carnegie Commission on Preventing Deadly Conflict, September 1997.

Glenny, Misha. *The Balkans, 1804–1999: Nationalism, War, and the Great Powers*. London: Granta, 2000.

Goulding, Marrack. *Peacemonger*. London: John Murray, 2002.

Gourevitch, Philip. *We Wish to Inform You That Tomorrow We Will Be Killed with Our Families*. London: Picador, 2000.

Gutman, Roy. "Big Atrocity: Serb Militia Chief Said to Have Role." *Newsday*, 8 August 1995.

———. *A Witness To Genocide*. New York: Lisa Drew, 1993.

Gutman, Roy, and Cabell Bruce. "How Troop-Hostage Talks Led to the Slaughter of Srebrenica." *Newsday*, 29 May 1996.

Halberstam, David. *War in a Time of Peace: Bush, Clinton, and the Generals*. London: Bloomsbury, 2002.

Halpern, Joel M., and David A. Kideckel, eds. *Neighbors at War: Anthropological Perspectives on Yugoslav Ethnicity, Culture, and History*. University Park: Pennsylvania State University Press, 2000.

Hamilton, Douglas. "Atrocity Film May Prepare Ground for Serb Arrests." Reuters, 3 June 2005.

Harding, Jeremy. "Short Cuts." *London Review of Books*, 6 May 2004.

"Hardly Radical, But It's a Start," *Economist*, 15 September 2005.

Heinlein, Peter. "UN Security Council Refuses Briefing on Darfur Atrocities," Voice of America, 11 October 2005.

Holbrooke, Richard. *To End a War*. New York: Modern Library, 1999.

Honig, Jan Willem, and Norbert Both. *Srebrenica: Record of a War Crime*. London: Penguin, 1996.

Hurd, Douglas. *Memoirs*. London: Abacus, 2003.

Joseph, Ed. "Bystanders to a Massacre: How the UN Failed Srebrenica." *Washington Post*, 10 July 2005.

Judah, Tim. *The Serbs: History, Myth, and the Destruction of Yugoslavia*. 2nd ed. New Haven: Yale University Press, 2000.

Karl, Jonathan. "The Darfur Disaster." *Weekly Standard*, April 2005.

Lane, Charles, and Thom Shanker. "Bosnia: What the CIA Didn't Tell Us." *New York Review of Books*, 9 May 1996.

LeBor, Adam. *A Heart Turned East: Among the Muslims of Europe and America*. New York: St. Martin's, 1998.

———. "How Omarska Drove Bosnians to Radical Islam." *Times* (London), 18 November 2005.

————. *Milosevic: A Biography.* New Haven: Yale University Press, 2003.

LeBor, Adam, and Roger Boyes. *Seduced by Hitler: The Choices of a Nation and the Ethics of Survival.* Naperville, Ill.: Sourcebooks, 2004.

Maass, Peter. *Love Thy Neighbor: A Story of War.* New York: Knopf, 1996.

————. "UN Keepers of the Siege: Relief Troops Bar Escape from Sarajevo." *Washington Post,* 30 December 1992.

Malcolm, Noel. *Bosnia: A Short History.* London: Papermac, 1994.

Malone, David M., ed. *The UN Security Council: From the Cold War to the 21st Century.* Boulder, Colo.: Lynne Rienner, 2004.

McDoom, Opheera. "Accused Darfur Militia Leader Says Turns to Peace." Reuters, 19 May 2005.

Napoleon, Loretta. *Terror Inc: Tracing the Money Behind Global Terrorism.* London: Penguin, 2004.

Neuffer, Elizabeth. *The Key to My Neighbour's House: Seeking Justice in Bosnia and Rwanda.* London: Bloomsbury, 2002.

Norris, H. T. *Islam in the Balkans.* London: C. Hurst, 1993.

Owen, David. *Balkan Odyssey.* London: Victor Gollancz, 1995.

Paris, Erna. *Long Shadows: Truth, Lies, and History.* London: Bloomsbury, 2000.

Polman, Linda. *We Did Nothing: Why the Truth Doesn't Always Come Out When the UN Goes In.* London: Viking, 2003.

Power, Samantha. "Dying in Darfur." *New Yorker,* 30 August 2004.

————. *A Problem from Hell.* London: Flamingo, 2003.

Prunier, Gerard. *Darfur: The Ambiguous Genocide.* London: C. Hurst, 2005.

"Rebuilding Failed States: From Chaos, Order." *Economist,* 3 March 2005.

Rieff, David. *Slaughterhouse: Bosnia and the Failure of the West.* New York: Touchstone, 1996.

Rohde, David. *A Safe Area, Srebrenica: Europe's Worst Massacre Since the Second World War.* London: Simon and Schuster, 1997.

Rose, Michael. *Fighting for Peace: Lessons from Bosnia.* London: Warner, 1999.

Sanjuan, Pedro A. *The UN Gang: A Memoir of Incompetence, Corruption, Espionage, Anti-Semitism, and Islamic Extremism at the UN Secretariat.* New York: Doubleday, 2005.

Sell, Louis. *Slobodan Milosevic and the Destruction of Yugoslavia.* Durham: Duke University Press, 2002.

Shawcross, William. *Deliver Us from Evil: Warlords and Peacekeepers in a World of Endless Conflict.* London: Bloomsbury, 2000.

Silber, Laura, and Allan Little. *The Death of Yugoslavia.* London: Penguin and BBC Books, 1995.

Silverstein, Ken. "Official Pariah Sudan Valuable to America's War on Terrorism." *Los Angeles Times,* 29 April 2005.

Simms, Brendan. *Unfinest Hour: Britain and the Destruction of Bosnia*. London: Allen Lane, 2001.

Smith, Rupert. *The Utility of Force: The Art of War in the Modern World*. London: Allen Lane, 2005.

Stamkowski, George, ed. *With No Peace to Keep: United Nations Peacekeeping and the Wars in the Former Yugoslavia*. London: Volatile Media, 2002.

Stankovic, Milos. *Trusted Mole*. London: HarperCollins 2000.

Stephen, Chris. *Judgement Day: The Trial of Slobodan Milošević*. London: Atlantic Monthly Press, 2005.

Sudetic, Chuck. *Blood and Vengeance*. New York: Penguin, 1998.

Suljagic, Emir. *Postcards from the Grave*. London: Saqi, 2005.

Tanner, Marcus. *Croatia: A Nation Forged in War*. New Haven: Yale University Press, 1997.

Thesiger, Wilfred. *The Life of My Choice*. London: Flamingo, 1992.

Thompson, Mark. *Forging War: The Media in Serbia, Croatia, Bosnia and Hercegovina*. Luton: University of Luton and Article 19, 1999.

Vulliamy, Ed. "How the CIA Intercepted SAS Signals." *Guardian*, 29 January 1996.

Warrell, Helen. "Command Responsibility Convictions." IWPR Tribunal Update 444, 17 March 2006.

Wax, Emily. "Refugees Moved Before Annan Visit." *Washington Post*, 2 July 2004.

Wiebes, Cees. *Intelligence and the War in Bosnia, 1992–1995*. Münster: Lit Verlag, 2003.

Willum, Bjørn. "Legitimizing Inaction Towards Genocide In Rwanda: A Matter Of Misconception?" *International Peacekeeping*, Autumn 1999.

Zimmerman, Robert. *Origins of a Catastrophe: Yugoslavia and Its Destroyers—America's Last Ambassador Tells What Happened and Why*. New York: Random House, 1996.

Reports

Amnesty International. *Darfur: What Hope for the Future: Civilians in Need of Protection*. London, 2004.

————. *Recommendations on the Deployment of a United Nations Peace Support Operation*. London, 2005.

————. *Sudan: Looming Crisis in Darfur*. London, 2003.

————. *Sudan: Who Will Answer for the Crimes?* London, 2005.

————. *Sudan, Darfur: No One to Complain To*. London, 2004.

French National Assembly. *Report by the Parliamentary Committee on the Events in Srebrenica.* Paris, 2001.

Human Rights Watch. *Darfur Documents Confirm Government Policy of Militia Support.* New York, 2004.

———. "Exclusive Video Interview with Alleged Janjaweed Leader." September 2004. Transcript available at http://www.hrw.org/english/docs/2005/03/02/darfur10234.htm

———. *The Fall of Srebrenica and the Failure of UN Peacekeeping.* New York, 1995.

———. "Sexual Violence and Its Consequences Among Displaced Persons in Chad and Darfur." Briefing paper, 12 April 2005.

———. *Sudan, Oil, and Human Rights.* New York, 2003.

International Crisis Group. *Darfur Deadline: A New International Action Plan.* Africa Report no. 83. Brussels, 2004.

———. *Darfur Rising: Sudan's New Crisis.* Africa Report no. 76. Brussels, 2004.

———. *Sudan: Now or Never in Darfur.* Africa Report no. 80. Brussels, 2004.

———. *To Save Darfur.* Africa Report no. 105. Brussels, 2006.

Netherlands Institute for War Documentation (NIOD). *Srebrenica—A "Safe" Area: Reconstruction, Background, Consequences, and Analyses of the Fall of a Safe Area.* Amsterdam, 2002. http://213.222.3.5/srebrenica/

United Nations. "Report of the Independent Enquiry into the Actions of the United Nations During the 1994 Genocide in Rwanda." December 1999.

———. "Report of the International Commission of Inquiry on Darfur to the United Nations Secretary-General." January 2005.

United Nations, General Assembly. "The Fall of Srebrenica." November 1999.

United Nations, General Assembly, Security Council. "Report of the Panel on United Nations Peace Operations." August 2000.

United Nations, Security Council. "Report of the Secretary-General on the Sudan." June 2004.

Web Sites

www.amnesty.org	Amnesty International
www.bosnia.org.uk	Bosnian Institute
http://news.bbc.co.uk	British Broadcasting Corporation
www.cij.org	Coalition for International Justice
www.crimesofwar.org	Crimes of War Project
www.economist.com	*The Economist*

www.eyeontheun.org	Eye on the UN
www.fas.org	Federation of American Scientists
www.hrw.org	Human Rights Watch
www.iwpr.net	Institute for War and Peace Reporting
www.icc-cpi.int	International Criminal Court
www.un.org/icty	International Criminal Tribunal for the Former Yugoslavia
www.un.org./ictr	International Criminal Tribunal on Rwanda
www.icg.org	International Crisis Group
www.preventgenocide.org	Prevent Genocide campaign
www.pbs.org	Public Broadcasting Service
www.sudanreeves.org	Eric Reeves, Sudan activist
www.savedarfur.org	Save Darfur campaign
www.securitycouncilreport.org	Security Council Report
www.shashitharoor.com	Shashi Tharoor
www.un.org.depts/dpko	UN Department of Peacekeeping Operations
www.ushmm.org	US Holocaust Memorial Museum
www.willum.com	Web site of journalist Bjorn Willum

Archives

Collection of David Rohde Relating to Srebrenica. Open Society Archives, HU-OSA 377–0-1. OSA, Budapest, Hungary. http://www.osa.ceu.hu

Death of Yugoslavia, documentary television series, Brian Lapping Associates. Liddell Hart Centre for Military Archives, GB 0099 KCLMA, Kings College London. http://www.kcl.ac.uk/lhcma/home.htm

Index

Mukhabarat (Sudanese intelligence service), 145, 224, 253
Musa, Sheikh Hilal, 139, 147
Muslim Brotherhood, 139
Mussolini, Benito, 15

Naivasha accords, 10, 18, 184, 195; Arab and Muslim view of, 206; autonomy of south Sudan and, 143; Darfur refugees and, 207; implications for Darfur, 162; officials' fear of jeopardizing, 156, 163; oil interests and, 225; peacekeeping force and, 185; as template for solving Darfur crisis, 187–88; United Nations and, 211
Namibia, 13
Nash, Gen. Bill, 237, 241
National Islamic Front (NIF), 139–40, 159, 233
NATO (North Atlantic Treaty Organization), 17, 25, 48, 57, 202, 269; actions in wake of Srebrenica massacre, 129, 130–32; airpower in Bosnia, 54, 62, 64, 67, 69, 97; bombing of Serbia, 207, 251; Darfur crisis and, 246, 279; Dayton peace settlement and, 234, 237; fall of Srebrenica and, 95, 100, 102, 104; increasing role in Bosnian war, 67; relations with United Nations, 70, 81, 83–85; Rwanda genocide and, 180, 181; Serbian antiaircraft weapons and, 86; Serbian military equipment destroyed by, 67–68; split over Bosnia intervention, 251; UN troops held

hostage by Serbs and, 107; weaponry in Bosnia, 65
NatWest Markets, 235–36
Nazism, 11, 47, 77; Nuremberg trials and, 242; Rwanda genocide compared to, 181; Serbian atrocities compared to, 117, 121–22
Ndiaye, Waly Bacre, 166
Netherlands, 71, 94
Neville-Jones, Pauline, 235
New York City, 8, 18–19, 85
New Zealand, 18, 40, 63, 178–79
Nicolai, Maj. Gen. Cees, 94, 95
Nigeria, 6
no-fly zones, 46, 54, 79, 107, 212
No Power to Protect: the African Union Mission in Sudan (Refugees International report), 202
Non-Aligned Caucus (NAC), 35, 39, 52, 282; Franco-British policy in Bosnia and, 53–54; safe areas and, 45, 46
North Korea, 247, 260
Nuremberg trials, 242

O'Brien, Jim, 238
Office for the Coordination of Humanitarian Affairs (OCHA), 5, 155, 158, 164, 172
oil interests, 225–26
Okun, Herb, 26
Omarska concentration camp, 242
Operation Deliberate Force, 131–32, 158
Operation Flash, 89
Operation Murambatsvina, 259
Operation Turquoise, 186
Ordinary Men (Browning), 121